REVOLUTIONARY MELODRAMA

CHICAGO STUDIES ON THE MIDDLE EAST

Center for Middle Eastern Studies
The University of Chicago

Published on behalf of the
Center for Middle Eastern Studies

By

The Middle East Documentation Center

Revolutionary Melodrama

Popular Film and Civic Identity in Nasser's Egypt

Joel Gordon

Chicago • Middle East Documentation Center • 2002

Published in 2002 by the Middle East Documentation Center
on behalf of the Center for Middle Eastern Studies,
The University of Chicago

Pick Hall 201
5828 S. University Avenue
Chicago, IL 60637
http://ChicagoStudiesOnTheMiddleEast.uchicago.edu

ISBN 0-9708199-0-0
Library of Congress Control Number: 2002108997

Manufactured in the United States of America

Let the projectionist rewind the scene
I want to see myself in the old days – young
among the ranks of the revolution – proud,
Impressed by neither king nor father
I want to see again and remember
Why one of my blows hit,
one of them missed
And one stopped the film, froze it.

Salah Jahin, "September Tunes"

CONTENTS

INTRODUCTION

"We've Lost a Lot"
Cinema and Longing since Nasser

Stop acting like Clark Gable, we'll miss Tom and Jerry!
—*Alexandria. . . . Why?*, 1978

The era of the Arab has begun, and with it their sweetest days. Days of perfection marked by the consciousness that they have attained unity and embraced happiness. Days in which they have sworn fealty to 'Gamal'— a leader. They have sworn fealty north and south, and he has accepted the homage and made a covenant with them.
—*al-Musawwar*, February 28, 1958

Voice of a Generation

Nasser's Egypt had many voices, but perhaps none as instantly recognizable as Galal Muawad. Muawad was a young broadcaster lured to the adventure of radio in the waning days of the old regime. Like other young nationalists in the profession he paid the price for partisanship. After the collapse of Egypt's last freely elected government and the imposition of martial law in late January 1952, he was reassigned to a desk job in the supply ministry. Five months later he returned to the air, and it was he who read the Free

Officers' first message to the nation on the morning of July 23. For the next eighteen years Muawad remained a mainstay on Egypt's primary station, notably as the announcer who presented Gamal Abdel Nasser to the radio audience. He prefaced Nasser's most famous addresses through good times and bad, none worse than the leader's resignation following the June 1967 "setback" *(al-naksa)*. In September 1970, choked with tears, the voice of the people, Muawad broadcast Nasser's funeral to those who were not amongst the millions in the streets accompanying the corporeal body of the "Boss" *(rayyis)* to his grave.

Like many others too closely associated with the Nasser regime, Galal Muawad did not survive the transition to the contested successor, Anwar al-Sadat. According to an oft-told anecdote, Muawad introduced the new president live and to the collective ears of the nation as "the glorious leader *(al-za'im al-khalid)*, Gamal Abdel Nasser." The script, delivered so often, had not changed for nearly two decades, and Muawad, consumed with grief, forgot to announce a new cast. Sadat, eager to emerge from Nasser's shadow, was neither amused nor sympathetic, and ordered Muawad dismissed. Even if embellished, the story says much about the changing nature of power in Egypt. Muawad and others too closely associated with the Nasser regime found themselves suddenly out of work. Some, like Muawad, found haven in neighboring states, another wave of brain drain; others accepted sinecures in the bureaucracy. Some, but not Muawad, would work in broadcast again under Sadat's successor, Hosni Mubarak.

When I met Muawad in December 1995 much of the fire seemed to have vanished. The voice was deep and melodious, familiar from his introductions to cassette recordings released since the early eighties of famous Nasser speeches and Nasser-era anthems sung by Abd al-Halim Hafiz. But weary. Perhaps it was the early morning hour and the informal setting, his home, where he greeted me in pajamas and bathrobe. Muawad was not an easy interview. I prodded for details that had either slipped from memory or were guarded for more intimate ears. I sensed I was hearing an oft-recited script and only later realized its intrinsic value. The underlying theme was loss, of close friends in broadcast and music, pioneers, giants. Abd al-Halim, Umm Kulthum, Farid al-Atrash, Muhammad Abd al-Wahhab, Nasser. And, although not clearly stated, of an Egypt that no longer exists.

"We've lost a lot," Muawad sighed. Our discussion was broken by long pauses, emotional reprieves. Within the week another old radio comrade, Hemat Mustafa, passed away, and I imagined Muawad's grief.[1]

Muawad and I did not discuss Egyptian movies. His will be one of the few voices in the pages that follow that is not rooted in acting, directing, scripting, designing, or analyzing the cinema. Muawad, however, had personal links to the world of the silver screen, not only via the musical stars he mentioned—all of whom made movies—but also his wife, the actress Layla Fawzi.[2] If his relationship to the film industry was primarily via personal connections, he was, of course, a viewer. I have never met an Egyptian, certainly of his generation, that did not grow up on movies, especially those who lived in the city.[3]

Icons

Films and filmic images have pervaded Egyptian cultural and intellectual life throughout the twentieth century. These include imported images, particularly from Hollywood. They are to be found in political cartoons, popular picture magazines, print and broadcast advertising, and are often embodied in filmed cross references. By the early 1950s the leader of Egypt's largest political party, the Wafd, and his heir apparent, were regularly caricatured as Laurel and Hardy. The sketched parody captured—and appropriately exaggerated—both physical resemblances and a sardonic slapstick vision of the state of national politics.[4] When Turkey and Iraq signed a treaty in 1953 that Egypt opposed, the same cartoonist drew Turkish prime minister Adnan Menderes a la Douglas Fairbanks as "The Thief of Baghdad," carrying off a young woman who represents "Iraqi freedom." [5] Weeklies like *al-Musawwar* and *Akhir saa*, which often displayed local beauties on the front cover—the exceptions being issues with more immediate political photos or cartoons—generally featured Hollywood starlets on the back. On rare occasions—Raquel Welch, the "Woman from *One Million Years B.C.*"—the foreign starlet might even make the cover.[6]

Hollywood set fashion trends—clothing, hairstyle, makeup—and fostered images of glamour throughout the Arab world. Hind Rassam Culhane, who grew up in urban Iraq, recalls "play acting" Hollywood films, imitating the "manner and dress" of American film stars, "Audrey Hepburn's swirling cloche skirt; Grace Kelly's white gloves" (1995: 4–5). For the middle class teenage girls in Latifa al-Zayyat's 1960 coming-of-age novel, *The Open Door (al-Bab al-maftuh),* adapted shortly thereafter for the screen, the benchmark for romance is also imported:

> But where would she meet him? At a dance party, that was it. She would be wearing a white dress just like the one Audrey Hepburn had worn in *Sabrina*. . . . He was elegant. Dark. Tall. He looked a lot like Gregory Peck, in fact (al-Zayyat 2000: 36–37).[7]

> Before falling in love with Mahmud she had been enamored of Robert Taylor. Fourteen years old, she had taken a razor and carved the first letter of his name into her hand. She let the blood well from the cut so that the letter "R" would still be there when the wound dried. And whenever the scar began to disappear she cut herself again (ibid.: 209).

Likewise, although the majority of Egypt's great directors, editors, and set designers trained in Europe, Egypt's "Hollywood on the Nile" borrowed more heavily from its American counterpart, adapting stories, borrowing scores, reenacting classic scenes.

In the opening scene of *Alexandria . . . Why?* (*Iskandriya lay?* 1979), Youssef Chahine's nostalgic look at his home town during the Second World War, a group of prep school boys go to the movies. Yahya (Muhsin Muhyi al-Din), Chahine's autobiographical self, stands transfixed in front of a poster for *An American in Paris*.[8] "Stop acting like Clark Gable," one of his friends shouts out. "We'll miss Tom and Jerry!" Climbing over seats and asking patrons to move to accommodate their group, the boys, all in school blazers, draw the sarcastic reproach of one audience member: "To come early, like the rest of God's creatures, must be beneath Victoria College!"[9] The theater darkens, the curtain opens, the MGM lion roars, and the assembled crowd is transported into the magical world of the movies: Georges Guetary singing "Stairway to Paradise" in *An American in*

Paris, then Eleanor Powell hoofing in the battleship deck finale of *Born to Dance*.[10]

Not all of the iconography is derivative. The Egyptian cinema created its own giants, whose personas, figures, and voices provided a "reference point, reflecting the general attitudes, perceptions, ideas, and self-definitions—the concept of *me and the other*" throughout the Arabic-speaking Middle East (Culhane 1995: 5). If Egyptians learned elocution from the stars, other Arabs "perfected the Egyptian dialect"—in addition to American slang—at the movie theater (ibid.: 4). Egyptian films produced by younger directors often allude, directly or indirectly, to earlier works from their own local canon. For viewers, casting choices, whether deliberate or not, play upon what Lila Abu-Lughod has called an "encyclopedic knowledge" of actors' past roles and private lives (1995: 204). When an aged star comes out of retirement or reprises a classic characterization yet again, the response can be ecstatic.

The best recent example is the brief, but powerful role played by Amina Rizq in the widely popular *Nasser 56* (*[Nasir 56]*, Muhammad Fadl 1996). Playing an antique peasant woman who comes to call on the president, Rizq lends not only dramatic, but self-referential historical weight to a key scene. With a career stretching back to the 1930s, the octogenarian actress is an iconic presence. Cast as a maternal figure early in her career—often playing women well beyond her age, and most often in the traditional "veiled" garb of a widow—she is most intimately associated with the black-and-white classics produced before color became the norm in the early 1970s. Most of all, she is associated with motherhood—despite the fact that some of her mother-roles were less than noble. The economist Galal Amin (2000: 135–36) recalls that his own mother "was a great one for crying, particularly in films starring Amina Rizq."

> My mother would go to the cinema dressed in black, covering her hair with her black veil, almost exactly like what Amina Rizq wore in most of her films. After each film, my mother would recall the film's exhortations and pieces of wisdom, often concluding, "By God, this film tells no other story but my own."

During the 1999–2000 Ramadan television season, when the movie theaters are closed and the most celebrated dramatic serials and entertainment specials are aired (Gordon 1998), Egyptians enjoyed a popular program called *This Woman is My Mother (al-Sitti di ummi).* The show, which aired shortly after *iftar* (the breaking of the fast at sundown), featured interviews with "exemplary mothers" who had been nominated by children and husbands, some celebrities, but most not. The opening credits, backed by a sentimental theme song, highlighted snippets of past and upcoming interviews. The final frame froze on a movie still of Amina Rizq, the ultimate maternal icon, as film star and filmic character.

Actors and actresses have been utilized to even greater extent by the media in recent years. Increasingly they appear in television advertisements to sell commercial products—from luxury villas in gated communities to mops and cleaning equipment—always playing on their screen images. In what to an American audience may seem a quaint throwback, they have started to appear as panelists on television quiz shows. Another popular early evening program during the 1999–2000 Ramadan season, *Clapstick (Klakitt),* featured two teams of actors competing over movie trivia.[11] For kids, the most popular show was *"Cut!" (Farkash!),* a nightly compilation of out-takes from the recent Muhammad Hinaydi blockbuster comedy, *Hamam in Amsterdam* (*[Hamam fi Amsterdam],* Said Hamid 1999). When the show began, the theme song, *"Ay, ya,"* a hit from the film, blared from apartment windows, accompanied by thousands of unseen young boys and girls.

Such manifestations of local film culture may well lend some optimism to the generally bleak vision of contemporary Egyptian cinema. The fact remains that an industry that once produced upwards of fifty films a year has produced fewer than twenty per year over the course of the last decade. Some of this is related to the globalization of the film market, a phenomenon that has impacted other world cinemas, from Bombay to Hong Kong.[12] Whatever the causes, wherever fault may lie, whatever the proposed panaceas (most notably the $300 million Media Production City constructed in October 6 City as a combined studio-theme park),[13] and notwithstanding an upsurge in production since the millennium's turn, the Egyptian film industry cannot break free of the general assessment expressed by Galal Muawad.

The iconic mother: Amina Rizq with Anwar Ahmad in *Mustafa Kamil.* Courtesy of *Ruz al-Yusuf.*

We've lost something that can never be recaptured. It is not only Muawad's generation, or the Nasser-born generation that followed, that expresses such sentiments. Younger Egyptians may flock to a Hinaydi comedy, a yuppie love story (such as the recent *Snakes and Ladders [al-Sillim wa al-thu'ban],* Tariq al-Aryan 2001), or safari adventure (*Africano,* Umru Arafa 2001). But they still would much rather see the Hollywood pyrotechnics of *Speed, Tornado,* or *Titanic.* What future, then, is there for newer artistically-inclined, even "scathingly original," directors like Usama Fawzi (*Asphalt Demons [Afarit al-asfalt]* 1996; *Fallen Angels' Paradise [Shayatin al-ginna]* 2000), Magdi Ahmad Ali (*Life, My Passion [ya Dunya ya gharami]* 1996; *Girls' Secrets [Asrar al-banat]* 2001), or Atif Hatata (*The Closed Doors [Abwab al-mughlaqa]* 2001) whose socially-driven, controversial, and deliberately under-starred works become instantly labeled as "festival films"? [14]

And yet, amidst this dismal prognosis, younger Egyptians, fed a steady dose of classic films on television—programming greatly enhanced by satellite options—seem to have imbued a degree of their parents' and grandparents' nostalgia for the "golden" black-and-white oldies. Their parents do not always feel so assured. Galal Amin muses:

> When I sit today in front of the television to watch an old Egyptian film produced in the 1940s, with a beginning, an end, and a straightforward story in the middle, I sometimes catch myself on the verge of tears in sympathy with one or another of the characters in the film, exactly as my mother would when she saw the films of Amina Rizq. I find myself quite willing to forgive some excessive sentimentality if the film has what I consider to be the right message. I try to win my children over to my point of view and to have them share with me the pleasure of seeing these old films, but my efforts are usually in vain. They may pretend for a few minutes to be enjoying the film, but it is abundantly clear to me that they are watching it only for my sake, exactly as I used to do with my mother fifty years ago.

This book is not about the younger generations. It is about their elders, people like Galal Amin and Galal Muawad, the writer Muhammad al-Bisati, who recalls fondly going to see action B-flicks at outdoor rural theaters in the fifties, the actress Samira Abd al-Aziz, who has played against some of Egypt's most handsome men, but still thinks none hold a candle to Gregory Peck. They and their children and their children's children all participate in an ongoing discourse about Egypt's past, present, and future that is very much linked to a cultural sense of being rooted in backward longing and forward confusion, with the cinema, as art and industry, a primary focus.[15]

Revolutionary Genres

Revolutionary Melodrama explores intersections between cinema and politics during the Nasser era, a period in which an authoritarian military regime embarked upon the construction of a new civic identity for an independent Egypt. The way in which filmmakers participated in this venture, inspired by the new regime—and later very critical of its shortcomings—provides the focal point, with their cultural production as the central texts. These texts both shaped and were shaped by an emerging sense of a new Egypt as artists took advantage of the toppling of artistic and thematic taboos (and, of course, the imposition of new taboos), working with (and at times against) government bureaucrats and ideologues to depict an Egypt that was modern, progressive, and at the forefront of the national liberation struggles of the late colonial and post-colonial eras in Africa and Asia.

This book grew out of my own ongoing interest in Nasserist revolutionary civic identity. This represents, for me, an effort to move beyond the political machinations of conspiracy and counter-conspiracy, the seizure and consolidation of power by young reform-minded officers that became the foundation for earlier work (Gordon 1992), to look at the meaning of the Nasser era to Egyptians who lived—and remember—it. A casual encounter with a bold and rather bawdy caricature of Nasser wielding a club but wearing a brassiere chalked (along with other anti-Israeli and pro-Islamist sketches) onto the back wall of the Qasr al-Ayni hospital complex in 1992 further sparked my interest in the ongoing and oft-changing legacy of the man and the political-ideological system that came to bear his name (Gordon 1997). Nasserism, I postulated, has been studied in myriad aspects since it began to take form in the mid-1950s. Early students of Nasser's Egypt, their attitudes shaped by images of a decadent old regime, depicted a youthful, well-intentioned, if impatient new order. Social scientists stressed relations between the military, a modern middle class, and the state. The socialist transformations of the sixties prompted studies of state ideology and class formation, as well as a leftist critique of Nasserist shortcomings. Sadat's reforms, a counter-revolution to some, generated a comparative political economy of two eras. Under the Mubarak regime, a more open discussion of recent history has afforded scholars—Egyptians and foreigners alike—the opportunity to revisit Nasserism and reexamine its origins. Still largely missing, however, has been an effort to analyze and understand the meaning for Egyptians of the society fashioned by Nasser and his associates.

I began with a general set of questions rooted in the supposition that the Nasser era fundamentally changed the way Egyptians looked at themselves as citizens. To what extent did the Nasser regime succeed in propagating a revolutionary ethos? What popular manifestations of that ethos captured the imagination of Egyptians? How did Egyptians view themselves differently than they had under the old regime? How did popular culture reflect the abolition of formal class lines, expanded educational opportunity, women's suffrage, Arab socialism, independence? How was religion or religious expression manifested in a civic culture that was avowedly secular? How did Nasserist culture utilize Egyptian history from the pharaohs to Farouk to articulate its vision of a new Egypt? The Egyptian cinema is not the only avenue or medium that might be utilized to answer such questions, but it is, because of its ongoing impact, an extremely important place to start.

The co-joining of revolution and melodrama may strike some as contradictory, even fantastic. It has been a staple of film criticism to posit studio-based genre cinema—which the Egyptian cinema has always been—as an inherently conservative, if not reactionary, art form, both aesthetically and politically (Wright 1995), one that is "opposed to experimentation, novelty, or tampering with the given order of things" (Sobchak 1995: 112). This, so the argument goes, is because genre-driven films, definable in relation to an identifiable corpus, share "a set of conventions . . . certain themes, certain typical actions, certain characteristic mannerisms" (Tudor 1995: 3) that "regularly oppose cultural values to counter-cultural drives" only to validate the predominant values (Altman 1987: 330). Thomas Schatz (1995: 99) argues that film genre must be understood from a dual perspective:

> It is, on the one hand, a product of a commercial, highly conventionalized popular art form and subject to certain demands imposed by both the audience and the cinematic system itself. On the other hand, the genre film represents a distinct manifestation of contemporary society's basic mythic impulse, its desire to confront elemental conflicts inherent in modern culture while at the same time participating in the projection of an idealized collective self-image.

One of the premises underlying this book, however, is that the Egyptian scenario, at least under Nasser, provides an alternate reading of genre.

What happens when a self-proclaimed—and at times highly acclaimed—revolutionary regime, working closely with a genre-driven film industry—personified by corporate financiers and creative artists, many of whom have been chafing at the constraints of old regime censorship—sets out to overturn old values, redefine collective self-identity, and, ultimately, re-script (and film) myth?

Whether or not Nasser's Free Officers really did foment a revolution or whether in actuality they forestalled one has been an ongoing debate. Leftist critics of the regime have argued the latter, at times persuasively (Abdel-Malek 1968; Riad 1964). This, however, begs the essential point, which is that the regime, which began referring to itself as "revolutionary" shortly after assuming power, clearly saw itself—as did many followers—as forging a new path. Whatever the shortfalls, the Free Officers coup *(inqilab)* became the July Revolution *(thawra),* eradicated the aristocracy, redistributed land, nationalized key sectors of the economy, and instituted free education for the masses. A key element in the Free Officers' program for national development was the active patronage of the arts, of which the cinema remained a key component.

Despite the steady outcry against the formulaic, genre-driven cinema produced by Egypt's studio system, the Nasser regime's program, at least for its first decade, did not entail fundamentally restructuring the studio industry. Revolution would be heralded within the existing confines of an established order. And when in the 1960s the state intervened more directly to influence and guide production of a more socially relevant cinema, it continued to rely on an established order of producers, directors, writers, and stars. Following this, many of the films that will be treated in the following pages are not revolutionary—or even necessarily extraordinary—in terms of text, script, or *mise-en-scène.* They do, however, reflect a bold, youthful spirit that may be called revolutionary, a spirit that transcended regime propaganda to embody a dynamic sense of social change, or at least its potentiality.

I use melodrama in its broadest sense to refer not to a specific genre, but rather to an "expressive code" (Elsaessar 1995: 359) or a "formula" that is "the model, the archetype, for genre itself" (Lang

1989: 46–48). What Thomas Elsaessar (1995: 359) says about Hollywood, applies equally to the Egyptian cinema:

> Dramatic situations are given an orchestration that will allow for complex aesthetic patterns: indeed, orchestration is fundamental to the American cinema as a whole (being essentially a dramatic cinema, spectacular, and based on a broad appeal) because it has drawn the aesthetic consequences of having the spoken word more as an additional "melodic" dimension than as an autonomous semantic discourse.

"Revolutionary melodrama" therefore refers to a vast corpus of studio and state-funded films—musicals, comedies, romances, thrillers, historicals, social and psychological dramas, beach romps, crime stories—produced between 1952, the year of the Free Officers coup, and the mid-1970s, when color became the norm, and when Anwar al-Sadat's consolidation of authority at the expense of many of the Nasserist faithful allowed for, or provoked, a new reading on celluloid of some aspects of the revolution and its shortcomings.

My "reading" of Egyptian films is based on an ever-growing familiarity with an enormous corpus of cinematic output. Egyptian filmmakers made some 900 movies between 1952 and 1970. Fortunately, a great majority of these films are available on video, and may be purchased in Egypt (LE 25, approximately $6.00, in downtown Cairo, slightly higher in the tourist market or hotel video shops).[16] An additional important source is Egyptian television, now featuring nine terrestrial channels, which runs an average of three to four films daily, and occasionally broadcasts films that are not available for sale. If I tell colleagues that I spent a great amount of funded research time not in state archives, but rather in front of the "little screen," often frustrated that posted listings in three daily papers and the weekly *Radio and Television* guide corresponded to no broadcast reality, they should rest assured that when I watched, it was with notepad in hand, my senses honed for sight and sound, dialogue, soundtrack, and camera pans. The films that I have seen, many multiple times, discussed and read about, constitute the primary texts from which I work. I have supplemented them with musical soundtracks (available on cassette and, increasingly, compact disc); stories, advertisements, and interviews in the contemporary popular press; published memoirs, biographic and photographic sketches, and critical film studies; and interviews with people involved in various aspects of film production, criticism, dissemination, or related fields of television and radio broadcast.

I will confess at the outset that I am a fan of Egyptian films, particularly, although not exclusively—Galal Amin's penchant for 1940s tear-jerkers notwithstanding—from the Nasser era. This bears noting because for many the industry has been forever scarred by genre conventionality, the "customary gulf that comes to exist in a film industry between commerce and art" (Armes 1987: 199), and, at times, by woeful inadequacies in production facilities. My purpose throughout, however, is not necessarily to champion particular films as works of art rather than craft, but rather as works of immense, lasting cultural power and, in many cases, of great creative endeavor.

ACKNOWLEDGMENTS

Only a fraction of those who were willing to speak with me are credited in the bibliography. Some of those noted, and many others, gave me far more time than indicated there. I am grateful to them all for inviting me into their homes and offices, their public, and at times private lives. Of the many, Louis Greiss, Mahfuz Abd al-Rahman and Samira Abd al-Aziz, Salah Mari, Ahmad Said, Khayri Bishara, and Tawfik Salih deserve special thanks. Some friends and colleagues also rate particular notes of gratitude: Walter Armbrust, who encouraged me to plunge into the film world, and who shared his personal Cairo phone book; Ahmad Abdalla, intellectual interlocutor and social activist par excellence, whose range of networks and depth of insight never cease to amaze; and Jacob Arback, without whom I might never have had the guts or wherewithal to navigate the Radio and Television Building. Our crack Zamalek electrician, who I know only as Ahmad, kept our television antenna, mounted on the roof of the building across the street, fine-tuned in the proper direction. And my regular video suppliers at Hamraa on Shawarbi Street have gone out of their way to help me build my collection. Susan Jelly, Ted Swedenburg, Jacob Arback, and John Calvert all graciously filled video shopping lists, at times having to persuade my vendors to sell recently-released productions at prices that they insisted "the Doctor" would not pay. Walter Armbrust, Israel Gershoni, Martin Stokes, Abd al-Wahhab Bakr, Bouthayna Kamel, Robert Vitalis, Jane Hathaway, Juan Cole, Donald Reid, Arthur Goldschmidt, Carl Petry, Didier Moncier, Rela Mazali, Ted Swedenburg, Yasin al-Khalesi, Charles Stewart, Ernest Dawn, and Jerold Simmons read, commented, validated, criticized, prompted revisions and new directions, sent relevant clippings and/or helped bring sections of this work to print in other venues.

Translations from written and film texts, unless otherwise indicated, are my own. In a few cases where films came with French or English subtitles, I have worked from, but amended, the work of others. On more than one occasion I found myself in need of more native eyes or ears. I want to thank Mohamed Sawaie, Abd al-Rahman al-Gibali, and Farid al-Salim for help turning a colloquial phrase, deciphering a fuzzy soundtrack, and/or conjugating a verb form that Hans Wehr apparently never encountered.

The project was supported initially by the Fulbright Foundation and the Social Science Research Council, both of which funded field research in Egypt in 1995–1996. Supplemental support has been generously provided by Fulbright College and the Middle East and Islamic Studies Center at the University of Arkansas. Former colleagues at the University of Nebraska-Omaha, and current colleagues at Arkansas deserve untold thanks for providing a scholarly environment I have not always found in the academy. Bruce Craig, Marlis Saleh, and Olaf Nelson have been marvelous editorial collaborators; it is an honor to help them inaugurate the new Chicago Studies on the Middle East series. John Sinno and his staff at Arab Film Distribution (www.arabfilm.com) graciously supplied me with many of the illustrations utilized; here's hoping their collection of films continues to grow.

Galal Amin (2000: 133–45) recalls fondly his first childhood visits to the theater, accompanied by one or both parents. His is an experience that many of us share worldwide. What I remember discovering most vividly—and what I am ever amazed by—is my parents' own "encyclopedic knowledge" of the film world, particularly the precision with which they are able to dissect the "golden oldies," from directors and stars down to the smallest bit players (and blacklisted screen writers). I am fortunate to have two addicted fans in my own household. JoAnn D'Alisera, combining the ethnographer's gaze with the insight gleaned from years of exposure to "Early" and "Late" shows (and her parents' encyclopedic knowledge), quickly developed the knack to help me "read" Egyptian films even before the colloquial began to take. And Alexander D'Alisera-Gordon (Iskandar al-akbar), who is not quite ready to really appreciate Magda, Nadia Lutfi, or Abd al-Halim, but who still laughs out loud at Shkuku, Ismail Yasin, and Naima Akif. This book is for him. . . .

. . . And for Suad Husni, Cinderella, for whom I wish I had searched harder.

TRANSLATION AND TRANSLITERATION

This book is written for the generalist, as well as the specialist, the film afficionado as well as the student of Middle East politics and culture. With that aim in mind, I have chosen to utilize English-language titles for movies, books, and songs. All are ultimately my own translations. Titles have been rendered in various ways by authors or publishers/distributors, and this can be confusing: Abd al-Rahman al-Sharqawi's novel *al-Ard* was translated as *Egyptian Earth,* but the subtitled video is listed and marketed—truer to the original—as *The Land,* which is what I use; Naguib Mahfouz's *Tharthara fawq al-Nil* I render as *Chatter on the Nile,* even though the English translator of the novel has aptly dubbed it *Adrift on the Nile;* Youssef Chahine's *Sira' fi al-Wadi* was released and is available subtitled as *The Blazing Sun,* but since there are so many film titles utilizing the word *sira'* (struggle) or the construct *sira' fi* (struggle in), it seems more apt to translate it as *Struggle in the Valley,* and so on.

I have also endeavored to render Arabic names, titles, and terms in a format that is most accessible to the general reader, while trying to find a happy medium for the specialist. Diacritics are not included for any names, titles, terms or phrases utilized. Medial and final (but not initial) hamzas (') and ayns (') are utilized only in cases where they will be of bibliographic use to the specialist: in expressions, titles, and names of authors (the latter only in the bibliography). These emendations aside, I have followed the transliteration system adopted by the *International Journal of Middle East Studies*—except, again, for those personalities whose names will be more recognizable in more common popular literary or journalistic renderings. Thus Omar Sharif but Umar al-Hariri; Naguib Mahfouz but Mahfuz Abd al-Rahman, Youssef Chahine but Yahya Shahin, Hassan Fathy, King Farouk, and Gamal Abdel Nasser. Egyptian films, reflecting their primary setting, urban Cairo, utilize—and have taught Arabic film viewers everywhere—colloquial Cairene, however stylized for the medium. That means, above all, the substitution of a "g" for the more classical and widely spoken "j." Nasser is, thereby, Gamal; and Abd al-Halim's father is "up" a *shagara.* Of course, when local dialect necessitates—Fatin Hamama's uncle in one film is Jabir, not Gabir—the "j" will be utilized. Otherwise I have everywhere—including formal titles of books and articles—utilized the spoken dialect of Hollywood on the Nile. Stubborn Syrian friends and the linguistically correct may refer to Najib al-Rihani and Anwar Wajdi, but to Arabs the world over they are Nagib and Wagdi.

NOTES

1. Muawad, himself, died within the year.

2. Fawzi's career stretches back to the early 1940s. She made her last film in the early 80s, but, ever beautiful, continues to act in television serials.

3. Theaters did not become widespread outside of the main metropolitan centers until after the Free Officers revolution. A primary public sector goal in the 1960s was to establish a cinema in every village (Mahfouz 1995).

4. Mustafa al-Nahhas, party chief since 1927, was Laurel, while the portly, mustached Fuad Sirag al-Din was Hardy. See, for only one example, the cover of *Ruz al-Yusuf,* February 18, 1952.

5. *Ruz al-Yusuf,* February 21, 1953, cover.

6. *Akhir saa,* October 26, 1966.

7. My own informal conversations with women who came of age in the late forties and fifties suggest that Gregory Peck was far and away the most alluring male lead. Their male age mates are less unanimous, but Audrey Hepburn, Susan Hayward, Marilyn Monroe, and Sophia Loren tend to head the cast.

8. The poster, and a brief film clip from the 1951 film, are playfully anachronistic since the setting is 1942.

9. Chahine attended the exclusive, all-boys English-language prep school, founded in 1902, and renamed Victory College after Suez. The school's most famous alumnus, amongst a panoply of cultural, intellectual, and political leaders (including Jordan's King Hussein), is still Omar Sharif (né Michel Chalhoub), although he attended the smaller Cairo branch. For the history of the institution, see the web-site operated by a later graduate, Samir Raafat (www.egypt.com).

10. Chahine, Egypt's most celebrated auteur (Armes 1987: 243–54; Fawwal 2001), is the first major director to have trained in Hollywood, although he studied acting rather than directing (ibid.: 29–33). See Farid (1993: 87) for a photograph of the young Chahine with screen greats Anthony Quinn, Yul Brynner, and Cecil B. DeMille. This is far more important in many respects than Chahine's Coptic background, which is more often noted by foreigners. As Fawwal (2001: 1) notes, "His Christianity in a predominantly Muslim country has not been problematic for him, his clashes with the Muslim fundamentalists notwithstanding." Known for his serious treatment of social and political themes, Chahine's frequent resort to elements of the musical has at times confused critics and viewers (ibid.: 202–4). The staged musical numbers throughout his "Alexandria Trilogy" (*Alexandria . . . Why?* 1978; *An Egyptian Tale,* 1982; *Alexandria Again and Forever,* 1990) all reveal his everlasting love for the grand studio style. His recent historical spectacle, *Destiny* (1998), a politically charged attack on recent religious taboos couched as historical epic, also also contains a variety of musical interludes (see, for example, Stephen Holden, "Philosophy as Hotblooded Adventure," in *The New York Times,* October 16, 1998).

11. Hosted by Ashraf Abd al-Baqi, a talented character actor, the show featured film clips and culminated in competitive charades based on film titles.

12. Legislative efforts to combat these trends have not proven successful. See Gamal Essam El-Din, "Cinema under siege," *al-Ahram Weekly,* 1–7 June 2000.

13. Heba Saleh, "Clouded view of grand design," *Financial Times,* May 9, 2001 (globalarchive.ft.com), provides a recent assessment.

14. "Scathingly original" (*al-Ahram Weekly,* August 5–11, 1999; ahram.org.eg/weekly/1999/441) refers specifically to Fawzi and the more senior Yusri Nasrallah, but fits for the others as well. Ali's *Girls' Secrets* recently won top prize at the Beirut Film Festival.

15. Most popular articles on the cinema inevitably point to the past as an era of classics. One film, panned in a recent review, "is based on the classic tale of the menage a trois, but, unlike many Egyptian films made during the 1950s and 1960s, it falls far short of its aim to present us with a plausible, let alone finished story (Adel Abdel Moniem, "Shaheen film enough to drive anyone mad," *Middle East Times,* metimes.com/2K/issue2000–21). A survey of the National Film Festival, held in June 2000, spoke to the "sorry state of Egypt's film industry." Of seventy-seven documentary and feature offerings, "only eight could be described as serious movies living up to the festival's main goal: upgrading the movie industry in Egypt and providing a forum for serious, underexposed movies" (Maha Khalil, "Festival mirrors film industry," *Middle East Times,* metimes.com/2K/2000–27). Even the recent upsurge in film production—some twenty films were scheduled for the summer 2001 season—is decried for the focus on two seasons—summer and Ramadan—with the predictable formula comedies, action films, and, increasingly, video-inspired youth movies (Mohamed El-Assyouti, "A successful formula?" *al-Ahram Weekly,* 21–28 January 1999, and "The children's hour," ibid., 7–13 June 2001).

16. A smaller, select group of videos subtitled in English may be purchased from a variety of US-based distributors, such as Arab Film Distribution, based in Seattle, and Facet's, based in Chicago. In addition, some Arab satellite television channels that are widely available as part of subscription packages broadcast Arabic language films, increasingly with English subtitles.

ONE

Playing to the People
Studios, Stars, and Social Texts

I was referring anyway to the foreign comedies. As for the home-grown versions, they usually end in a sudden character change on the part of the lead in a facile, preachy manner. That's why the third act is usually the weakest in the play; it is usually written for the censors.

—Naguib Mahfouz, *Adrift on the Nile*

I believe in the place of fine artistry in the cinema, but I believe more in art that the critics and audience both like. . . . Whoever fails to respect the pleasure of the public will not succeed.

—Magdi al-Imrusi, *A'azz al-nass*

Imagined Scenarios

In July 1953, on the first anniversary of the Free Officers coup, a popular Egyptian picture magazine asked several prominent movie personalities how they would film the revolution. Veteran director Kamil al-Tilmissani, who had pushed the bounds of artistic taboos in pre-revolutionary films, offered the grim story of a poor man compelled to murder his own family. Fatin Hamama, a beloved child star who was just coming into her own as a romantic lead, offered a sunnier scenario. She would play a *fellaha* (peasant woman), the owner of a single feddan (roughly an acre), who faced eviction at the hands of a large land-owning family, now saved by land reform. Izz al-Din Zulficar, one of the new generation of filmmakers to emerge in years prior to the coup, and a former officer, suggested wryly that he would direct Salah Salim, the most publicly prominent junta member after Gamal Abdel Nasser, in his by now infamous Sudanese "war dance." [1] Comic director Fatin Abd al-Wahhab, also a former officer, offered either Nasser or Salah Salim reproaching the British, demonstrating that "our movement was undertaken not merely to change Egypt's name from kingdom to republic, but to raise the spirit of all Egyptians from servility and ignominy to glory and honor." [2]

In the most specific scenario, Salah Abu Sayf, on his way to becoming one of Egypt's great directors, outlined a detailed montage of the military operation. He set his scene at six a.m. on July 23:

> The camera pans across Cairo neighborhoods capturing the tranquility. Young lads open the cafes. The camera stops outside the door of a gambling club, focusing on the drivers who spend the night hours waiting for the pashas and beys inside. Then the camera cuts to the armored cars that have moved into position to encircle the central broadcast building. Soldiers and their officers, carrying their weapons, leap from their vehicles to storm the building. We see the fear on the face of the doorkeeper, then Major Anwar al-Sadat as he and two other officers quickly climb the stairs. They enter the studio and broadcast the proclamation. The scene shifts to Montazah Palace, where we see the ex-king staggering in a drunken stupor, still in his clothes, collapsing on his bed after a night of gambling. His valet knocks at the door and the ex-king becomes enraged. As the announcement is read, Farouk trembles. Half asleep, he cries, "Sack the announcer! Shut down the station, so I can sleep!" Then the camera roams into the streets and squares. We see the people who have gathered around their radio sets—in Cairo,

> Alexandria, everywhere—clapping, exulting at this surprise which no Egyptian dreamed possible.

The responses, al-Tilmissani's excepted, all reflect a cocksure optimism. In this respect it is important to remember that in July 1953 the future of the regime was far from clear.[3] Nonetheless, the film world had embraced the spirit of a "new era" *(al-ahd al-gadid)* and hastened the toppling of taboos that had constrained the representation of social ills: poverty, class distinction, political cronyism, profiteering, tradition. Sensitive topics had been broached in the years immediately prior to the Free Officers coup, but still with palliative conclusions. After July 1952, with the blessing of a new regime, the leaders of which both adored and saw political potential in the cinema, filmmakers redefined their roles and eagerly carried the banner of revolutionary change.

This book is about the relationship between cinema—films, filmmakers, and, ultimately, the viewing audience—and the "new era" instituted by the new Nasser regime. Specifically, it is about how "Nasser's New Egypt" found expression on the silver screen.[4] It is not simply a history of Egyptian cinema; rather, it is an exploration into the relationship between film and revolution, art and public culture, national imagination and star power, and, finally, the remembrance of a golden age—or remembered golden age—of civic pride and cultural production.

NASSERISM TURNS FIFTY

The Free Officers revolution will this year (2002) mark its golden anniversary. Nasser has been gone thirty years, a premature victim of poor health, and his close associates are dwindling in numbers (as I write, only three of his thirteen fellow Revolutionary Command Council members survive). The cohorts who comprise a self-styled "Nasser generation," younger men and women who came of age with the revolution, today wield considerable political, intellectual, and cultural power, and have so for nearly two decades. Their ranks are divided, as the generation has found itself caught in a Manichaean world of Nasserists and Sadatists, the latter having followed Nasser's collaborator and successor in his dismantling of the Nasserist political, economic, and social order.[5] Yet as they script and rescript their lives in personal memory, policy formulations, and, in some cases, big (movie) and little (television) screen productions, many recall with ever glowing warmth the spirit that fired their youth.

The Nasser era has become the benchmark for public recollection and debate, even as young Egyptians, like young people everywhere, seem to grow ever distant from any appreciation of their recent history. With a majority of the population now born well after Sadat's assassination in 1981, Nasser has become a particularly distant image.[6] He had been the epitome of the iconized Arab ruler (Ossman 1994: 3), but Sadat quickly set out to dismantle the public iconography, leaving the country with no official memorial. Where images could not come down, such as the soon-forgotten monument to Soviet-Egyptian friendship at the Aswan High Dam, the successor superimposed his own likeness over that of his predecessor. Private icons remained—and remain—in homes, shops, local cafes, but generally under a protective layer of dust, seemingly forgotten in the rush of counter-revolutionary iconoclasm.[7]

Nasser and Nasserism mean many things to different people, which is quite natural for so formative a moment in Egypt's post-colonial history. As such, the legacies are numerous and justly debated, often still with great emotion. Nasser's political experiment never paved the way for "sound" democratic rule, the immediate goal enunciated by the young mutineers. Under Sadat (1970–81) and then Mubarak (1981–) the system opened dramatically, but the authoritarian ruling party, whatever its appellation, has yet to cede its monopoly of power. After the very suspect parliamentary elections in the Fall of 1995, the ultra-cynical noted, with full recognition of the irony, that at least "Gamal" warranted "his" 99.9% electoral victories. The Arab socialist experiment produced economic stagnation and an unwieldy state bureaucracy, swollen with the ranks of underemployed, listless graduates. Yet, argue many, it shone a human face that has been vanquished in the rush to privatize. Pan-Arabism put Egypt center stage in regional and world affairs. At the same time, Nasser's foreign and military policy produced a shameful rebuff from Syria, entangled Egypt in a still-forgotten quagmire in the Yemen, and culminated in the disastrous "setback" of June 1967.

As time has passed the emphases of these varied legacies have shifted. In the early 1980s, as the revolution turned thirty, the focus of public discourse remained the political disappointments, sparked ironically by renewed hopes of democratic progress. A decade later, with those hopes largely dashed and the country rent by sectarian discord and political violence, another aspect of Nasser's legacy—the dream of a progressive, united, forward-looking, socially just society—took precedence. For many, Nasser and his comrades again became the progenitors of an era in which Egyptians shared a sense of community, in which common, enlightened aims predominated, and in which religion did not create barriers (Gordon 1997). There are certainly counter-discourses. The Islamist camp from the outset considered Nasser a traitor, a renegade Muslim Brother who usurped authority from within, then savagely attacked their movement. Sons and daughters of pashas, financiers, and industrialists still regale foreign friends and clients with tales—some too tall—of midnight expulsions from villas and other properties. Some hold Nasserism accountable for virtually every social ill facing the nation, from traffic snarls and pedestrian anarchy to the fall of social graces. Yet, to others Nasser remains a savior, warts and all. The man who opened education to sons and daughters of the lower orders, less the comic book hero of legendary proportions (Douglas and Malti-Douglas 1994: 27–45) than a simple man of simple tastes, a man whom you might have met and approached on the street—or at the cinema.

A fundamental tenet of what follows is that Nasserism changed forever the way Egyptians have looked at self and country. The vision has never been static. The images—positive and negative—are powerful, and many will resound throughout this work: military might complemented by civil defense; factories working at full capacity and heavy construction equipment moving the earth; proud, self-confident peasants, the *tarahil,* reclaiming agricultural land; working women, some with authority over men; students, clean-cut, then increasingly shaggy, optimistic, ambitious, and openly intimate; wicked landowners, traitorous pashas, ignorant peasants, dishonest shaykhs, tradition-bound parents, lecherous uncles, corrupt officials, social climbers, and secret police.

Underscoring a sense of revolutionary civic pride, and recalled increasingly, are memories of a golden age of popular and civic culture.

The Nasserist state promoted and subsidized cultural production on many levels: classical Western dance and music, Upper and Lower Egyptian folklore, cinema, theater, radio and television drama, fiction, poetry, comedy, the fine arts.[8] In retrospect, much of it may have been hackneyed, too ideologically driven, too often in the hands of bureaucrats rather than creative artists. But such assessments beg the issue of popular nostalgia for popular icons, whose faces, bodies, voices, lyrics, melodies, scripts, and camera shots embody an unassailable pantheon of cultural production. This pantheon may well prove to be the lasting legacy of Nasserism, one that lives on in Egyptian popular consciousness—even among those who are highly critical of and working to undo the other legacies—continually reshaping a self-view that for many transcends politics and economics, religion and class.

Hollywood on the Nile

Of these golden cultural icons it should not be surprising that most either hail from the world of the cinema or, if their talents were multi-faceted, saw their careers intersect with the world of the silver screen. The Egyptian film industry celebrated its centenary in 1996, one hundred years after the first cinematographic shows screened in Cairo and Alexandria. The theme of the Cairo International Film Festival that year was "100 Years of Cinema," kicked off by an Oscar-like musical revue.[9] The past few years have marked the passing of great stars and directors who began their careers in the late 1940s, some even earlier, many of whom continued to work well into their latter years. Some living icons have long since retired, but others still appear with some regularity in films and/or television dramas.

The cultural power of the Egyptian cinema has been immense, both for the national community and the broader Arabic-speaking world. The Egyptian media—film, broadcast, and print—has simultaneously shaped both national Egyptian and regional Arab identity throughout the past century, and more recently exerts considerable imaginative influence on diaspora communities that find Egyptian films accessible on video and via satellite television. Proof of this cultural power is the widespread familiarity with the Egyptian dialect of spoken Arabic, the predominant language of the motion picture industry (the exceptions are rare historicals in which a cumbersome "classical" dialect has been attempted, or the occasional venture to adapt other dialects to the screen when a non-Egyptian setting is staged), as well as television and, before that, Nasser's radio. The industry, rooted in the cosmopolitan world of early twentieth century Cairo and Alexandria, provided a venue for established and aspiring artists from all over the Arabic-speaking world, many of the original stars making a transition from the stage and cabaret.

Looking back now, many Egyptians bemoan the demise of that cosmopolitanism during the Nasser years when economic nationalization, pan-Arabism, and the intensification of the Arab-Israeli conflict led to the dispersal of minority populations and a more narrow focus on what it meant to be Egyptian (Beinin 1998). The old films remain a testimonial to that cosmopolitanism, sometimes in thematic content, even more often in the presence of players from diverse backgrounds: Farid al-Atrash (and his sister Asmahan), related to the Syrian Druze chieftain; Stefan Rosti, the son of Viennese nobility; Asya Dagher, Mary Queenie, and Mary Munib, all Lebanese Christians; Abd al-Salam al-Nabulsi, a Palestinian; Layla Murad, Nagma Ibrahim, the comic Shalom, and the early director Togo Mizrahi, all of whom were Jews. Until the mid-1950s at least, ethnic, religious, or national background—always public knowledge—never proved an impediment to attaining or maintaining stardom. Layla Murad almost became a striking exception. In 1946, a year after marrying Anwar Wagdi, the singer-actress publically announced her conversion to Islam. In the early fifties, however, she faced accusations that she had sent financial contributions to Israel, and was blacklisted in Syria. Yet in Egypt her recordings and films continued to draw huge audiences and the young Nasser regime persuaded the Syrians to relent. There is, thus, no convincing proof (and evidence to the contrary) to suggest that her precipitate retirement and Garbo-esque disappearance after her final film in 1955 could be linked to ethnic-religious politics. As Joel Beinin has concluded (ibid: 84–85), "There was (and continues to be) a substantial commercial market in Egypt for star-gazing gossip of this sort, and the Jewish origins of several of the stars did not diminish the public's interest in them."

Likewise, until the mid-fifties comedic ethnic-religious stereotypes, rooted in an intimate knowledge of the "familiar" rather than the "other," were not uncommon. The most popular and enduring of these films is *Hasan, Marcos, and Cohen* (*[Hasan wa Marqus wa Kuhayn]*, Fuad al-Gazayirly 1954). The three skinflint businessmen of the title, wickedly loveable shysters, are played by vaudeville-trained actors (Nagib al-Rihani as Hasan, Muhammad Kamal al-Masri as Marcos, and Stefan Rosti as Cohen) who were fluent in ethnic accents and conventional exaggerated character traits. The impersonations are rooted in an affectionate self-social parody, cross-ethnic dressing, reminiscent of Chico Marx, the child of Jewish immigrants, playing Chicollini, Ravelli, et al. with perfectly garbled Italo-English. The portrayals are neither vindictive nor demeaning, and the real mockery is modernist, with the three businessman depicted as ridiculously out of fashion with modern Cairo.

Even during the heyday of pan-Arabism, the Egyptian film industry remained fundamentally Nilocentric. The studio system was financed by national capitalists, led by the preeminent financier, Talaat Harb, who founded Studio Misr (Studio Egypt) in the mid-1930s. After an early flurry of silent Valentino-inspired desert romances, Egypt's filmmakers, whatever their origin—and they came increasingly from the national population—set out to film Egyptian stories in Egyptian settings, many of them scripted by and/or adapted from the pens of Egypt's great writers, or to Egyptianize Western literary and film classics (Kassem 1995). From the end of the Second World War, when the industry really took off, until the troubles of recent years, Egyptian studios produced some fifty films per year.

The cultural power of the Egyptian cinema is also demonstrated in the "encyclopedic knowledge of Egyptian films and serials . . . and private lives and previous roles of actresses and actors" (Abu-Lughod 1995: 204) that Egyptians and fellow Arabs exhibit, and which extends to directors and even scenarists. This attests not only to the extent to which Egyptian films have pervaded popular Arab-world culture, but to the somewhat limited pool of artists involved and the nature of the studio system as it evolved from the 1930s. A plethora of studios followed on the heels of Studio Misr, and in most respects the Hollywood model best describes the industry. Egyptian film was, as critics often remind us, a genre-driven project. Movies were shot primarily on elaborately constructed sound stages which, to the sharply discerning eye, reappear in countless venues. Neither actors nor directors were contractually bound to particular studios, but most found themselves regularly typecast to play stock characters or shoot predictable films with predictable, usually happy, endings. The statements that open this chapter, one spoken by a character in a Naguib Mahfouz novel (subsequently filmed), the other by Abd al-Halim Hafiz's business manager, both speak, albeit from different perspectives, to the constraints of the industry.

Given the nature of the Egyptian industry and the tenor of international film criticism since the 1960s, it is not surprising that, despite its import to Egypt and the Arab world, few studies of world cinema have noted it other than in passing, and that such mention has generally been dismissive. The most widely available monographs and reference works have rarely indexed Egyptian, or even Arab, film as a category. Initially this was rooted partly in a lack of widespread distribution beyond the immediate linguistic region, something for which Egypt's media moguls may be faulted. Thus, in a 1960 study, one author observed only that "Egypt has a flourishing industry according to accounts, but its work is confined to the Arabic-speaking world" (Rotha 1960: 618). This despite a series of successful entries to European festivals throughout the prior decade.[10] Third Cinema studies only further marginalized Egyptian film output. Teshome H. Gabriel made only passing reference to "Hollywood on the Nile" (Gabriel 1982: 122), positing the Egyptian cinema, not unlike the more widely treated Indian industry, as the antithesis of radical, national, artistic, and above all, critically interesting production. In those rare instances when treatments of African cinema traversed the Sahara, the largest, most influential industry on the continent also found itself confined to the margins. The author of the "Africa" section in one anthology of post-World War II international cinema did refer to "the forty-odd films produced each year in Egypt, films noted for their employment of fabulously glamorous stars, sensational plots laced with musical interludes, and a decidedly commercial orientation" (Clyde Taylor in Lohr 1987: 6). When this critic pointed to several works of artistic merit, however, he situated them "apart from a developed entertainment film industry that has earned Egypt the name of the Hollywood of the Arab world" (ibid: 17).

The appellation, with all its negative baggage, has been difficult to shed. The first major English account of Arab cinema was published in Beirut in the mid-1960s (Sadoul 1966); the second, by Muhammad Khan (Khan 1969), soon to emerge as one of Egypt's major, and critically acceptable directors, has gone largely unnoticed. Recent years have witnessed the beginnings of a reevaluation (Wassef 1995; Armbrust 1996; Shafik 1998), more importantly a willingness to finally evaluate Egyptian cinema on its own terms. As such, foreign and Egyptian critics and scholars seem poised finally to address the conundrum best expressed by Roy Armes over a decade ago. The commercial cinemas of India, Egypt, and Brazil, he postulates (1987: 65), remain difficult to evaluate because there exists "no acceptable critical methodology with which to handle such films." On the one hand, "the sheer volume of material is immense . . . on the other, the fact is that very little of this production has ever been shown outside the national or regional boundaries and so tested against standards other than those implicit in its manufacture." Local response may well have been enthusiastic. Still, "Created for a mass audience and apparently fulfilling no more than an entertainment function, these films are the cause of great unease on the part of Third World critics and film makers, even—and perhaps especially—those concerned to define and promote a 'national' cinema."

Armes, who has been among the first to address the Egyptian film industry in other than patronizing terms, has been heavily influenced nevertheless by the very criticism he recognizes as problematic in approaching commercial cinema. Like others with a greater penchant towards the revolutionary artistic, independent—or at least autonomous—auteur, he seeks out those filmmakers and films that break rather than exemplify cinematic paradigms. The commercial cinema should, he hopes, break free of its "multiple refusals," grounded in the petty bourgeois nature of its majority practitioners, "to look directly and critically at contemporary society, to adopt a standpoint rooted outside the particular class position of the artist, to make real use of local traditions of narrative . . . or to break with formulas designed to do no more than extract a commercial return from the audience." A few filmmakers do break free, those "who have accepted the challenge of working within the industry and who have used its accumulated skills as the basis for conveying their visions." And they should certainly not be overlooked. "Their work in the mainstream of commercial production, often full of immense visual excitement and always emotionally engaging in its use of melodramatic forms rewards re-viewing today" (ibid: 72).

But how should we re-view them, and how limited are their ranks? Armes, not unlike others, celebrates a small circle of artists and an even smaller corpus of their work. His argument raises broader questions of mass culture, globalization, and post-colonialism, especially for film industries like those of Egypt or India. Does the popular, genre-based cinema reflect the ultimate loss of cultural distinctiveness? So argues Indian film critic Ziaddun Sardar (1998: 85), who bemoans the fact that "when contemporary Indian films surrendered their Indianness they lost their potency as cultural communication." Or, as Ashis Nandy counters (1998: 12), is popular cinema reflective of a much more dynamic, interactive cultural process?

> . . . popular cinema creates a space for the global, the unitary and homogenizing, but it does so in terms of a principle of plurality grounded in traditions. As a result, the homogenization such cinema promotes is not a unilinear movement from diversity to uniformity, but a multi-layered affair with the global mass culture which itself takes weird new forms as a result.

Nandy, also writing of the Indian cinema that is often vilified like the Egyptian (or praised only for its exceptions), introduces a degree of active agency to film audiences that fits well within the theoretical framework of "viewer activity" (Naficy 1993: 92), an approach that attempts to "foreground the spectator's role in the production of meanings" (Mankekar 1993: 471; also Ang 1985; Wilk 1993; Abu-Lughod 1995, 1998; Armbrust 1996). If we take as a starting point that the Indian cinema "has a built-in plurality that tends to subvert mass culture even when seemingly adapting to it passively" (Nandy 1998: 13), we can begin to develop tools to look beyond the constraints, compromises, and commoditization of the studio, and thereby begin to envision what Thomas Schatz, defending the Hollywood metropole, has boldly called (after Andre Bazin) "the genius of the system." For Schatz, "the quality and artistry of all these films were the product not simply of individual human expression, but of a melding of institutional forces" (1996: 6).

The call is not simply to take Egyptian films on their own terms, but that is not a bad place to start. Too often Egyptian film has been subsumed within broader, unwieldy constructs—Arab (Shafik 1998), Arab and African (Malkmus and Armes 1991), or even Third World (Armes 1987) cinemas—constructs in which the Egyptian industry, despite its immense commercial and cultural power, cannot compete critically (Armbrust 2000a). There are several other charges. First is to rethink common schemas of periodization and genre designations. Next we need to re-view a far greater corpus of films than is usual, with a greater eye toward historical audience reception, popular rather than critical acclaim. Finally, we need to ground our understanding of Egyptian films and film industry in the very factors that have lent it such cultural—and commercial—power, primarily the star system. Re-viewing each of these categories entails rethinking much of the standard critical analysis of film, politics, and the intersection between art and social change.

Periodization

It has long been accepted by scholars that the onset of the Nasser era ushered in major changes in the content and style of Egyptian film production. Yet, cultural eras, like political eras pass through a liminal phase; they do not begin and end smoothly in conjunction with specific events, in this case a coup d'etat (July 23, 1952) and a leader's passing (September 28, 1970). While the Free Officers hastened the toppling of taboos and threw open wide the limits of acceptable plot convention (albeit with their own imposed constraints), we should not forget that some filmmakers had already taken major steps in this direction. Egyptian films have classically been periodized across a spectrum that shifts from the artistic to the political. We traditionally move from the first Cairo and Alexandria nickelodeons to two-reelers to the first full-length features, produced and directed by a variety of Europeans and immigrant Arabs. Most consider Muhammad Karim's *Zaynab* (1930) the first "true" Egyptian full-length feature.[11] Then comes the shift to talkies, the founding of Studio Misr in 1934, with it a professional Egyptian industry, and the fluorescence of entertainments (with the few noteworthy exceptions) throughout the 1940s, especially after World War II—the so-called "war profiteer" boom—and into the 1950s. When we reach 1952 the focus suddenly becomes political.

The Nasser era has been subdivided according to the degree of state influence and/or interference. A recent study (Abu Shadi 1998: 35) designates three periods: guidance (1952–56), subsidy (1956–62), and nationalization (1962–71). Most critics designate the period after June 1967 through Nasser's death a period of "thaw" in which government censors allowed a greater degree of more explicit political criticism of the regime. But whether this represented a safety valve to dissipate real political pressure or a noble effort to promote more open discussion remains hotly debated (ibid.: 18).

While I generally accept the validity of such Nasser-era designations, it is important to recognize that just as the political situation in Egypt remained vital—and, in the eyes of many, viable—prior to July 23, 1952, with myriad political options promoted by a variety of countervailing forces (Gordon 1989a, 1989b), so the film industry found itself moving in new directions. Without the Free Officers coup and subsequent revolution one can still postulate—or at least not rule out definitively—the growing tendency towards a cinema of social realism, perhaps even a government-subsidized film sector. Likewise, and more readily recognized, the cinema that we can designate Nasser-era did not suddenly transform with the passing of the leader. If nothing else, the legacy of the Nasser-era Cinema Institute continued—and continues—to resound in the films produced, whatever their "political" orientation, by its early graduates. I end the Nasser era from a cinematic perspective not with the re-privatization of the film industry in 1972, but with the proliferation of a series of highly popular works that not only called into question, but boldly decried the abuses of the Nasserist state. That such films coincided with the consolidation of power and re-articulation of national identity by Anwar al-Sadat, rather than with his ascension to the presidency, is not surprising.

The very designation of a cinematic "golden age" warrants clarification, for the appellation has had multiple meanings in multiple contexts. When scholars and critics have traditionally spoken of a golden age of Egyptian film they have covered the time span from the 1930s through the 1960s. Here "golden age" corresponds to the popular parlance of "golden oldies" or "classics," with the emphasis on a bygone era designated primarily by black-and-white production. Others will invert the designation. Samir Farid, a leading Egyptian critic for three decades, sees 1958 as a watershed year, an apex of creative potentiality, after which the film world retreated into convention and complacency (February 7, 1996), while Walter Armbrust, playing off a countervailing attitude, that "serious" film comes only with the public sector in the 1960s, denotes the entire period prior to nationalization a "golden age before the golden age" (2000a). Deeply attuned to what critics too often deride as "the misguided tastes of uneducated people suddenly thrust into the unfamiliar role of culture consumers" (ibid: 292), Armbrust is right on target. If I bracket Egypt's golden age within different parameters, I do so in order to underscore and understand a different dynamic in Egyptian popular culture and cultural memory. A fundamental underpinning of this work is that Nasser-era films constitute and reflect a particular golden age, one that is perceived as separate from what preceded (and certainly from what followed), however blurred the boundaries.

Genre

More than with periodization we need to expand our field of vision to include entire genres of film that have been long ignored, even derided, by several generations of critics and scholars. In a very real sense, to study Egyptian cinema at all in an international context is to study the popular, the "vulgar," rather than high cinema (Armbrust 1996). As noted above, when foreign and Egyptian scholars have turned their gaze to Egyptian films, the emphasis has generally been on the few films, directors, and moments that more closely approach the artistry of post-war European and post-colonial auteur cinema. In their pioneering synthetic analysis of Arab and African cinemas Lizbeth Malkmus and Roy Armes recognize that the Egyptian film industry

> is customarily attacked for its triviality and indulgence in melodramatic excess. But any consideration of its output over seventy or so years shows that it has genuine popular appeal throughout the Arab world and the work within the mainstream of such film-makers as

> Salah Abou Seif, Yusuf Chahine, and Tewfik Saleh shows clearly that it offers those film-makers willing and able to work within its confines as much scope as any other commercial film industry elsewhere in the world (1991: 47).

This is, of course, faint praise in some quarters. Like others who have observed and analyzed Egyptian cinema, Malkmus and Armes share a predilection for the boundary pushers who "rework the genre conventions, invert the cliches, and offer radically new roles to the popular stars of the day" (ibid.: 56). Consciously or not—and despite their comparative respect for the industry—they ignore an obvious problem: in Egypt these films are often not those that have influenced the public. Scholarly myopia is certainly not unique to the Egyptian cinema. In his study of Hollywood biopics, George Custen (1992: 27) cautions us that we "reframe the masterworks at the expense of overlooking richly informative minor efforts." For Egyptian film it is not simply a matter of looking beyond the masterworks, but defining what exactly constitutes a film worth viewing for anything other than diversionary "entertainment" or worth analyzing for social-cultural import.

Scholars with a political focus have discussed in great detail films that speak directly to a politic, regardless of whether or not these films ever attained what most directors and producers seek, an audience. For the closing years of the Nasser era, the two films that have generated the most print are Salah Abu Sayf's *Case 68* (*Qadiya 68* 1968) and Tawfiq Salih's *The Rebels* (*al-Mutamaridun* 1968). Both are intelligent, politically potent, and extremely cynical films that reflect declining faith in Nasser's socialist experiment in the mid-1960s and the crisis of confidence that followed Egypt's military defeat in June 1967 (Baker 1974; Abu Shadi 1998: 11–18). They are, to put it simply, the most directly political films of the Nasser era. Still, whatever their artistic merits and/or intellectual contributions to post-defeat social criticism, these films did not resonate far beyond the intelligentsia. While I will treat both in Chapter 6, I pay far more attention to other films made by these directors that were more widely accessible and, therefore, more influential.

Egyptian critics, with foreigners close in tow, also persist in defining cinematic genres in extremely limited terms: political, social, melodrama, musical, comedy, dance. The critics recognize the constraints they perpetuate, but find it difficult to break out and redefine them. Political cinema, as Ali Abu Shadi, a former chief censor, has written, is a "vague and confusing term . . . because every film is political in one way or another." True enough, but to root this genre he then falls back upon a comfortable convention: "films which engage with contemporary political conditions directly without resorting to the historical" (1996: 110). The problem here for the Nasser era is that with few exceptions—and these appear after 1967 (even if produced beforehand, like Salih's *The Rebels*)—the only way to approach political or even certain types of social criticism was to couch them in historical garb. Throw in an official royal portrait, the old crescent flag, a tarbush, and you can say, as does a character in Salah Abu Sayf's influential *Cairo 1930* (*al-Qahira 30* 1966), "We live in such filthy times. . . ."

Social films are even harder to pin down. Abu Shadi (ibid.: 85) recognizes that the "overlapping of different genres and the merging of artistic forms, such as melodrama, with genres, such as realism" makes this a dubious project. We run into real problems when we move from the realm of serious drama toward melodrama and musical comedy. The problem is rooted in part in the "problematic" nature of Egyptian films. Not all films have the requisite song-and-dance pause-for-entertainment sequence, but many do, even films that otherwise treat serious issues. The latter have been categorized inconsistently in official listings, such as the comprehensive *Directory of Egyptian Films* (also known as the *Panorama of the Egyptian Cinema*) published by the Cinema Development Fund in 1983. As Egyptian films have rewound their way to video format in the past two decades, the taxonomy persists.[12] One consequence is that we do not focus on parallel developments in the industry that are of paramount importance, for example the arrival of a whole new generation of leading men and women who would personify Nasser's new Egypt. And we move further away from serious study of popular film genres that while not at the cutting edge of social commentary, certainly reflected, promoted, and contributed to the promulgation of a new Egyptian sense of self.

This is where the recent work of scholars of popular Indian cinema has been so revealing. Starting from the postulate that commercial cinema is an "immensely successful but slighted industrial product" (Nandy 1998: 1) and that "debates on Third World filmmaking . . . are sadly lacking an engagement with the popular" (Chakravarty 1993: 8), Indian film specialists have taken on both the hegemony of Hollywood and the hegemonic discourse of Third Cinema criticism to defend the popular film as a vital determinant of national and cultural identity. If the "history of film culture intersects with discourses of nationalism in highly volatile ways" (ibid.: 14), and if Hollywood remains the "locus of envy and resentment" (ibid.: 15), we may still pose the question, "So what exactly is there to choose between Arnold Schwarzenegger and Amitabh Bachchan?" (Sardar 1998: 85)—or, for our present purposes, Hind Rustam and Marilyn Monroe or Farid Shawqi and Robert Mitchum—and find a satisfactory answer that does not reduce to the negation of Indianness or Egyptianness or Arabness. That answer, however, is to be found not in the literate columns of an art journal, but in the crowded balcony of a movie house (Armbrust 1998) or, perhaps more apt in today's world, in a smaller gathering around a television set, where a far broader catalog of films is appreciated, albeit on a multitude of different levels (Abu-Lughod 1995, 1998).

The call is not to be encyclopedic—Egyptian filmmakers made nearly 1100 films between 1952 and 1975—but rather to highlight movies, directors, and stars most representative of the fundamental trends in filmmaking that helped define and, in turn, reflected an era. Following on Chakravarty (1993: 10), my choice of films "is meant to reflect both the range and diversity . . . as well as [the] singularity" of Egypt's cinema between the early 1950s and mid-1970s. "The choice is not restricted to box office hits alone but is fairly eclectic, encompassing works of different genres and styles, popular successes and failures, works by established and esteemed directors . . . as well as those by unknown and forgotten figures, products of both the 'new wave' and the 'formula' film."

STAR POWER

For an industry so rooted and appreciated in terms of its luminary players, the near complete backgrounding of star actors and directors in most academic treatments is startling. Anyone who watches half a dozen films from a given decade will instantly begin to recognize familiar visages and voices, and will soon develop a sense of how primary and secondary actors were generally typecast. Thus, to attempt to understand the impact of these movies without reference to players—and in many cases directors—is to miss a primary component of the film going or viewing experience and, ultimately, the potential power of a given film to move an audience. George Custen, who has explored Hollywood's "rhetoric of fame" (1992: 34), the onscreen performances inextricably linked to offscreen lives captured and/or manufactured by fan magazines, publicity agents, and gossip columnists, might well be treating any studio system in which stars are instantly recognized by viewers and their screen personas fixed in place. Implicit in his understanding is the chemistry between leading players who may be or have been married, or who have had an off-screen romance; who may have co-starred in prior hits; who may be making the leap from second lead to star or playing the aging mentor to a bright new face; who may be undertaking a rare role that is out of character or building upon a well-honed screen reputation for decency, profligacy, lechery, or sagacity.

As in any genre-based cinema, Egyptian film "characters are conveyed through iconographical means—costumes, tools, setting, and so on," not least the iconography of recognizable stars and character players:

> Typecasting in the genre film is a bonus, not a debit. It is just one more way of establishing character quickly and efficiently. John Wayne is the character type John Wayne. . . . Other performers like Bela Lugosi, Peter Lorre, and Vincent Price are instantly "knowable" as genre figures (Sobchack 1995: 107–8).

In these regards, and especially the star system, the Egyptian cinema truly merits its "Hollywood" reputation:

> If the system functioned so well, it was because the cinema was a lucrative industry, sporting at the end of the 40s nearly 150 production houses. Pygmalion

> producers launched the careers of stars . . . in the manner of a Selznick of Hollywood. Ramsis Nagib was one of the most illustrious of them: he "discovered" talents, made them sign contracts for one hundred films, and occupied himself with their image and artistic choices. Would Nadia Lutfi have had the same career without Ramsis Nagib? Would Shadia have been so shrewd without Hilmi Rafla? Certain actors, such as Amina Rizq, Farid al-Atrash, Layla Fawzi, or Madiha Yusri even had their own production houses. Specialized publications like *al-Kawakib (The Stars), al-Shabaka (The Net),* and *al-Mawad (Rendezvous)* played a non-negligible role in launching a star. Mary Ghadban, a journalist for *al-Kawakib,* recalls the grand epoch of the journal: "The power of Hasan Imam Umar, the editor-in-chief of *Kawakib,* was unimaginable. Actors feared him most of all. Journalists played an essential role in the careers of stars, like Abd al-Nur Khalil, film critic for *al-Musawwar,* who launched the films of Fatin Hamama with frightening efficiency (Ayad 1995: 136).

Many Egyptian film stars, like their Hollywood counterparts, crafted images by taking on stage names to enhance star power. Common or old-fashioned names gave way to glamorous new identities. The screen's two greatest belly dancers transformed themselves from Zaynab Ibrahim and Tahia Karim into Samia Gamal and Tahiya Carioca (for the Latin dance); screen beauties Fadwa al-Baytar and Paula Shafiq became Zizi al-Badrawi and Nadia Lutfi. Common nicknames replaced more formal appellations: Rose Abu Madi and Aziza Imam became Zuzu Madi and Zuzu Nabil. For some women, single names became the rage: Janet Faghali became Sabah, Fatima Shakir became Shadia, and Afaf al-Sabahi became the incomparable Magda. Men tended to shorten longer family names (Farid Shawqi Abduh became Farid Shawqi, Hasan Yusuf Hasan became Hasan Yusuf, and Mahmud Yasin Taha became Mahmud Yasin) in order to attain a better ring, more star-like, more macho. Some fashioned new last names or changed their name entirely, sometimes to evoke a greater Egyptian-ness, more often to shed the commonplace: Anwar Wagdi was born Anwar al-Fital, Nur al-Sharif was Muhammad Abdallah, and the brothers Husayn and Muhammad Shafiq, borrowing different parts of their lineage became Husayn Riyad and Fuad Shafiq. In the most famous star turn of all, Michel Chalhoub blossomed into Omar Sharif.[13] Part of stardom also included publicity: endorsing products and penning memoirs, appearing at public functions (Armbrust 2000b), embracing political initiatives (al-Hakim 2000), and in some cases leaving the country when greater opportunity shone elsewhere or when political constraints proved choking (Fayid 1999: 47–49).[14]

For these reasons we must pay particular attention to casting when assessing many of the films treated in the pages that follow. Here it is not inconsequential that a new generation of film stars came of age with the Free Officers takeover. Their arrival was in no way politically motivated; there were no purges in the cinema community. Rather, they were the byproduct of the industry's natural turn toward a new crop of fresh young faces, voices, and bodies. By the early 1950s some critics cried desperately for the transition. There are only fourteen stars in Egypt, complained the popular picture magazine *Akhir saa* in late 1953.[15] Consequently, actors over forty continue to play young lovers. Directors have no time to train new faces, and are thus forced into numerous takes. Second-rank players, who claim to be infinitely more talented, find their roles restricted. Compounding matters, too many leading men and women play only specialized characters. Mahmud al-Maligi, Farid Shawqi, and Mahmud Ismail always play heavies, while younger stars like Shukri Sirhan, Umar al-Hariri, and Nur al-Dimardash cannot break out of secondary villain parts. Imad Hamdi is always "the young man who loses his sight or a limb in an accident," Muhsin Sirhan the "husband who doubts his wife but lacks proof," Kamal al-Shinawi the "lover who sweeps the young woman from the arms of Ismail Yasin," and Yahya Shahin the miscast "young lover." Anwar Wagdi, who debuted as "the young lover who steals his friends' wives," has now turned great profit in musicals featuring the child star Fayruz or playing off comedian Ismail Yasin. The article, a snapshot in time of motion pictures, is revealing both for its contemporary critique and, in retrospect, the rapidity with which it became dated as a new generation, both secondary players (Shukri Sirhan, Farid Shawqi, and others) and stunning fresh

Star power in one name: Magda.

faces (Omar Sharif, Lubna Abd al-Aziz, and others), quickly came to dominate the silver screen and to play the lead roles in so many films associated with the "new era."

It is incontrovertible that this new generation, many of whom had started their careers under the old regime but now emerged as stars, happened to be formed and helped fashion over time the new cinema. The changeover was in some cases gradual. Imad Hamdi remained a romantic lead throughout the fifties, even as Omar Sharif's and Shukri Sirhan's stars rose. But by the early sixties he began playing elderly, paternal roles. Concurrently, Muhsin Sirhan and Husayn Sidqi disappeared from the screen, while the untimely death of Anwar Wagdi left a gaping hole in the comic-action realm. Among the starlets, Fatin Hamama, Magda, Maryam Fakhr al-Din, Shadia, and Huda Sultan (born Bahiga al-Haw) replaced an earlier generation of female leads who now became more matronly. By the end of the 1950s a new cohort arrived on the scene, preparing to supplant their elders: Rushdi Abaza, Ahmad Mazhar, Hassan Yusuf, Hind Rustam, Nadia Lutfi, and Suad Husni.[16] By the end of the next decade, Husayn Fahmi, Nur al-Sharif, Mahmud Yasin, Mervat Amin, and Nagla Fathi comprised a newer "brat pack" who helped lead the film industry into a new phase. The same held for supporting players: heavies, buddies, cheeky servants, parents and step-parents, wisecrackers, bad girls. Here the elders tended to hang on longer, but by the early 1970s many had reached the end of their careers.

Star power in Egypt extends beyond the players to include a cohort of major directors whose work, if not immediately recognizable to the average film viewer, is nonetheless cataloged as a popular corpus. In a continuum from Hollywood to the independent director-identified cinema of post-World War II Europe or today's Iran, the Egyptian industry stands somewhere in the middle. Producers, and later state production sector officials, wielded great power. Perhaps not with the ultimate authority of a Zanuck or Selznick, but as the studio bosses and financial backers they could, and often still do, dictate cast, plot resolution, and at times project. Salah Abu Sayf and Tawfiq Salih were each noted for their penchant to cast secondary players in leading roles. Salih, however, recalls how difficult it was to persuade the higher authorities to accept such risks (January 7, 2000).[17] Abu Sayf and Youssef Chahine both directed musical romances starring Farid al-Atrash. Yet, whereas Chahine has always admitted—and demonstrated—a fondness for musicals, Abu Sayf only inserted songs in early films out of commercial necessity. Not inconsequentially, after Chahine's dark, European neo-realist inspired *Cairo Station* (*Bab al-Hadid* 1958) bombed, he briefly returned to more commercial endeavors (Farid 1993: 82).

Still, relative to Hollywood in the heyday of the studio era, Egyptian directors in the 1950s and 1960s retained a greater sense of artistic control. The same *Akhir saa* piece that complained of a limited star pool laid considerable blame for the lack of creative casting at the foot of Egypt's directors: " The director, as 'chef,' is used to presenting particular dishes. So if queried as to a new taste, he replies that he is afraid to try it. . . ." The ongoing debate about the "state of the industry" is complex. Given the far greater constraints of limited capital outlay, even major productions were filmed within exceedingly short time spans, leaving little time for rehearsal or retake (Tawfiq Salih, January 7, 2000). Despite such conditions, a sizable cohort of directors were able to put their own distinct imprint on their work, auteurs working within the bounds of a commercial genre-based cinema.

Within the panoply of glamour, the on-screen and behind-the-camera stars of the fifties and sixties remain paramount in popular memory and ongoing appreciations of fame, fortune, and fantasy. It is a common maxim that Egypt's golden age ended in the early 1970s, when color became the dominant medium. Color had been introduced in the late fifties, but had been used sparingly due to excessive costs (even many black-and-white productions suffered from low production quality).[18] The great majority of works, however, were still black-and-white and, many argue, the better for it. So it is in black-and-white that Egyptians still imagine their greatest film stars, as well as the visual history of the Nasser era. For Nasser and his generation this is the natural shade of the medium; for successive generations, particularly those that have come of age with color television it represents a fount of residual nostalgia into which a vast majority are schooled from a very early age.

NASSER AND FILM, NASSER ON FILM

Movies play a particular part in the lore surrounding the Free Officers coup. Anwar Sadat nearly missed the operation due to a family film outing the night the tanks rolled.[19] Two years later, in late March

1954, amidst a debilitating struggle for power within the revolutionary council, Khalid Muhyi al-Din, the "red major" who found himself on the losing end, claimed to be at the movies when his dissident armor corps met in their barracks with Revolutionary Command colleagues (Gordon 1992: 130). Had he sought sanctuary as an alibi or merely to lose himself in the crowd for a few crucial hours?[20] The young officers had been raised in a world of matinee idols: debonair leading men, femme fatales, comic sidekicks, and enticing belly dancers. Nasser and Sadat both remained active, visible cinema-goers, whose appearances at Cairo cinemas represented an important part of their early public personas, and Abd al-Hakim Amr married screen seductress Berlanti Abd al-Hamid. If the officers did not share Lenin's maxim, "Of all the arts for us the cinema is the most important" (Taylor 1979: 155), they certainly saw the silver screen as a palette for depicting a new polity and society. If they loved the escapist melodramas of the thirties and forties, they later proved committed to promoting a cinema that would engage serious issues, at times proffer unhappy endings, and later, with nationalization of the industry, liberate movies somewhat from the entertainment-driven constraints of profit margins and audience expectation.

It is therefore fitting that the lasting monument to Nasser and the spirit of his revolution may well prove to be a full-length feature film, a meticulously researched epic on the Suez crisis starring one of the great actors of the last two decades, Ahmad Zaki (Gordon 2000). *Nasser 56* opened in the late summer of 1996, forty years after the events it recreated, and immediately set attendance records (since surpassed) for an Egyptian film production.[21] It also created a buzz throughout the Arab world and among diaspora populations who eagerly awaited its release on video and satellite television. After a gala premiere to an invite-only crowd at the 1995 Egyptian Radio and Television Festival, the film had sat in the censor's office for over a year. Everyone had an excuse for the precipitate disappearance. Broadcast officials insisted the film needed further sound work and expressed legitimate concerns about video piracy. Most observers, however, sensed that the film, produced by the state-run Egyptian Radio and Television Union (ERTU) to celebrate a particular moment—and, by extension, an era—of national unity, ingenuity, and perseverance in the face of grave crisis had inadvertently reflected poorly on present political leadership. After a full year of hints—the face of Ahmad Zaki as Nasser continued to dominate the televised logo for all ERTU dramatic productions and his picture headlined festival marquees that remained in place around Cairo—the film finally received a green light and energized a national rediscovery of hero and era.

Nasser 56, which grew out of plans for a one-hour biographical sketch, is primarily a political thriller, with emphasis on the secret plan to nationalize the Suez Canal while Nasser addressed the nation on the fourth anniversary of the expulsion of King Farouk (July 26). Nasser, however, remains the center of gravity, and the most popular scenes are those in which he plays not the committed Egyptian nationalist wrestling with superpower intransigence, but a loving father struggling to balance national interest with familial duties, a common man of simple tastes, a president who one might hail in a crowd and be recognized (Hasan Husni), or on whose doorstep one might camp out and successfully gain an impromptu audience (Amina Rizq). Such scenes, products of scenarist Mahfuz Abd al-Rahman's creative imagination, encapsulate persistent memories of the populist hero, "a man of the utmost simplicity and modesty . . . a man of simple dreams" for whom "the pleasures of life consisted of olives and cheese, going to the cinema, listening to Umm Kulthum" (Abd al-Rahman 1997: 6–7).

A veteran of historical dramas, Abd al-Rahman masterfully balanced the verifiable, as well as the visual detail, with the invented, crafting an historical recreation that is, for many who lived the period, authentic, and for those who came afterwards may well prove to be authoritative. He has also, along with director Muhammad Fadil and actor Ahmad Zaki, whose impersonation drew rave reviews, apparently swept away imposing taboos against reenacting recent history and depicting national political leaders. Nasser has appeared more recently in a television bio-serial of Umm Kulthum, also scripted by Abd al-Rahman (Ramadan season 1999–2000), and Ahmad Zaki has more recently played Nasser's successor in *Days of Sadat* (*Ayyam al-Sadat* 2001), a sweeping epic biopic directed by Muhammad Khan (Gordon 2002).

The linchpin of the Abd al-Rahman-Zaki-Fadil film is the Suez Crisis. Consequently, some have suggested the creative team took too easy a path. Suez remains a key symbol of Nasserism: the bold reassertion of Egyptian sovereignty over its territory and the defiant opposition to the subsequent Tripartite aggression. Abd al-Rahman's script serves a dual purpose as historical text, to recall not only the recent leader and his unified nation at a supreme moment of triumph, but also to educate—or re-educate—the nation about its historical claims to its sovereign territory. A leader and his people endeavor together to address historic grievances and guide the nation forward. As Nasser (Zaki) reads historical and legal texts, queries judicial and technical experts and, in one melodramatic touch, watches a film documentary with footage reenacting the Canal's construction, the film audience also learns of the waterway's influence on Egyptian history and the inextricable link to foreign exploitation. Abd al-Rahman has elsewhere underscored the importance of the Canal to his generation.[22] His celebrated dramatic television series, *Halawani's Gate (Bawwabat al-Halawani),* which screened during the Ramadan season prior to the film's public release and which has been through two sequels, is set in the court of Khedive Ismail (1863–79) and revolves around the complicated politics that produced the British occupation that ultimately set the stage for Suez. At the same time, Abd al-Rahman opened himself to the challenge, taken up by some of his critics, to script a more controversial episode in the "glorious" leader's career: why not *Nasser 67,* some chided.[23]

The film's author is quick to assert that he never has been a Nasserist. A secondary school student with leftist inclinations in 1952, he mistrusted the officers' motives and demonstrated against the regime. He never joined the Party in any of its guises, even though he worked for state media. Yet, like most of his generation, he was consumed with a desire for national liberation, social justice, and dreams of Arab unity, and was captivated by Nasser's charisma as symbol of the nation. He admits that when he embarked on the bio-project he deliberately chose the Suez Crisis because it was the one period about which there is little, if any dispute, and because it was with Suez that Nasser's star rose. Implicit in this choice, in the references to Nasser's modest character—olives and cheese, a wife without political ambition, a simple domicile without a swimming pool, even thoughts of a retirement vacation—Abd al-Rahman seeks to recapture and re-impart a sense of lost community and moral polity.

Mahfuz Abd al-Rahman is not alone. As noted above, while Nasser's legacies remain multiple and ever-controversial, one discourse, an emergent meta-narrative, recalls fondly the forward spirit of national purpose. In a recent stage play that captured much less equivocal government support, Muhammad Salmawi echoed similar themes.[24] *Chains (al-Ganzir),* the story of a family held hostage by an Islamist gunman, addresses contemporary religious extremism and the growing proclivity towards violence in a forthright, nuanced manner. Backdrop to the action is a portrait of the family patriarch, twenty years deceased, an engineer who worked on the Aswan High Dam. His absent presence dominates the stage, a reference point for lost hope on familial and national scales. Speaking to her dissolute younger son, a drug addict, the captive mother (played in the initial run by long-time screen star Magda al-Khatib) invokes the loss of national will and of a patriarch who clearly might be Nasser:

> If your father was alive he would instill in you a concern for your country. Your father was an unbending nationalist; that was the reason for his success—his love for Egypt. He was not only a great engineer, he was a leader who believed in his country and its mission. Do you know how he moved all those working with him on the project? He inspired them to love their country and believe in it, like he did. . . . Your father always said that the real value of the High Dam was far greater than a giant engineering project. It was a test of national will, the embodiment of a cause, a symbol of honor and freedom (Salmawi 1996: 78–79).

Salmawi recognizes the multi-vocality of symbols; to the young Islamist the High Dam represents "apostasy and prison" (ibid: 80). Like Suez, however, it remains a key symbol of Nasserist hopes and aspirations, and our dramatist clearly tilts the scales toward nostalgia.

What makes Mahfuz Abd al-Rahman's *Nasser 56* ultimately more important than Salmawi's *Chains* (and this is by no means to judge artistic content) is that the former is a full-length cinema production that screened in seventeen Cairo movie houses, other Middle Eastern and diaspora venues, then worked its way to satellite television and video, whereas the latter has been confined to one Cairo stage. More than anyone might have reckoned, *Nasser 56* underscores the power of the big screen to mold public culture. For all the ground that television has invaded, including the usurpation of historical drama (Chakravarty 1993: 157; Custen 1992: 214–32), and despite the ever-heightened attraction of the Hollywood product, the national cinema retains its elemental allure.[25] Television dominates Egyptian public attention during Ramadan, the month during which the most eagerly awaited dramatic serials are aired. After Ramadan, however, the theaters are again packed as people line up to see the latest Adil Imam comedy or Nadia al-Gindi potboiler.[26] Attendance records set by a black-and-white historical docu-drama with little action, no sex, no musical/dance numbers, and understated suspense say something about the vitality of the cinema in public imagination, a thirst for good historical drama on the big screen, and the lingering social-cultural power of Egypt's golden age to excite interest. The power of *Nasser 56* is that it presents a history lesson (however shaded) in a medium—not just film, but black-and-white film—that touches directly a popular public chord. Nasserism should be reenacted in black-and-white, because that properly reflects its original incarnation (likewise, the newer Sadat biopic should be—and is—filmed in lush colors). There is considerable poetic justice in the likelihood that a well-conceived, well-acted biographical film treatment of Nasser at his finest hour may become his lasting testimonial, a monument preserved on celluloid rather than granite.

Public Memory and Rushdi Abaza Eyes

Public memory, as John Bodnar suggests (1992: 15), "is a body of beliefs and ideas about the past that help a public or society understand both its past and present, and by implication its future." He continues: "The major focus of this communicative and cognitive process is not the past, however, but serious matters in the present such as the nature of power and the question of loyalty to official and vernacular cultures." In the past two decades, during which Egyptians have been free to openly debate their history, public—and published—memory has been dazzlingly multi-vocal. Vernacular anti-Nasserist histories—leftist, old regime parliamentary, Islamist—all at one time illegal, have

The idol's gaze—Rushdi Abaza with Fatin Hamama in *No Time For Love.*

emerged from the underground to become standard counter-orthodoxies to the Nasserist official history. The Nasserist response, also fragmented, has become just another vernacular tradition competing for public space.[27] Nostalgia in Egypt is subsequently a particularly complex phenomenon. Demographics, the passing of the old regime generation, the rise to cultural predominance of the Nasser generation, and "serious matters of the present" all point Egyptians ever more toward Nasser and his era. The foundations of this nostalgia are a complicated construct of political cynicism, uneven development, glaring social inequities, unfulfilled material aspirations, the spread of globalized mass commoditization and the vise of Islamist and state-sponsored violence.

Amidst all this, Egyptians are confronted daily by an alternative vision. Radio and television waves remain dominated by the cultural production of what was by all accounts a golden age of artistry. The songs, concert and stage clips, TV shows and, above all, the movies that captivated a generation still work their charms amidst all that is new and alluring. Young boys in the street still croon Abd al-Halim Hafiz songs, teenage girls still fall for Rushdi Abaza's Italian-Egyptian eyes. They may lack historical context; in this respect they differ little from age mates elsewhere. Yet, if their loyalties are divided between and by younger—and foreign—stars, they, not unlike their parents and grandparents—who adored Susan Hayward, Elizabeth Taylor, Tony Curtis, and Jack Lemmon—still recognize the genuine articles for what they are. And for what they were.

Cinema is, when all is said and done, when the final cut is printed, about experience. As Teshome H. Gabriel has stated (1999: 79), "Cinema should not simply be images printed on celluloid, but what those images refer to—the memories, the lived experiences, the dreams, the unseen realm of myths and spirits that hovers beyond and between the images." In that spirit, this book seeks to situate a particular place and time—Nasserist Egypt in the 1950s and '60s—within the context of cinematic production. *Revolutionary Melodrama* is comprehensive, entailing comedies, tragedies, romances, musicals, and thrillers. The approach will be both thematic and chronological. For in addressing shifts in genre or plot convention we must also pay diligent attention to social and political transformations. Egyptian film during the Nasser era needs to be viewed against the shifting scenery of revolutionary upheaval and enthusiasm, post-colonial ambition, social machination, diplomatic victory and military defeat, national and pan-Arab dreams, and, at times, local and regional nightmares, disillusion and malaise. However constrained by studio convention and market demands, Egyptian films did change dramatically between 1952 and the early 1970s. At times government guidance set the tone; at other times the power of creative artists led the way. Egyptian films may not quite qualify as revolutionary auteur Third Cinema. The great majority still look "Hollywood," although many creative artists chafed at the bit. Happy endings remained the norm, but an increasing degree of ambivalence is striking. These films did, nonetheless, reflect, and at times refract the changing spirit of a changing Egypt

NOTES

1. On a diplomatic mission to the southern Sudan in early 1953, the charismatic Salim stripped to a makeshift loincloth and, mugging for the cameras, participated in a local ceremony.

2. *Akhir saa,* July 22, 1953, pp. 24–25.

3. On June 18, 1953, the Revolutionary Council abolished the monarchy, proclaimed a republic and appointed Muhammad Nagib president. Tensions within the Council and ongoing confrontations with opposition elements, however, regularly threatened the forward momentum of the regime (Gordon 1992: 79–91).

4. Constructs with "new" found a multiplicity of associations with Nasser's Egypt, arising out of the regime's own early propaganda. One such reflection is Wheelock (1960).

5. A by-now classic treatment is Waterbury (1978).

6. Young Egyptians seem to share the fundamental ahistorical perceptions of age mates elsewhere. This should not surprise, but it struck me particularly in July 1996, the fortieth anniversary of the Suez crisis, when a TV-listing for the propaganda film classic about the war, *Port Said* (1957), described the historical context as if a much more distant set of events.

7. For the idea of revolutionary iconoclasm, see Stites (1985).

8. For a detailed treatment see the memoirs of two-time culture minister Tharwat Ukasha (1990).

9. The theme song was penned by poet Bahaa Jahin, son of the now legendary poet, lyricist, cartoonist—and sometime actor—Salah Jahin. Jahin wrote many of the most popular nationalist anthems of the era in addition to songs for one of the most popular musical films of all time, *Watch Out for Zouzou* (1972).

10. Festival entries do often reflect a particular process of selection, one that tends to favor films that "travel well" across cultural boundaries at the expense of more locally nuanced and, often, more locally appreciated works. In his comparison of a New York audience's response to an Egyptian musical from the late 1940s and a more recent Tunisian "art" film, Armbrust (2000a: 298) has suggested that the latter film fared better "not so much because of its inherent sophistication or its refusal of Hollywood genres but because it understood film festival genres so well." He refers to a unique festival dedicated solely to Arab film, but his analysis holds for general international festivals to which only select films from a select few are submitted.

11. Armes (1987: 197) gives that credit to Wadad Urfi and Stefan Rosti's *Layla* (1927), but Karim was the first native Egyptian to direct a film from start to finish.

12. I have perused catalogs from the major video companies in my favorite Cairo video outlet.

13. Chalhoub/Sharif came from Lebanese Christian roots, and announced his conversion to Islam in 1955, upon his marriage to Fatin Hamama. Nonetheless, rumors persist that he was born Jewish (Beinin 1998: 85).

14. The most notorious cases were Fatin Hamama and director Henry Baracat; neither produced anything of lasting artistic merit or popularity abroad. A different

case was that of Omar Sharif, who, after becoming a major international star following his role in *Lawrence of Arabia,* stayed away for some fifteen years. As he has recounted, "Politics at home were getting more and more tense back then, and I was working with many Jewish people in the film industry [abroad]. In the Nasser days, you needed an exit visa to leave the country, and I was afraid one day I would come home and find myself barred from leaving again. So I stayed away. . . . ("A Land of Mysteries," *Egypt Revealed,* March–April 2001, p.10).

15. They were Fatin Hamama, Kamal al-Shinawi, Layla Fawzi, Muhsin Sirhan, Shadia, Yahya Shahin, Raqiya Ibrahim, Husayn Sidqi, Madiha Yusri, Imad Hamdi, Magda, Mahmud Zulficar, Anwar Wagdi, and Maryam Fakhr al-Din (October 14, 1953, pp. 28–29).

16. See the spread on "Twenty New Faces" in *Akhir saa,* November 9, 1960. Of the twenty, only three (Suad Husni, Nadia Lutfi, and Shweikar) really hit it big.

17. There is a touch of irony in my comparison because in the early 1960s Abu Sayf, as chief of the public sector, represented those authorities.

18. Those I can identify are: *Dalila* (1956), *Return My Heart* (1957), *I Can't Sleep* (1957), *Saladin the Victorious* (1963), *Bride of the Nile* (1963), *Dawn of the New Age* (1965), *Too Young for Love* (1966), *The People's Idol* (1967), *Father's Up a Tree* (1968), *The Mummy* (1968), and *The Land* (1970).

19. Sadat had been recalled to Cairo from the north Sinai coastal base at al-Arish on July 22. Uncertain of the specific timing for marching orders and too agitated to sit at home he took—depending on the story—either his wife (Sadat 1977: 105–6) or his children (Sadat 1957: 139) to the movies. Only upon his return did he learn that the operation had commenced, an innocent mishap that antagonists would hold against him in later years (Heikal 1983: 28; Mohi El Din 1995: 103–4).

20. In his memoirs, Muhyi al-Din says only that he "deliberately remained out of sight," disconnecting his phone and staying away from home "so that no one would ask for my opinion" (Mohi El Din 1995: 188).

21. The comedy hit *A Saidi at the American University* (1998), starring Muhammad Hinaydi, surpassed the Nasser film two seasons later.

22. "To my generation the Suez Canal was the core of Egyptian politics," he said in a special program marking the fortieth anniversary of nationalization on the *Sawt al-Arab* radio station, July 26, 1996.

23. When Abd al-Rahman expressed public willingness, perhaps playfully, he was contacted immediately by lawyers representing the heirs of Abd al-Hakim Amr, who were concerned about how the Field Marshall would be depicted in such a controversial episode (*al-Idhaa wa al-tilifiziyun,* November 4, 1995; personal conversation, April 11, 1996).

24. Salmawi's play was heavily advertised on state-run television. The playbill contained review extracts from a variety of officials, including Esmat Abdel Magid, secretary-general of the Arab League, Osama al-Baz, President Mubarak's chief foreign policy advisor, the governor of Giza, and a former minister of culture. All echo the sentiments expressed by tourism minster Mamduh al-Baltagi: "When a work of art serves the interest of the state, when dramatic creativity serves

enlightenment... and delights the audience... the work is great, the evening is enjoyable, and Egypt is well."

25. Robert Vitalis (2000) argues that by the 1940s, when the Egyptian industry began to really take off, and into the 1960s the local product always competed more successfully with Hollywood than we have traditionally been led to believe. As a counter-reading to the usual statistics detailing the far larger number of foreign features distributed in local theaters, he suggests that audience demand may have outstripped the industry's ability to supply enough Egyptian films.

26. For the 2000 post-Ramadan season, "out of 120 cinemas in Egypt, 55 will be showing Imam's new Hello America.... and 35 cinemas will have Bono Bono, Guindi's new film" (Awad Al Adawy, "Battle of the aging cinema titans," *Middle East Times* (metimes.com/2K/issue2000–2).

27. One manifestation has been the Nasserist Democratic Party, officially sanctioned and allowed to contest elections in 1992. The party has, however, suffered from repeated schisms and has failed to excite any public enthusiasm. After the 1995 elections, the party paper, *al-Arabi,* ceased daily publication and returned to its original weekly format.

TWO

God and the Censor
History and Politics in Revolutionary Film

I'll tell you tomorrow's news: July 23, 1952—"Good Tidings for Egypt and the Egyptians! The Intrepid Egyptian Army rises up in a 'Salvation Movement' against Oppression and Tyranny!"
Uncle Abduh's Ghost, 1953

You may have the Big Man, but God is on our side!
With God on Our Side, 1955

Spontaneous Exhortations

If the proclamations above are scripted inventions, they are nevertheless rooted in reality. Even the prediction of a justly vengeful ghost found utterance after the coup undertaken by the Free Officers in the early morning hours of July 23. Few in power had actually anticipated a military operation, despite a proliferation of signals: pamphlets, manifestoes, and a successful bid by disgruntled dissidents to capture the governing board of the Officers Club. Even after "Black Saturday" (January 26, 1952), when mobs ran riot in Cairo, torching symbols of foreign occupation and elite recreation—including several movie palaces—King Farouk assured the British ambassador there were only "about twelve unsatisfactory officers and these would be got rid of" (Gordon 1992: 56).[1] Now the pashas scrambled to grasp the implications of armored vehicles in the streets, palaces blockaded, a king deposed by "revolutionary jurisprudence," and pledges delivered by a military junta to restore "sound" democracy. The rest of the country watched anxiously, many hoping for a quick restoration of order, others for the unfolding of a more sweeping radicalism.

Egypt's motion picture artists proved no exception. Professionally, they would find themselves buffeted by shifts in the pendulum of power. The first years of military rule were marked by uncertainty. How far would—or should—Egypt's new administrators go in purging and transforming the old order? Was this in fact a revolution, and if so, when and how should that revolution end: with the officers back in the barracks, having handed power to trustworthy, like-minded civilians, or with their own consolidation of state authority? Few mourned the demise of the monarchy, but just what kind of republic did the young officers envision? And what role might the intellectual or the artist play?

At the outset much remained vague. Egypt's new rulers clearly appreciated the power of celluloid images to help fashion the new society they set out to create, even if—as in so many other sectors—they hesitated to intervene directly. On August 18, 1952, less than a month after their uprising, Muhammad Nagib, leader of the junta, issued a statement lauding the cinema as an important instrument of education and acculturation. "When we misuse it," he announced, "we consign ourselves to a state of decay . . . and a generation of youth to the abyss." The following November he asserted that the regime "cannot accept from artists and those who supervise the arts anything as it occurred in the past." The state did not yet intervene directly. Wagih Abaza, the Free Officer assigned to oversee the film industry, met with producers to underscore the need for a fresh start, and noted directors trumpeted their work as reflecting the new age (Abu Shadi 1998: 35–36).

The idea of a "cinema of the past" has ever after skewed discussion of the motion picture arts, as critics and filmmakers have debated the value of artistic production, always viewed in contradistinction to "entertainment." Whatever the film industry was or was not prior to July 1952 cannot be squarely laid on the shoulders of people working in the industry, certainly not to the exclusion of royal censors and the foreign legates who ultimately called the shots. Whatever the proclivity of box-office-conscious producers, it is not fair to claim, as one critic has, that the industry stood as a neutral party toward social questions or even in the camp that stood against the social goals of the revolution, then hastened to "conclude a truce" and martial the emerging slogans of the new regime (Abd al-Al 1984: 15).

Several films already in production when the officers seized power were hastily rescripted in order to insert invocations supporting the military movement. Two of the more obvious—and entertaining—addendums screened in comedies starring Ismail Yasin. A clown with immense physical and verbal talent, Yasin had started out in films as the consummate comic buddy of the romantic lead (often played by Farid al-Atrash). He worked prodigiously, averaging fifteen films a year between 1951 and 1953, many of these in secondary roles. By the early 1950s, however, he had emerged as a lead player in low budget comedy romps.[2]

In *Uncle Abduh's Ghost* (*[Afrit Amm Abduh]*, Husayn Fawzi 1953), two low-level office workers, Fistuq (Yasin) and Ahmad (Shukri Sirhan), find themselves caught in the middle of an inheritance battle between a beautiful young woman whom they meet by chance on a public bus, and her villainous uncle, who just so happens to be their boss. Habaib (played by the singer of the same name), her uncle (Mahmud al-Maligi), his henchman (Abd al-Salam al-Nabulsi), and the vixen who pretends to love both (Lola Sidqi), all search for an engagement ring on which is written instructions to an abandoned desert villa where a treasure has been hidden in a pharaonic chest. The script provides innumerable opportunities for slapstick, including a scene in the unlit basement of the villa in which the villains dress as spooks and skeletons, a routine right out of an Abbot and Costello film or Three Stooges short.

Extra comic relief is provided by Uncle Abduh (al-Sayyid Badir), a small-time newspaper publisher with a penchant for the spirit world. When our heroes first visit him, the portly, bearded Abduh sits hunched over a crystal ball reciting humorous, nonsensical incantations. Snapped out of his trance, the publisher forewarns them that he will break a major news story the following day. Halfway through the film, after his murder at the evil uncle's hands, Uncle Abduh appears at the desert villa—his friends are unaware that he is a shade, but the villains scatter in terror—and reveals the next day's headlines:

> Good Tidings for Egypt and the Egyptians! The Intrepid Egyptian Army rises up in a "Salvation Movement" against Oppression and Tyranny!

Later, after coyly pitting the villains against each other, he shows his friends the soon-to-be-printed newspaper:

> *Uncle Abduh:* Didn't I tell you yesterday about the glorious coup that will occur in Egypt? Please, read the paper. . . .
>
> *Ahmad:* Good Lord, this is the best news . . . the era of evil and oppression and tyranny has ended! . . .
>
> *Fistuq:* Yes, the era of talk has ended, and the era of order begun. . . .[3]
>
> *Uncle Abduh:* Listen, there's more. Tomorrow's news: the Egyptian army will demand in the name of the people that King Farouk abdicate the throne and leave the country at 6 o'clock on July 26, 1952. . . .

In a later scene the three friends sit side by side on a divan while Ahmad reads a newspaper aloud. By now the headlines note the king's abdication and departure from Egypt, and the formation of a regency council. Ahmad praises God and invokes the Quran (3: 26):

> *Ahmad:* How wonderful! Praise God! "Say Praise be to You, God, the Sovereign. You give power to whomever you wish and take it from whomever You wish, honor whomever You wish and bring low whomever You wish. All good lies in Your hands, and You are capable of all things."
>
> *Habaib (looking at the camera):* "This news will make the whole world look upon Egypt with the utmost respect and reverence!"

Fistuq (looking skyward with his hands raised in supplication): Yes, a victory from God, with more to follow!

As precipitately as the scene intruded, it cuts back to the action, setting up the final chase scene that will resolve the original story.

In Ismail Yasin's next feature, *The Noble Thief* (*[al-Liss al-sharif]*, Himada Abd al-Wahhab 1953), the revolutionary insertion is more abrupt, even less tied to plot. This film is a vehicle for Yasin to play dual roles: the classic schlemiel with designs on the pretty girl next door (Shadia), and his look-alike, a ruthless underworld boss. When the gangster removes his goatee to elude a police dragnet, he sets in motion a comedy of mistaken identities. Bumbler is taken for boss by both his hapless gonzels and bewildered gun moll (Lola Sidqi). Before the inadvertent imposture is discovered, Yasin reprises the classic double-Groucho Marx mirror scene (played by Groucho and Harpo) from *Duck Soup,* although here he plays both sides of the "mirror." On the run from the mob, the confused hero returns to his working class neighborhood, where a festival is underway. Whose wedding? All of Egypt is celebrating, his buddy informs him: "The army has triumphed; the oppression has ended; there are no more pashas or beys. The entire neighborhood is rejoicing!" Exhorting God's blessing, the comic calls for music, and leads the crowd in a spirited number. The lyrics capture an immediacy of the moment, the populist sentiment that the Free Officers invoked, especially through their symbolic and rhetorical assaults on class structure and ill-gotten financial gains, and the expulsion of an abhorred monarch.

Twenty million and more were living here as if they were dead.
All for the sake of their excellencies, the masters, the beys and pashas.
Twenty million or more. . . .
The peasant used to toil, running back and forth, all for those who were idle.
And the big-bellied [rich], behaving like bankers in Europe, they would beat any tourist at that!
Spending their money on gambling and women.

Spend all you have, more will come!
There is no happiness beyond his [Farouk's] own, that's because he's the privileged one, backed by the masters, the beys and pashas.
Twenty million and more. . . .
The rich were so rich, owning thousands in cash and thousands of feddans.
He [Farouk] was the master, the others the slaves.
His words absolute, he locked up free men in jail, while the fat rich engaged in excess.
He steals and they say he is honest; he grows larger and they say "Amen!"
And they say he is pious, one who performs miracles![4]
The masters, beys, and pashas deceived him into believing it.
Twenty million and more. . . .
It was an era of corruption and injustice against a good and generous people.
But God, by His will, stood guard and heard the victims' complaints.
His blessing was near at hand; He listened and answered their prayers.
Nagib and the army made plans, and with God's will, victory was theirs.
The people now control their destiny, with a will that defies all power.
We have all become masters—there are no more beys or pashas!
Twenty million and more. . . .

As the number ends, the chase continues to its predictable happy end. The song never became a revolutionary anthem; Muhammad Nagib's spiraling fall from grace surely saw to that. Nonetheless, it remains a quaint, spontaneous presage of an emergent revolutionary ethos, in which such enthusiastic musical revues, always far more orchestrated and choreographed, would play so important a role in coming years.

Production Codes

While the two spliced insertions noted above may appear baldly opportunistic, the enthusiasm for the military takeover, with all the attendant hopes for "an end to the era of talk and the onset of order," should not be discounted. Films like *Uncle Abduh's Ghost* or *The Noble Thief* should be viewed through the prism of the moment, not (despite Uncle Abduh's clairvoyance!) in light of what followed. Nor should motion picture producers-directors-scenarists-actors, any more than any other artists or intellectuals, be overly criticized for caution or hesitating to jump into the fray. If the regime's future appeared unclear, its leaders, only recently becoming recognizable figures, still unsure of themselves and their agenda, the general thrust of their program reflected the concerns and answered the frustrations of many Egyptians, including many in the arts.

The Egyptian film industry had been fashioned from the outset as an entertainment industry, partly due to market forces, but also to the exigencies of working within a repressive political and social order. Performance artists found themselves watched much more closely and faced far greater restrictions than those, for example, writing literature. In 1945 Naguib Mahfouz could publish a novel like *New Cairo (al-Qahira al-gadida),* in which students promote socialism, nihilism, even Islamism, but politics was kept strictly off stage and screen, and social analysis allowed voice only within comfortable, watered-down genre conventions. With the country occupied by a foreign power and direct rule in the hands of an increasingly untenable monarchy (and, after 1936, an increasingly untenable monarch), with rising calls for "total independence," "social justice," and in some quarters "revolution," the cinema, especially, had been heavily monitored from the outset.

The power of visual filmic representation, whether realistic or symbolic, raised red flags on a variety of fronts. A silent-era project to reenact the rise of Islam, with stage (and later film) great Yusuf Wahbi playing the Prophet Muhammad, drew the ire of religious authorities, who preempted filming. *Layla the Bedouin* (*[Layla al-badawiya],* Bahiga Hafiz 1944), a costume-drama set in pre-Islamic times, drew censorial wrath when it was produced in the late 1930s due to the abduction in the film of a bedouin girl by a Persian king.

The trouble was that Farouk's sister had recently become engaged to the Iranian crown prince (and later Shah), Muhammad Reza Pahlavi. The film finally screened seven years later, after the couple's divorce.[5] Fritz Kremp's *Lachine* (1939), a medieval-era tale of an upright military commander serving a weak monarch and corrupt vizier, sat on the shelves for eight months until a new conclusion had been added, replacing a popular rebellion with the restoration of just rule. In 1943, *Those Who Missed Their Past* (*[Man fata qadimu]*, Farid al-Gindi), a social drama about abuse of power that contained unflattering depictions of Wafdist leader Mustafa al-Nahhas and his wife, screened only after 480 meters of footage had been excised (Farid 1995b: 105–7).[6]

Nonetheless, a series of films produced between 1939 and 1945 began to explore seriously issues of class inequity, labor, unemployment, and war profiteering. Kamal Salim's *Determination* (*al-Azima* 1939) is considered the first realist film produced by the Egyptian cinema. Kamil al-Tilmissani's *Black Market* (*al-Suq al-sawda'* 1945), completed in 1943 but banned for two years, bombed at the box office, yet retains historical importance for its grim depiction of wartime economic exploitation by neighborhood scoundrels. It is also, according to one critic, the "first and last Egyptian film to point seriously, in an almost inflammatory manner, to the role of the masses in defending their rights and interests" (Abd al-Al 1984: 14). In 1947, in response to what critic Samir Farid has dubbed this "other"—seriously analytic—cinema, the government issued a series of sixty-one specific ordinances that "hardened" the view of tolerable cinematic content (Farid 1995b: 107). The Egyptian equivalent of Hollywood's Production (or Hays) Code—in many cases seemingly copied outright—these ordinances struck out at films like al-Tilmissani's that, despite the conventional, expected happy ending, threatened to rile more than they entertained.[7]

The ordinances fell into two primary categories. Thirty-seven of the sixty-one prohibitions related to social mores and morals. This category, recalls Mustafa Darwish (1995: 93), chief censor in the mid-sixties, "began with religion and ended with sexuality and violence." Religious restrictions centered on inflammatory or derogatory depictions of faith and the faithful. Corporeal depictions of God's power or the prophets, recitation of—even possession of—the

Quran by insincere or villainous characters, and any satirical or negative depictions of religious actions such as prayer, pilgrimage, fasting, or funeral processions were strictly forbidden (religious figures, however, could be mocked). National and Arab pride mitigated against depictions of urban or rural deprivation: squalid alleys, hand carts, peddlers, the inside or outside of ramshackle peasant huts, or beggars. Consequently, as most critics have agreed ever since, no realistic depiction of Egyptian society—not only anti-social behavior and social ills, but social relations in general—proved filmable. The ordinances even banned direct allusions to titles, ranks, or decorations, as well as any exhortations that served to belittle the power of government ministers, religious, judicial, or medical officials. In the realm of sexuality, the code banned full or partial nudity, discussion of or reference to sexually transmitted diseases, childbearing, or other medical affairs "of a private nature"; similarly, the code forbade depictions of suicide, torture, hanging, suffering, or scenes of excessive violence or cruelty (ibid.; Darwich 1987: 102).

The second category related to national security and public safety. Politically inflammatory issues topped the list: communism or any anti-establishment ideologies; expressions of popular mass dissent, such as mass gatherings, demonstrations, strikes, or even discussions—and certainly speeches—related to incendiary issues like labor rights. Political violence and the depiction of anti-social behavior such as drug abuse were also strictly forbidden. The code went so far as to outlaw the depiction of historical personages and any historical depiction of resistance to foreign occupation, even in pharaonic dress. *Lachine* had obviously taught the censors a lesson. Historicals, if they can even be called that, remained glittery costume pageants, devoid of political allusion.

Despite the sweeping scope of the regulations, some filmmakers continued to push boundaries, and on occasion those boundaries receded. Salah Abu Sayf, a child of Cairo's working class Bulaq quarter, brought to his work a heightened sense of social consciousness and a desire to portray a more realistic, broad-based urban world. Abu Sayf dated his own love affair with the cinema to a spontaneous decision, while playing hooky from elementary school, to attend a matinee (he recalls staying for three features, including a Tarzan film and a Chaplin short). As a high school student he sent a screenplay to actress-producer

Daisy al-Amir, and received a letter of encouragement. Upon graduating from the business school to which he had transferred, Abu Sayf went to work for a textile company, directed a company play (under an Italian pseudonym), and got his lucky break when the director Niyazi Mustafa came to shoot in the factory and wound up talking movies in the young secretary's office. After working as assistant director to Kamal Salim on *Determination,* Abu Sayf went to study film in Paris (al-Nahhas 1996: 34–42).

His first half dozen films fit safely into established genres of comedy, romance, and costume drama. Then in the early 1950s he moved from his "experiments" into "the popular quarter" (al-Nahhas 1996). In *Day of the Unjust* (*Laka yawm ya zalim* 1951), which he co-wrote with Naguib Mahfouz and produced himself, Abu Sayf adapted Zola's *Therese Raquin* into a local setting—and set key scenes in the local bath house (ibid: 68–69). The film marked his arrival as a major director and "a turning point in Egyptian cinema art" (al-Sayyid Sadiq in Yusuf 1992: 83–84).

A year later, in *Boss Hasan* (*al-Usta Hasan* 1952) he went further. The film, which opened exactly a month before the Free Officers coup, concerns a laborer (Farid Shawqi) who abandons his family and the communal solidarity of Bulaq to become the kept man of a sugar-mommy (Zuzu Madi) across the river in upper-crust Zamalek. In this film, Abu Sayf portrayed urban deprivation and the disparities between the poor "who own nothing" and the rich "who own everything" in ways heretofore unseen on the screen (al-Nahhas 1995: 7). Sensing upcoming troubles with the censor, he deliberately filmed a series of steamy scenes as a diversion. A week into the film's screening, however, the censor insisted he insert the slogan which opens the film—"temperance is an imperishable treasure" *(al-qina'a kinz la yanfi)*—at the end, after Hasan has returned to his former life (al-Nahhas 1996: 71).

BIOGRAPHY AND SEDITION

The boldest challenge to the production code prior to July 23 was Ahmad Badrakhan's 1951 biography of the early twentieth-century nationalist firebrand orator Mustafa Kamil (1874–1908). *Mustafa Kamil* followed in many respects the formula of a classic Hollywood biopic (Custen 1992; Gordon 1999). The movie begins with a flashback from the 1919 anti-British revolt as an elderly teacher (Husayn Riyad), inspired by the oration of one of his students, delivers a history lesson detailing the story of—and his relation to—their school's namesake. The script then follows the young Mustafa from headstrong student days to his founding of the Nationalist Party, and his premature death at age thirty-four. Formulaic biopic cliches include a nurturing domestic sphere—an ailing mother (Amina Rizq) who longs for her son to marry and settle down, an officer brother (Mahmud al-Maligi) who is court-martialled for nationalist sympathies—and the dramatic tension of an unrequited love interest, the teacher's beautiful daughter (Magda), who sews the Egyptian flag which Mustafa will carry abroad, but who can never quite be the partner that she—or his mother—envisions.

Punctuated by excerpts from Kamil's spellbinding oratory, delivered with conviction by acting novice and striking look-alike Anwar Ahmad, the film is the first to depict the British occupation, as well as nationalist resistance to it.[8] In an early scene the hero encounters a servant who has suffered corporeal punishment, and who recalls earlier Egyptian resistance to foreign rule. The 1906 Dinshawy incident, in which British authorities executed four villagers and publicly flogged many others after an altercation with a hunting party, is recreated while a voice-over narrates a letter informing Kamil of the event. After the hero's death, the action returns to the present of 1919. Students file out for a new round of demonstrations. As the teacher urges them on, shots ring out and he is struck. Collapsing at the base of a statue of Kamil, he looks up and invokes the nationalist slogan, "You taught us Egypt for the Egyptians," before succumbing to fatal wounds.

Breaking virtually every public safety taboo, the film never cleared royal censors, and screened only after the Free Officers coup, in November 1953.[9] By that time work had begun on several fictionalized representations of military heroism and political activism. The most important example is *Down with Imperialism* (*[Yusqut al-isti'mar]*, Husayn Sidqi 1952), which deals with resistance to British rule in Egypt and the Sudan after the Second World War and through Egypt's abrogation of the 1936 Anglo-Egyptian treaty in October 1951. The film's very title resounded in advertisements in the print media, although because of its focus on the immediate pre-revolutionary struggle, a period that had yet to be sorted out by the new official historians, it soon found itself confined to the margins.[10] The experience of producing, then screening dramatic works such as *Down with Imperialism* and *Mustafa Kamil,* far more serious political ventures than comedy vehicles that were enhanced with political platitudes, underscored the tenuous nature of politicizing the arts in a time of revolutionary upheaval, as well as the ongoing limits of open discourse at a time of political transition.

In the early months following the coup much remained at the discretion of individual officials, either officers or civilians who had officers looking over their shoulders. Anecdotes abound about overzealous purveyors of public good. A song that Muhammad Abd al-Wahhab had performed before Farouk was banned from the radio; so was a religious number by Umm Kulthum that referred to Muhammad as the "prince" of prophets *(amir al-anba'),* a reference that to one official's ears smacked of royalist allusions. Quick protests further up the chain of command led to the reversal of such interdictions, and in the latter case prompted the offending censor's transfer. Umm Kulthum had even found herself briefly on a general blacklist. In an oft-told yarn—which Mahfuz Abd al-Rahman has scripted into his highly successful 1999–2000 Ramadan television serial—Nasser intervened personally, expressing dismay as a fan and proclaiming that banning the great lady was tantamount to inciting a popular counter-revolution. "The sun also rose and set before the revolution. Are we going to do away with it too?" goes another account of his reaction (Danielson 1991: 195).[11] According to Ahmad Said (January 24, 1996), director of the newly-founded *Voice of the Arabs,* the censor who banned Umm Kulthum's religious song was not replaced, leaving radio officials to exercise self-censorship.

The film industry did not fare so well. Still, although the 1947 ordinances remained in place, and would until the mid-1970s, the rules of the game clearly began to change. This is not to say simply that "what was forbidden was allowed and what was allowed was forbidden" (Mustafa Darwish, April 17, 1996). Rather, the regime hoped and sought means to encourage the industry to facilitate the production of films that evoked a social conscience, legitimated the present vis-à-vis the past, and broke out of "old" patterns. Before 1955 this meant primarily establishing a "revolutionary" voice, largely at the behest of ace propagandists like Ahmad Said and Fathi Radwan, chief of the national guidance ministry, and through growing control over the print media.[12] Movies, too, were now supposed to rally the masses to support the regime and its program. But how, and to what specific ends? If most in the industry reacted with caution, they had good reason to lay low—or at least to work within conventional genres in order to test the waters.

God Versus The Censor[13]

Ahmad Badrakhan's *With God on Our Side* (*Allah ma'ana* 1955), scripted and shot in the heady days following the Free Officers takeover, is a particularly interesting example of the problematic: how to film a revolution that is still unfolding. A fictional account produced within the textual framework of conventional melodrama by a major studio director working with a star-studded cast, and reflecting the official narrative of the revolutionists, it nonetheless failed to clear censorship. When it finally screened, two years after completion, it failed to make any significant impact, then faded into oblivion. The project thus raises intriguing questions not only about the process by which pro-revolutionary artists frame and shoot revolutionary events—including classic historical issues of casting and constructing a manageable plot line—but of the politics behind the ultimate phase in the telling, the actual screening of the narrative before a general audience (Gordon 2001a).

Given the complex, often dangerous politics of artistic production in a revolutionary setting, Badrakhan's risk appears both bold and foolhardy. There is no presumption of docu-dramatic reconstruction. None of the leading characters are historical figures. Some secondary roles, particularly palace cronies and a dissident journalist, have recognizable counterparts. King Farouk, whose face is unseen (except in prominently displayed portraits), is never named until the very end. The story is loose historical fiction at best. Nevertheless, because of its particular imprint, its pedigree, its immediacy to the military rising (in terms of production if not screening), and the particular focus of the social grievances represented, the film clearly was meant to be "read" as an official textual history. Filming began shortly after the coup, with official blessing or, as skeptics would later claim, under order.[14]

The Revolution onscreen—the pasha (Mahmud al-Maligi) between young patriots (Imad Hamdi and Fatin Hamama) in *With God on Our Side.*

The film tells the story of Captain Ahmad Gamal al-Din (Imad Hamdi), a young officer who loses an arm in the Palestine War and returns home to organize a coup d'etat with fellow officers. Ahmad is the prototypical Free Officer, hailing from a modest, lower middle class background. But there is a dramatic twist: his father died in the 1919 anti-British uprising, leaving the family to live below their social standing. This is something of which Ahmad's paternal uncle, Abd al-Aziz Pasha (Mahmud al-Maligi in a classic villain role), a man with close links to the palace, continually reminds him. His uncle is also the father of his intended, Nadia (Fatin Hamama), and looks askance at the young couple's attachment. When Ahmad visits to bid them adieu, the pasha chastises him for not seeking his influence to arrange a deferment and refuses his outstretched hand, a premonition of Ahmad's upcoming injury. He then retires into his office, where he phones the palace to report the arrival in Alexandria of black market hand grenades due for the front.

After a series of farewells, replete with promises of a short "vacation," then a panoramic view of Jerusalem, the movie cuts to a combat montage.[15] In a brief interlude junior officers listen to dance tunes on Cairo radio. While we fight with defective weapons, our leaders back home drink whiskey, one comments. A quick break in the combat montage finds Ahmad's uncle and the chief of the royal cabinet, Zakur Pasha (Husayn Riyad), discussing arms sales. Back on the battlefield, disaster strikes when a battery backfires. Ahmad awakens in hospital, muttering about treachery. When his roommate tries to cheer him up, promising a hasty return to battle, Ahmad reveals a political conversion:

> *Ahmad:* Return to the front! I have no business at the front! We'll fight on without weapons. What, so we can be killed by broken down guns?
> *Sharif:* Remember, we fight above all for Egypt.
> *Ahmad:* So we must fight here, in Cairo. First, we must clean up the home front. . . .

Ahmad punctuates his outburst by decrying the high command as "merchants of death" and "thieves and criminals." When he tries to sit up, he discovers that he has lost his left arm.

In subsequent scenes Ahmad and his comrades meet secretly, swear fealty on Quran and pistol, and discuss how to reveal the treachery to the public. They approach an opposition leader, who backs off when Zakur reads him the riot act. Nonetheless, the Senate debates the propriety of an investigation. In the gallery sits the young, maverick journalist, Muhsin Abd al-Mugud (Shukri Sirhan), who takes up the officers' crusade. Based on details they provide, he pens columns accusing palace and military figures of trafficking in defective arms. Soon, a palace courtesan fingers Abd al-Aziz Pasha as the prime culprit. Ahmad tells Nadia, who opens her father's secret office safe and turns incriminating papers over to the journalist.

Matters now move quickly. The conspirators distribute leaflets in the name of the Free Officers that Ahmad and Nadia print on a machine in her father's villa. A brief montage depicts the leaflets in the hands of workers, professionals, and soldiers. Zakur receives one in the mail, as does Abd al-Aziz.[16] When the pasha discovers the print machine he informs the palace. Police agents gun down Ahmad in the street, wounding him seriously. In the late night hours of July 22, while Ahmad recovers at home, the Free Officers secure Cairo. The next morning, as their initial announcement is broadcast, Abd al-Aziz Pasha prepares to flee. Despite his entreaties, Nadia refuses to accompany him. When soldiers arrive to arrest him, he retreats to his study, then returns wielding a hand grenade. Pulling the pin, he holds the bomb aloft, but the grenade explodes prematurely, and as Nadia shrieks, her father collapses at the bottom of the front stairs.

A final montage ends the film. Ahmad and Nadia stand in a balcony window. The king, seen for the first time in full figure but too distant to discern any features except his girth (the actor is much too short), heads toward the yacht that will carry him to exile, as a final voice-over intones the moral:

> And so, the tyrant was expelled and his oppressive emblem torn down. Raised in its place was the lofty flag of intrepid Egypt. So that history will record that this people and this army refused to remain blemished by submissiveness to the tyrant's will which had poisoned their very existence. So Egypt spoke: to expel the king, the traitor, the ravisher, the merchant of death, the murderer, the tyrant. And so the tyrant departed, so that Egypt might embark upon her new era. And God is with us til . . . "The End."

With God on Our Side is replete with revolutionary rhetoric that echoes the Free Officers' early published accounts of their movement. The specific grievance highlighted, the purchase of defective munitions for use by Egyptian troops in Palestine, was first raised in the press in mid-1949 and debated in the Senate a year later. Although in retrospect the matter proves to have been primarily a case of plausible culpability (Bakr 1982: 213–23; 1988: 26–31), the scandal came to define royal corruption and military ineptitude, fuel for an explosive challenge to the integrity of an entire order.[17] It was the topic of the first Free Officers leaflet, printed and distributed in the fall of 1950 (Mohi El

Din 1995: 48–49), and became the focal point of official print narratives of their movement following the coup (Bakr 1988: 32; Nasser 1955: 21–23; El-Sadat 1957: 108).

No one was better placed, politically or professionally, to bring the story to the screen, or to write himself into the script as the fictional journalist than Ihsan Abd al-Quddus. Editor of the influential weekly *Ruz al-Yusuf,* he had raised the clarion call loudest, naming names, spelling out details of contracts, and demanding legal action (al-Quwaysni 1991: 50–126). Like the fictional Muhsin, Ihsan faced harassment, physical attack, and death threats (Abu al-Futuh 1982: 96–119). Thereafter he played a major role in shaping the discourse of disillusion rampant among his civilian and military contemporaries in the years leading to the Free Officers coup. In the months prior to their coup, Free Officer leaflets were heavily influenced by his line. It was Ihsan to whom they turned in the early morning hours of July 23 to help them contact their prime minister designate, Ali Mahir, and he collaborated closely with the mutineers for a crucial period thereafter (Gordon 1992: 33–36, 60–66).

The background to the arms question is the depiction of the ex-monarch and his entourage. Farouk's foibles were the bread and butter of both tabloid and serious journalism well before the coup, even when camouflaged behind innocuous reports and rumors (McLeave 1969: 208–12). After his deposition all wraps came off. Opening credits to *With God on Our Side* note that scenes were filmed on location at five palaces, as well as the Pyramids Rest House and the royal yacht.[18] The opportunity to reenact the "nights of Farouk" *in situ* must have been exhilarating. There is a noticeable verve to the performances, part comic, part insidious that points not only to a moment of enthusiasm, but also perhaps to an uncertainty as to whether to play the old regime as comedy or tragedy.

The royal voice is spoken primarily by Zakur Pasha, a thinly veiled characterization of Hafiz Afifi, chief of Farouk's cabinet, who is played by Husayn Riyad as a devious, omnipotent villain. The opening scene, in which the camera follows him up the stairs, down the hall, and through a doorway into the throne room recalls Kerensky's famous climb in *October,* another ill-fated state-sponsored revolutionary epic (Goodwin 1993: 80–82, 94; Dickinson and De la Roche 1972: 28). The second most influential figure in the palace, Monsieur Tony

(Stefan Rosti), modeled on the Italian electrician and palace procurer, Anton Pulli, is really played for laughs, with an exaggerated foreign accent and a touch of effeminacy.[19] Until the final montage when he sails into exile, Farouk is always shot from behind, an oversized figure with rosary or cigar dangling from an outstretched arm. The few words he speaks off screen are in a shrill, childish cackle.

As the plot thickens, the film takes a somber turn. An important subplot concerns efforts by Palestine war widows to hold public memorial services to honor their fallen. Huda (Magda), the journalist's wife, organizes the ceremonies, which are held in large funerary tents. Nadia, after learning of her father's complicity in the tragedy, also attends. The climactic confrontation between Nadia and her father is a classic heart-tugger. Discovering that his safe has been pilfered, Abd al-Aziz Pasha runs from his office shouting her name. Nadia calmly descends the stairs to the foyer. Her father meets her halfway and looks up beseechingly. They embrace, both weeping, until Nadia broaches the subject of compensating the victims of his illicit arms sales. The pasha suddenly explodes with anger, asserting caustically that the "Big Man" will protect him. Nadia retorts quietly, "You may have the Big Man, but God is on our side!"

Like most historicals, *With God on Our Side* conflates the motivations driving characters and events to manageable cine-text dimension. Here everything is reduced to the Free Officers battlefield experience and their resentment at being sent to the front ill-prepared. That said, images of young officers closeted in a darkened room, speaking in hushed tones at the Officers Club, or composing and printing secret leaflets, reprise the Free Officers' own descriptions of their movement's origins. They are at times portrayed as ingenues: in one scene, critical to plot development, they leave an apartment window open and are overheard by agents of the political police. But there is method to the script. Caught between the corrupt and insidious palace and the ineffective parliamentary establishment, the young officers ultimately find no alternative to mutiny.

First advertised in the fall of 1953, *With God on Our Side* did not reach the screen until March 1955. Given such an artistic and political recipe for success—and for official acclamation—why did the movie sit unseen for so long, then vanish thereafter? Standard screen histories speak only of unsettling "rumors" and "unexpected obstacles" surrounding the film that kept it from the cinemas until leading members of the revolutionary council, Nasser and Sadat in particular, reappraised the film and found it acceptable (Saad 1975: 86; Abd al-Al 1984: 15).[20] Given their initial enthusiasm for the project, such casual assessments appear to belie far more pressing and problematic matters.

First, the story's author, whose name featured prominently in opening screen credits and movie ads, had fallen from favor. After July 1952 Ihsan Abd al-Quddus pressed consistently for a more precipitate return to civilian rule than others who urged the officers to extend their authority. As they increasingly heeded the latter call, Ihsan grew critical. In late March 1954, at the peak of the crisis surrounding the dismissal of Muhammad Nagib, and with the film already on hold, he called upon the "secret society that rules Egypt" to return to the barracks (al-Quwaysni 1991: 136–41). When the RCC restored martial law they instituted a thorough purge of institutions of civil society that had stood against them: the press, the universities, labor unions, professional organizations. Ihsan spent several months in prison (Gordon 1992: 127–56).

Particularly problematic, Abd al-Quddus had written a fictional counterpart to Muhammad Nagib into the script. In the flush days after July 23, with the thrice-wounded Palestine hero as figure-head leader of the junta, this made perfect sense. Nagib was the officer most associated in the public eye with breaking the defective arms scandal (McLeave 1969: 197), and he lent a gentle, comforting demeanor to the military junta. He—or a character "whose performance resembled [his] deportment and demeanor" (Abu Shadi 1998: 170)—was played by the well-known stage director-actor Zaki Tulaymat. However, by the time of the film's advertised opening, even before his appointment as the new republic's first president, Nagib's relationship with fellow junta members had steadily soured and coexistence proved impossible. To dismantle his integrity, Nasser and his colleagues first cast him as a reactionary, amenable to the restoration of corrupt party politics, then set about re-writing his place in the history of their movement.[21]

For immediate propaganda purposes he could be simply spliced from the film's final cut. There are no obvious holes in the scenario or dangling references to a sympathetic senior officer, and Zaki Tulaymat's name does not appear in the credits. Consequently his role in *With God on Our Side* is difficult to ascertain. In one surviving still from the film (Shusha 1978: 98; Gordon 2001a), Tulaymat cuts a striking image of Nagib, in general's uniform and with the characteristic pipe in hand. In this scene he plays opposite Fatin Hamama, who is also in uniform, an outfit she wears on only one occasion in the final film version, an early scene in which she visits Ahmad at the hospital.

If a fallen character might be nimbly excised, the guiding premise of the film could not, and by 1953 the focus on defective weapons raised an adjunct set of problems. In January 1953 the ruling junta outlawed all political parties and announced a three-year transition period of martial rule. Two months later, a court handed down acquittals in the defective arms case, which was later upheld in appeal.[22] In now positing themselves a revolutionary council, the officers sought to rally the nation around a broader consensus that superseded, even downplayed military grievances. Nasser spoke to this point in his manifesto, *Egypt's Liberation* (in Arabic *Falsafat al-thawra*/*The Philosophy of the Revolution*), which first appeared in 1954:

> It is not true that the successful revolution of 1952 stemmed from what happened in the Palestinian War; nor is it true that it was due to the defective weapons which caused the death of our men and officers. . . . In my view, the real cause must be sought further and is more profound. Had the Army officers attempted the revolt in their own account because they were inveigled into the Palestine War, or because they had been shocked by the defective weapons scandal, or because of the attack on their honor in the [officers] club elections, it could not have been called a revolution—mutiny would have been a more appropriate name (Nasser 1955: 15).[23]

Although the film does transcend military grievances toward the end, the July 23 morning broadcast in the film speaks virtually only to the defective arms as the motivation for the uprising.

With God on Our Side merits the distinction of being the only film banned by the military regime during its period of consolidation

(Farid 1995b: 108). As with Eisenstein's *October,* precipitate shifts in revolutionary mission undermined, then buried, the Egyptian narrative of revolution. In the Soviet case, a decade's distance from events did not lessen the political risk involved in celebrating the Bolshevik seizure of power. In Badrakhan's case the revolution's grip on power was not yet absolute. Party line remained very much in flux, and dissident, even counter-revolutionary currents retained vitality. The film had been scripted, acted, and shot in a moment of optimism, but emerged out of production in an atmosphere of "anxiety, unrest, intrigue, instability, rumors, and political intrigue" (Saad 1975: 86). Consequently the performances, even the comedic turns, convey a particular power. Yet because there was no perspective from a distance the film did not age well. When it finally opened in 1955 Badrakhan's film proved somewhat archaic, creating barely a ripple despite Nasser's presence at the Rivoli Theater in downtown Cairo for the premiere.[24]

New Narratives for New and Old Orders

By the time *With God on Our Side* made its way to the big screen, key Egyptian filmmakers had adopted different modes of revolutionary narrative. Sensing an opening after July 23, they hastily began breaking old taboos against depicting colonialism, poverty, dirty politics, and insidious pashas. The "realist" cinema pioneered by Salah Abu Sayf just a few years earlier took off with rapid speed, as he and others began to explore social underpinnings of anti-social behavior. Abu Sayf followed up with two crime-thrillers, *Raya and Sakina* (*Raya wa Sakina* 1953), about real-life serial killers who terrorized Alexandria in the early twenties, then *The Monster* (*al-Wahsh* 1953), based on a contemporary underworld ring in Upper Egypt. Save for some superfluous melodramatic touches, both films underscored Abu Sayf's new direction.[25]

The directions charted by Abu Sayf and colleagues like Atif Salim, Ahmad Dia al-Din, and Tawfiq Salih speak to a growing sense of artistic enthusiasm for a social and political movement in an era that predates nationalization and the socialist decrees. In 1955 the regime embarked on a series of institutional initiatives designed to facilitate government supervision of the film industry and promote higher production standards. Administration of the cinema shifted from the ministries of social affairs and interior, where the power had resided since 1945 (prior to 1945 the interior ministry exercised sole control over censorship) to the Ministry of Information and Culture. Law 430 aimed to reinforce social mores, maintain public order, and protect the interests of the state. Details would be left up to the censor. All films required approval at three stages in order to be successfully produced and distributed: the script, prior to shooting, and prior to release (Darwish 1995: 91). In 1956 the Arts Administration *(Maslahat al-funun)* was founded and charged, among other things, with the production of documentary films. In 1957 the Cinema Development Fund *(Sanduq da'm al-sinima)* was established to promote higher artistic standards and international distribution of Egyptian films. In 1958 the new Ministry of Guidance and Culture assumed authority for the film industry, and a year later inaugurated the Cinema Institute *(Mu'assasat al-sinima)* which was intended to facilitate production at all levels from script writing to technical aspects of film production.

With all the institutional transformations and legal amendments, the 1947 production code remained in place, even as younger filmmakers chipped away at its vitality. Censorship during the first decade of the revolution constituted both the toppling of old and raising of new taboos. Crime films, so long as they did not touch on political dissent, became widely popular, especially in the hands of Kamal al-Shaykh, Egypt's young master of film noir and suspense (Adli 1995). Nudity and depiction of sexual activities remained taboo. Yet, in the Marilyn-like persona—and body—of Hind Rustam (and later Nadia al-Lutfi), and with a franker treatment of obsession by Youssef Chahine in *Cairo Station,* Egyptian movies, like Hollywood and European new wave counterparts, did steam up considerably. The regime looked more favorably on historical re-enactment, on the condition it validated the establishment of their new era. Negative depictions of reactionary elements, serious investigations of social problems relating crime to poverty, and depictions of the harsh price paid by those who clung to outmoded ideologies and customs were allowed, if still marked by a touch of comedy, a song-and-dance or two, and a happy ending. In practice, a political or social film might even transcend traditional boundaries by being situated historically as old regime, via an official portrait of the king behind the desk of a corrupt official or the pervasive sporting of the fez (which passed out of fashion shortly after July 1952) by employees or neighborhood dignitaries, often in conjunction with the old green crescent and star flag.[26]

Politics and history remained perilous undertakings for filmmakers in the aftermath of the Badrakhan fiasco. Soldiering retained a certain place of pride, but now, after a series of crackdowns on dissident elements within the military (Gordon 1992: 109–26, 128–33, 138) and the retirement of revolutionary command members from the ranks, kept within limited contexts. A series of military heroes emerged throughout the 1950s and into the 1960s. Soldiers figured in several notable films, but now as constituent parts of the new society, promoting social reform—Anwar Wagdi as the benevolent director of a girls' reformatory in *Four Girls and an Officer* (*[Arba' banat wa zabit]*, Anwar Wagdi 1953)—or battling organized crime—Farid Shawqi as an unjustly demoted coast guard non-com in *Platform Number 5* (*[Rasif nimra khamsa]*, Niyazi Mustafa 1955). Immediate concerns led to the scripting and production of a series of patriotic combat films. Here military valor was expressed on the battlefield—even if, as during Suez, that field was the streets of Egyptian cities—not in subversive pamphleteering or conspiracy. Corruption, treason, and betrayal remained the primary themes of such films, but soldiers and civilians—citizens—now struggled side by side on behalf of legitimate government, flag and country, against foreign and fifth column elements rather than against a decrepit old order.

Soldiering — Suez and Beyond

The 1956 Suez crisis naturally demanded, and received, cinematic treatment. Before the enemy occupation had ended, government authorities, with Nasser's personal approval, granted former officer turned director Izz al-Din Zulficar and an all-star cast permission to commence filming a heroic tale of underground resistance to foreign aggression. Production team and cast fashioned a script as they proceeded, then returned to the studio to fill in the gaps. *Port Said* (*Bur Sa'id* 1957) opened one month after a more traditionally filmed studio piece, *The Prisoner of Abu Zaabal* (*[Sijin Abu Za'bal]*, Niyazi Mustafa 1957). The latter, billed as "the first film about the Tripartite Aggression," proved a far greater success, even though later critics would praise the realistic touches and raw emotional chords of *Port Said* and chastize *Prisoner of Abu Zaabal* as "artificial." In later years several other movies found their way to the screen, some full-fledged war stories, while in others the war served more as melodramatic backdrop (Ramzi 1984b: 82–88). Unlike the recent *Nasser 56,* or even the troublesome *With God on Our Side,* these films rarely depict high politics or seek to provide analytical background. Each focuses on small groups of individuals struggling and persevering against great odds: foreign troops, spies and traitors in their midst.

Port Said opens to a rousing chorus of the Suez battle anthem "God is Greatest" *(Allahu akbar),* while screen credits roll upward against the clouds. With Nasser's July 26, 1956, speech (in which he nationalized the Suez Canal Company) in the background, the camera focuses in on a dark Port Said street. The cafes are filled with people quietly listening to the radio broadcast. A young boy stops to greet various patrons, then enters an apartment and hugs a blind woman who is listening with her family. In Canal Company offices a mixed group of Egyptians and foreigners hear the decisive statement of nationalization. The foreigners are consternated, their Egyptian subalterns passively jubilant, until one foreigner, a woman, turns to them, raises a glass and offers congratulations. Suddenly people pour out into the streets. The blind woman, singing from her balcony, leads the crowd in another anthem:

> Go Ahead and Nationalize, Gamal—have no fear! We are here, a solid front!
> With our weapons and our will, we will conquer the injustice of our enemies.
> Nationalize, Gamal (3x)—have no fear!
> Nationalize, Gamal (3x)—have no fear!
> Give us the good news; whatever God wills will be.
> For the Canal is my canal, my own right throughout history.
> It will remain mine, all my life, it is our proven right.
> Nationalize, Gamal—have no fear! We are here, a solid front!
> By our weapons and our will, we will conquer the injustice of our enemies.

> Nationalize, Gamal (3x)—have no fear!
> O Egypt, by nationalization let us renew the ages.
> You have been the victim and martyr of the Canal throughout history.
> Today you have achieved your dream,
> O Egypt (3x), dearest of all homelands.
> Nationalize, Gamal (3x)—have no fear. We are here, a solid front!
> No foreign power now rules over you, O Egypt, mother of the Pyramids.
> Your name is now recognized; your glory has become known among the nations.
> Our wealth has become ours.
> O Gamal (3x), your son has now assumed command!
> O Gamal (3x), your son has now assumed command!

The story that follows, patched together on the run, draws on a full run of Second World War and Cold War home front filmic cliches in an effort to mobilize audience emotion.

Action centers on two families living in a popular quarter of the city and a larger circle of neighbors who become ensnared in the crucible of a vicious assault on home and country. The two families have been touched by war before: both lost breadwinners in Palestine. The present conflict, as one character avers, is just another round in the imperialist struggle to dominate the Arab nation. Heading the cast is Farid Shawqi as Tulba, the rugged commander of the local National Guard, who loves the blind Wafiya, played by Huda Sultan (at the time Shawqi's wife). Shukri Sirhan plays her brother, Fathi, a naval officer in love with Pat (Layla Fawzi), the foreign beauty who, despite her earlier toast, works covertly for the British, and attempts to sow discord between the two male leads. Fathi, aware of her political and emotional deceit, has been feeding her misinformation. Soon after, however, he falls in battle. Tulba, who had nearly been taken in, now sets about organizing resistance to the expected invasion.

Some critics, like Kamal Ramzi, have read *Port Said* as a text starring the masses, highlighting communal rather than individual valor (ibid.: 83). Yet, while the main characters occasionally fade into the crowd, that crowd is filled with familiar faces. Filling out the cast are Amina Rizq (yet again) as a steadfast mother, Husayn Riyad as a patriotic cleric who is murdered by British agents, and Tawfiq al-Daqn as the traitorous barber who betrays most of Tulba's partisans. Surrounding this dramatic action is old World War II newsreel footage of carpet bombing and paratroop drops, cut back and forth against scenes of the terrified victims, partisan strikes against British units, defiant residents refusing to be evacuated, and a variety of scenes inside British headquarters, where Pat and her superiors grow increasingly frustrated at their inability to break the resistance.

Given the mode of production, the characters lack any real depth, and the film is marred by loose ends, not least an abrupt resolution. When Wafiya is apprehended and tortured, Tulba resolves to surrender himself. At the exchange point, out in the dark streets, a firefight ensues during which he and Wafiya are suddenly reunited, Pat and her fellow agents gunned down. After a brief restatement of unflagging resolve—the battle is not yet won—scene and film end. To a reprise of Huda Sultan's opening number, newsreel footage depicts the dynamiting of the massive statue of Canal builder Ferdinand de Lesseps. A final title announces "Victory is ours!"

More engaging, although less historically situated, is the action-thriller *Prisoner of Abu Zaabal,* one of the last star vehicles for Muhsin Sirhan, Egypt's Gary Cooper.[27] In the classic wronged-man-in-prison scenario, Hasan (Sirhan), the pure-hearted owner of a small launch, runs afoul of both a rich foreigner (Stefan Rosti), with whose young fiancée he is in love, and Abu Rus (Mahmud al-Maligi), a smuggler, whom he roughs up for improper advances toward his sister. Already partners in crime, Hasan's two antagonists now conspire to frame him for possession of narcotics. Abu Rus has the drugs planted on his bicycle, and Hasan finds himself in the notorious Abu Zaabal penitentiary. An outraged recalcitrant innocent, Hasan does time in solitary, but soon emerges as cell block leader. When a loyal cell mate, Said (Said Abu Bakr), is released, he infiltrates the Abu Rus gang and sets up the boss, who now finds himself in Hasan's block, forced to sleep with one eye open. When the two antagonists finally come to blows they are each placed in solitary.

Suddenly, without warning—thus the exploitative nature of the film, according to some critics—British planes bomb the prison, allowing the prisoners to escape. In the courtyard Abu Rus and Hasan together man an abandoned machine gun, firing at the enemy aircraft. Only after they carry off the wounded do they resume their private battle until, grappling on the floor, they are both knocked unconscious by a second air strike. Regaining his senses, Hasan tracks Abu Rus to a nearby field and threatens to kill him. Thinking fast, Abu Rus persuades Hasan to put aside past differences in order to confront a common foe. As the new-found allies make their way back to Port Said they pass a stream of refugees and enter a bombed out, dispirited city (some critics also lambasted the absence of popular resistance). Hasan is briefly reunited with his family, even lending his blessing when Abu Rus expresses true love for his sister. The next raid, however, kills the family. In yet another abrupt plot shift, Abu Rus now learns that his former employer, who is known throughout only as the "foreigner," is harboring British paratroopers. He informs Hasan and Said, who, now in military uniform, has dropped suddenly back into the picture. Together they storm the villa. Abu Rus is killed, but Hasan and Said capture the foreigner and free his fiancée, who now spits at his feet and departs with Hasan.

Criticized for exploiting patriotism within a commercial genre film, director Niyazi Mustafa rejoined by asserting that this gave the film a timeless, universal grounding. That he rushed the film to the screen, beating *Port Said* to the theaters, suggests that the Suez tie-in was somewhat gratuitous (ibid.). Nonetheless, given the film's popularity, the confluence of Suez with the prison flick transforms *Prisoner of Abu Zaabal* into a successful propaganda vehicle. By emphasizing the connivance of resident foreign elements in the Tripartite Aggression, the film, like *Port Said,* served to reinforce the "Egyptianization" of Egyptian society—the expulsions of foreigners and sequestrations of foreign property—that followed on the heels of the conflict. Both films in a way exonerate the common criminal, who is merely a pawn in a much larger sociological and political game. Abu Rus pays with his life for his proclivity towards corruption, but not before he repents and teaches Hasan a fundamental lesson in civic duty. In so doing, he provides means by which the once naive citizen, now a hardened combatant, can return to civilian life to help effect Egypt's transformation into a more equitable society. Likewise, in *Port Said* the deceitful barber is even allowed to turn double agent and help lure British contacts into harm's way. In this latter film, conceived as the bombs fell and shot primarily in the darkness of blackouts, resolution comes less easily, for the struggle continues as the heroes withdraw into the shadows—and the actors return to their studios.

BEYOND SUEZ—REVOLUTIONARY LINEAGE

Suez heralded a heightened sense of Arab solidarity, a sentiment to which *Port Said* certainly speaks. In the following years several films highlighting this and other Arab struggles found openings in the still bounded genre of political historicals. Kamal al-Shaykh's *Land of Peace* (*Ard al-salam* 1957), a romantic vehicle for Omar Sharif and Fatin Hamama, finds a lone Egyptian commando wounded behind Zionist lines during the 1948 Palestine war. Ahmad (Sharif), the only surviving member of a three-man team dispatched to sabotage an enemy fueling station in Gaza, is nursed to health then aided in his mission by a community of refugees from Deir Yasin, site of the April 1948 Zionist massacre. In the process he falls for Salma (Hamama), who helps hide him from Zionist patrols until, mission accomplished, the refugees move on further from home towards haven—and future battle-staging ground—on the Egyptian frontier. A year later Youssef Chahine released *Jamila* (1958), the story of martyred Algerian resistance fighter Jamila bou Hureida (Fawwal 2001: 81–88), played with Saint Joan righteousness—and a Jean Seberg haircut—by Magda, the decade's second—and more politically inclined—leading lady.

Following this first venture into historical drama, one that was covered widely in the popular press[28] and immensely successful with audiences, Chahine signed on to direct a sweeping color epic of the Third Crusade that was already scripted and ready to begin production.[29] *Saladin the Victorious* (*al-Nasir Salah al-Din* 1963), the largest Egyptian studio production to date, starred Ahmad Mazhar, a handsome officer who had turned to a movie career but not yet escaped villainous secondary roles, as the Kurdish Muslim hero.[30] Here Saladin is the stuff of legend, "the great leader who unites the Arabs and shows magnanimity to the foes he defeats as much by moral superiority as by tactical ingenuity" (Armes 1987: 247). The film's even-handed treatment of heroes and villains on both sides has ever after been over-shadowed by the equation of the Kurdish chieftain, flying the eagle of

Past as present—Layla Fawzi and Umar al-Hariri in *Saladin the Victorious.* Courtesy of Arab Film Distribution.

the contemporary Egyptian flag, with Nasser, the Arab nationalist champion.[31] The allusions, which resound throughout script and *mise-en-scéne* are unmistakable, even if they were, as Roy Armes notes (ibid.), already "wishful thinking" by 1963. In later years Chahine has remained defensive about the film for both its politics and its exorbitant costs.[32]

Post-Suez and into the early 1960s, with a politically secure regime embarking upon socialist reform, more frequent dramatic ventures into more recent political history would be tolerated in the spirit both of national unity and revolutionary justification. Izz al-Din Zulficar's sweeping treatment of Yusuf al-Sibai's epic novel *Return My Heart* (*Rudda qalbi* 1957) became, with the arrival of television in the early sixties, an annual Revolution Day matinee special that for many Egyptians, wherever they stand politically, retains a nostalgic glow. The melodramatic story of an estate gardener's son who joins the officer corps and helps make a revolution, the film features a particularly insidious array of aristocrats and the cross-class romance that had became the signature piece of revolutionary social cinema (Gordon 2001b; more on this in Chapter 3). Henry Baracat's adaptation of Ihsan Abd al-Quddus's *A Man in Our House* (*Fi baytina ragul* 1961) features a different type of explosive romance, one between a terrorist fugitive (Omar Sharif) and the young woman (Zizi al-Badrawi) in whose parents' flat he has taken refuge. Contravening normal censorial guidelines, the film begins with the political assassination—albeit off screen—of a pasha. In *Almaz and Abduh al-Hamuli* (*Almaz wa Abduh al-Hamuli* 1962), Hilmi Rafla's musical biopic of the nineteenth century court singers, the much-maligned Khedive Ismail (1863–79) is portrayed Farouk-like, as a lecherous buffoon, while disgruntled army officers debate nationalist politics in the barracks. Hussam al-Din Mustafa's *Adham al-Sharqawi* (1964), depicting the career of Egypt's most famous social bandit, features the hero at one point wreaking vengeance on foreign capitalist exploiters.[33] And in *Sayyid Darwish* (1966), Ahmad Badrakhan returned to the biopic genre to film the story of the foundational singer-composer, highlighting the musician's nationalist anthems and reusing some of the 1919 demonstration footage from the earlier *Mustafa Kamil* (Gordon 1999).

The 1919 "revolution" found its fullest fruition in Hasan al-Imam's much-maligned rendition of the Naguib Mahfouz classic, *Palace Walk* (*Bayn al-qasrayn* 1964). The selection of the veteran director, "as commercial a director as there has ever been in the Egyptian cinema" (Armbrust 1995: 85), by Salah Abu Sayf, then chief of the nationalized production sector, stirred considerable controversy, especially coming on the heels of Abu Sayf's dismissal of the critically regarded Tawfiq Salih, who had been initially assigned the project.[34] Many critics deplored Imam's finished product as cheaply sensationalist, focusing on sex and music, overstating comical elements, and ignoring the realism that is the hallmark of Mahfouz's work (Armbrust 1995: 86–90; al-Nahhas 1990: 29). Still, al-Imam gave lasting life to one of Egypt's most regarded works of fiction, especially by casting Yahya Shahin as Sayyid Ahmad, patriarch of the Abd al-Gawwad clan. For Shahin, the "Heathcliff" of Egyptian film, it was the role of a lifetime (Ramzi 1997: 361–62). And if Hasan al-Imam devoted too much energy to dance scenes, his choreography of popular rebellion, a ten-minute montage of mass demonstrations by students and women, punctuated by patriotic sermons delivered by priests and imams, and backed by a rousing chorus of the nationalist anthem, pealing church bells and the muezzin's call to prayer, recreated the spirit of national unity in a way that does capture the political sub-text of Mahfouz's novel.[35]

In *Palace Walk* and *Sayyid Darwish,* as with the earlier *Mustafa Kamil,* the 1919 revolution is clearly posited as antecedent to the Free Officers coup. With official sanction, a new generation of scholars set out to study 1919, producing a definitive official account of the nationalist movement and its failings (Gran 1978). If this revolution could be championed as an affirmative moment of nationalist enthusiasm, the "liberal experiment" that followed proved more problematic, less easily rehabilitated. Demonstrators in *Palace Walk* might carry twin banners of Mustafa Kamil and Wafd leader Saad Zaghlul; Sayyid Darwish might die in the film biography after completing an anthem celebrating Zaghlul's return from exile in 1923. But there would be no biopic during the Nasser years of Zaghlul or of any other liberal era politician. The parliamentary years, from 1924 to 1952, marked by corruption and disillusion, paved the path toward the July revolution, but treating them in any way as positive threatened to lend legitimacy to the discarded establishment. Occasional reminders of residual nostalgia for popular liberal era leaders—such as throngs chanting "No freedom since you," at the funeral in 1965 of former Wafd chief and four-time prime minister Mustafa al-Nahhas—only served to insure they would not get their cinematic due.[36]

Struggle against the old order, domestic or foreign, passed censorial muster so long as it could not be taken as subterfuge for contemporary concerns. A political assassin might even be romanticized, especially if he was Omar Sharif, so long as the film could be read only as historical fiction. Still, directors, even the politically powerful Salah Abu Sayf, acted with caution. Naguib Mahfouz's 1949 novel *The Beginning and the End (al-Bidaya wa al-nihaya)* makes no specific reference to particular events. At the outset of his highly regarded 1961 adaptation, however, Abu Sayf decided to overlay the year 1936 and create dialogue making several references to the stranglehold of British occupation (al-Nahhas 1990: 158).[37] The tenuousness of historical referencing could become more complex when a sophisticated text fell into the hands of artists who sensed an opportunity to turn history not into hagiography, a la *Saladin,* but rather into a backdrop for persistent political woes.

Cairo 1930s/1960s

Cairo 1930, Salah Abu Sayf's complex, open-ended adaptation of Mahfouz's 1945 novel, *New Cairo*—a novel which did contain specific political and historical references—poses such matters to dramatic effect. The director claimed long-term interest in an adaptation dating back to the start of his career in the late 1940s. Four times old regime censors rejected his bid, and Mahfouz, when serving as chief censor in the early sixties, also counseled against the project. Finally, in 1964 Abu Sayf secured approval to film a scenario that had originated in the scriptwriting division of the Cinema Institute and then worked its way through the hands of several leading writers, including the well-known leftist intellectual Lutfi al-Khuli, who provided dialogue, and veteran scenarist Ali al-Zirqani, who deserves primary credit for both the initial schema and finished product. To create a coherent script from a novel that focused on four Cairo University students—and to get past the censor—al-Zirqani and Abu Sayf all but eliminated the character of Maamun Radwan due to his Muslim Brotherhood leanings (Radwan appears in the background only in several early scenes and disappears thereafter). They also changed their working title from "Scandal in Cairo" *(Fadiha fi al-Qahira)* to *Cairo 1930,* setting time and place unquestionably—even with period costume and narrative references—in the liberal era (al-Nahhas 1996: 152–53; Rida al-Tayyar in Yusuf 1992: 325–26).

The script focuses on two of the four students, the socialist dreamer, Ali Taha, and the nihilistic Mahgub Abd al-Daim, who eventually becomes the novel's axis. Abu Sayf maintained that Egypt's socialist orientation mandated that he forefront Ali, whose ideological leanings he nevertheless supported (al-Nahhas 1990: 124). In the opening scene the young socialist dominates a philosophical conversation between three friends on campus; at the conclusion he foils the political police, avoiding an assassin by taking refuge in a crowd and managing to throw an armload of subversive leaflets into the air. This finale is, as one critic has suggested, "one of the most clever open endings in Arab cinema" (Ridda al-Tayyar in Yusuf 1992: 326). This because novel and film really focus on Mahgub, a problematic character who is at once the product of social corruption and his own inner being.[38] A child of poverty who scorns ideology—his philosophical watchword is "phooey" (or "crap"/*tuz*)—Mahgub finds himself forced to cower before Salim al-Ikhshidi, a successful village boy only a few years his senior who has patronage to dispense. After being handed a series of insulting journalistic assignments, Mahgub is then contracted in marriage to Ihsan, Ali's old girl friend, now the mistress of Salim's boss, Qasim Bey. The arrangement is one of mutual, if corrupting, convenience for all concerned. Poor and desperate to escape her vulgar, greedy parents, Ihsan abandons her true love and allows the rich Qasim to seduce her in an artful scene backed by hot stripper music that cuts between Ihsan preening in front of a mirror and Qasim preparing drinks and delicately slicing fruit.

While Abu Sayf's film lends Mahgub—as well as Ihsan and even Qasim Bey—more humanity than in the original text, the depiction of politics and society is marked by bold negativism.[39] Ihsan's impoverished parents, displeased with her potential engagement to a socially conscious, poor student, sink as low as Egypt's elites, who buy and sell mistresses as easily as political appointments. Yet the strength of the film is that the shared torment of Mahgub and Ihsan, who are thrown together by coincidence after a series of uncomfortable early encounters when she is Ali's girl and he leers a bit too openly (and in one scene gropes her), ultimately makes them sympathetic characters, whatever their ethical transgressions. When Qasim Bey becomes a cabinet minister (the background politics involve the restoration of the 1923 constitution in 1933 after a wave of political demonstrations), Mahgub displaces Salim as office director. His star seems on the rise, but shortly thereafter, Qasim's wife tracks the bey to Ihsan's bedroom and creates a public scandal that threatens to bring them all down. Distraught, yet cynically optimistic, Mahgub assures Ihsan that all will be well. "We live in such filthy times," he proclaims. "And the filthiest prevail!" The film then cuts abruptly to Ali's escape from the political police, a last-second suggestion, a bit forced, perhaps to pass the censor, that the struggle for good will continue. The closing title, "The Beginning of the End," suggests an effort to look ahead to July 1952, and to officially posit the story one last time in a comfortable past.

So is this history or contemporary criticism? The fact that the Free Officers coup is still another twenty years in the future dampens the euphoria of Ali's momentary triumph. Mahgub and Ihsan—and even Qasim Bey for that matter—actually might not suffer too much ignominy in the immediate present. Viewed less as history than as a contemporary moral fable, however, *Cairo 1930* becomes a powerful call not for Ali's socialist revolution—or even the overthrow of the old regime—but for cleansing Nasser's socialist experiment, the 1952 revolution itself. In this light, the character of the fourth friend, a self-proclaimed observer rather than a partisan, proves equally, if not more disturbing than Mahgub. A journalist with Wafdist sympathies, Ahmad seems a right-thinking, loyal, if somewhat timid friend who cautions Ali about police reprisals and, at the same time, maintains amiable relations with Mahgub. In private, his criticism of the state of the nation differs little from the others'. Yet, when the police raid Ali's office during one of his visits, he fails the test of friendship, attempting to extricate himself from the situation as an innocent apolitical bystander. If in the novel he leans towards the Wafd, in the Nasser-era movie he signifies more the "crisis of the intellectuals," criticized as fellow travelers with minimal commitments to regime, revolution, and nation.[40]

Part of the power of Abu Sayf's film resides in his unconventional casting. For the leading male roles the director selected three new faces: Hamdi Ahmad (Ali), Abd al-Aziz al-Makiwi (Mahgub), and Ahmad Tawfiq (Salim). The appearance of new players in an industry so dominated by the usual stars still lends a freshness to the film that few others can convey. None of the three leading men became major players, and Hamdi Ahmad never appeared onscreen again. Abu Sayf, who always championed rising talent, surrounded the three novices with major players (Sami al-Salamuni in ibid.: 318–19). Suad Husni, first in a breed of younger, harder-edged actresses who—unlike, say, Magda or Fatin Hamama—played good and bad girls with equal pluck, took the role of Ihsan. Ahmad Mazhar, by now a romantic lead, undertook a rare secondary role as Qasim Bey. The casting of Abd al-Munim Ibrahim, a comical character actor with penchant for fast talk, as Ahmad underscores his negative positioning relative to his friends.[41]

Cairo 1950s-1960s

A year after *Cairo 1930* hit the theaters, Hussam al-Din Mustafa brought to the screen a more recent Mahfouz novel that treated contemporary, rather than pre-revolutionary politics, albeit indirectly. *Autumn Quail* (*al-Siman wa al-kharif* 1967) is an elegy to an old regime politician with no place in the new society. Isa al-Dabagh (Mahmud Mursi) represents the young generation of parliamentarians who, blocked from advancement in party ranks by an entrenched old guard (Gordon 1989a), suddenly found themselves cast aside by the tides of revolution. In the opening of the film he serves as under-secretary in the last Wafd government (1950–52). He is seen first accepting a bribe, then, in a somewhat surreal scene, parlaying with nationalist guerillas in the Suez Canal zone. The frustrated fighters, supported through back channels by the government, demand sufficient armaments to carry out attacks on British targets. Action then shifts abruptly to Cairo. It is Black Saturday; Isa dismounts a train to find the city aflame, its citizens milling around robot-like. Making his way home, he meets his cousin Hasan (Abd Allah Ghayth), and the two argue politics. Hasan supports the anti-establishment and will be revealed later to be on good terms with the Free Officers. In a succeeding scene, shots of tanks rolling through the streets signal the military take over.

As in the novel, perhaps more so here, Isa proves to be a tragic character, caught between establishment, party loyalty, and an honest desire to work with progressive forces. He sparks only astonishment when he suggests to his senior minister, a cigar-puffing pasha lounging on the beach in Alexandria, that the party support the officers. Another quick cut places Isa before the purge committee founded after the Free Officers coup to root out parliamentary villains (Gordon 1992: 68–75). A hand-held camera closes in on faces, then wavers, creating a sensation of disorientation as Isa swoons, the indictment ringing in his ears. Romantic ignominy follows, as his fiancée throws him over for his cousin.

His career and personal future ruined, Isa retreats to Alexandria. Sitting drunk under the downtown statue of Saad Zaghlul, he encounters Riri (Nadia Lutfi), a prostitute with a heart of gold. After exchanging silent glances with the statue, he is distracted by a shadow, then framed by Riri's legs, exposed by a mini-skirt.[42] The two embark on a wild romance until Riri informs him of her pregnancy. Isa reacts violently, and ends the relationship. His life spirals further downward until the Suez crisis, when he volunteers for military drill and is reunited with Hasan at boot camp. After the war he gets married, but things devolve and he eventually regains contact with Riri. In the book, Isa finds Riri contentedly married to a kind older man who has adopted their daughter. When he tries to reestablish contact, she rebuffs him. Brooding again under the statue of Saad Zaghlul, he encounters a young revolutionary whom he had once interrogated. Surprisingly, the man greets him and tries to initiate a discussion of fate and politics. Initially dismissive, Isa suddenly changes his mind and chases after the young man. The film ends in a more uplifting, resolute manner. Isa sits morose under Zaghlul's gaze, but now he again encounters Riri and their daughter, and reconciles with them.

Mustafa's film, echoing Mahfouz's novel, resounds with ambivalence about the revolutionary project. Isa remains a troubling anti-hero. His corruption as an old regime grandee is undeniable; at the same time he is too young, virile and potentially productive to be banished to the fringes of society. Hasan, who jumps in and out of the action, a man of the revolution who lusts after, then steals Isa's fiancée, an unlikeable spoiled rich girl, proves equally problematic. Rasheed El-Enany (1993: 105) suggests that the novel be read, at least in part, as a criticism of the Nasserist penchant to adopt the trappings of the old regime elite. This, he holds, is contrary to the earlier, standard reading that had more simply highlighted Isa's lost footing in a society that had legitimately usurped power from and displaced the old regime. His re-reading of the book fits well with the timing and tenor of the movie. Isa is a character of many faults. Yet he proves a real patriot when the need arises. His boot camp reunion with Hasan highlights the unifying force of Suez, allowing both "sides" to share in the spirited defense of homeland—and system. And his final acceptance of his daughter and lover, which allows the film a happy ending, marks him at once as fallen and uplifted, in a strange way progressive.

Monuments

Twice in *Autumn Quail,* and especially at the end of the film, Isa al-Dabagh sits at the foot of the towering statue of Saad Zaghlul that dominates the sea front of Alexandria's business district. Zaghlul's was one of many pre-revolutionary monuments, both in Alexandria and Cairo, spared the fate of revolutionary iconoclasm in Egypt's two major cities. Uneasy reminders of an unflagging past, such monuments remained troubled "sites of memory" (Nora 1989) throughout the Nasser era. As such, they exemplify the uneasy relationship between the progenitors of Egypt's two twentieth-century nationalist revolutions. If liberal sites were generally spared, royal sites and symbols were either eradicated or appropriated. The statue of Farouk's father, Fuad I, destined for Ismailia (renamed Liberation) Square, stayed in mothballs. The royal anthem, the march from *Aida,* was replaced by a variety of patriotic anthems. Fuad I Avenue became July 26 Street, and Farouk's boulevard was renamed for the Army. But what of those sites already printed on celluloid, particularly the royal portraits that hung in studio sets—of government offices, courtrooms, police stations—in countless dramas?

At some point after consolidation of the revolution and prior to Farouk's death in 1965 censors working for the new regime thought to ban filmed royal portraiture outright. They first spliced the king out of, or darkened the background in, pre-revolutionary films earmarked for export. With the arrival of television and the instant recycling of old films into the rerun mill, Farouk was blacked out for local viewers as well (Mumtaz 1985: 38). However, for new films, from the first politically charged nationalist dramas to the more subtle films of the sixties, rather than disappear, Farouk's visage shifted context.

The monarch, who once looked on benevolently in government offices, courtrooms, and police stations, now hung stage center as an evil icon utilized to identify villainous characters and odious actions, as well as to mark the historical divide. Abd al-Aziz Pasha, the war profiteer in *With God on Our Side,* concludes his shady business dealings and later informs on his nephew from a darkened home study in which the royal portrait hangs prominently. In Anwar Wagdi's *Daughter of Nobility* (*Bint al-akabir* 1953; a film that will be discussed in Chapter 3), the royal portrait oversees the futile attempts of a lawyer to convince the commoner hero to abandon his romantic involvement with the pasha's daughter. In Salah Abu Sayf's *The Thug* (*al-Futuwwa* 1957), an apolitical and potentially ahistorical sociological study of power and corruption in an agricultural market, the king's portrait frames the passing of a bribe. A decade later, when Isa al-Dabagh accepts a bribe in the opening scene of *Autumn Quail,* the act is again framed by an official portrait of King Farouk, who stares approvingly in the background, already a common touch in films that either treated or wanted to appear to treat the old regime.

Portraits of Nasser, or any other Free Officer, remain strikingly absent from post-1952 films. When miscarriages of justice occur in a contemporary context, such as the investigation and sentencing of the innocent Hasan Sharif in *The Prisoner of Abu Zaabal,* the camera focuses down on the officials or shoots over their shoulders at the victim, literally avoiding the inevitable portrait of power. A rare exception to this rule occurs in *Port Said,* a film that foregrounds the leader in ways heretofore and generally thereafter unseen. The scene, filmed in the safety of a Cairo studio, intrudes upon the narrative which has until this point focused on the partisans' neighborhood and the unsuccessful efforts by the British to crush resistance. Suddenly British and French officials visit an Egyptian government official to demand the city's surrender. When the Egyptian (a cameo by Sirag Munir) politely refuses, a foreign officer asks about the portrait hanging on the wall behind him. "Is that your Colonel Nasser?" he asks sarcastically. Informed he is asking about the "president of an independent Egypt," the British officer suggests it be removed. "You think you can take this picture down here, but you cannot remove it from the hearts of twenty-three million Egyptians or eighty million Arabs," the Egyptian responds. As the foreign officers withdraw, the camera remains fixed on the portrait. Nasser looks forward, the new icon of popular will. Twenty million or more.

Port Said is one of a small number of films from the revolution's first decade that treat the contemporary moment openly, with a foreign enemy as dramatic antagonist. The utilization of his speech to open the film, the hagiographic anthem that brackets the action, and his official portrait in this short scene, a moment of high-level politics in a film that otherwise treats grass-roots guerilla activity, all herald Nasser's arrival as the man of the people, hero of the Egyptians and the Arabs. With only the rarest exception—one is the 1960 Suez war film *Giants of the Sea* (*[Amaliqat al-bihar],* al-Sayyid Badir)—his image would vanish thereafter from the screen, even as it proliferated throughout city and country, adorning public and private walls, and resonated in the lyrics of revolutionary anthems and school ditties. When Nasser finally reappeared on the silver screen in the last years of his rule, then after his death, it was as anti-icon, a tarnished portrait of power.

NOTES

1. Berque (1972) has a photograph of the Metro Cinema burning; the film is *When Worlds Collide.*

2. Soon after, he commenced work in a series of formula films that featured his name in the title: *The Adventures of Ismail Yasin; Ismail Yasin in the Army,* and so on. He released ten such films between 1955 and 1959. His output dipped sharply in the sixties. He died in 1972, reportedly broke. For further biographical information, as well as film and video clips, see the CD-ROM "Isma'il Yasin fi al-kumbyutur" (MetaMedia 1999).

3. His pronouncement echoes an early slogan of the new regime: "Unity, Order, and Work."

4. The allusion here is to Farouk's endeavors to assert spiritual authority over the Muslim world as caliph, and early popular references to him as "Farouk the Pious."

5. In 1996 a restored version of the film was screened at the National Festival for Egyptian cinema (*Egyptian Gazette,* May 11, 1996).

6. In the interim the Wafd came to power. The newly appointed government sought to ban the film outright, but reckoning that would be politically unwise, settled for the excisions. Director Farid al-Gindi made only two subsequent films, neither with any political content (Abd al-Al 1984: 14–15).

7. Samir Farid (February 7, 1996) says the Egyptian code was essentially the Hollywood code. Mustafa Darwish (April 17, 1996) agrees that "Mr. Hays influenced us—we consider him holy!" For the Hays code, see Leff and Simmons (1990).

8. Badrakhan, who had worked with many major stars, cast a former law school mate as Kamil and reportedly wrote into his contract a clause stating that he would not act again. After his well-regarded performance, Anwar Ahmad "retired" into the civil service (Shusha 1978: 141; Saad 1975: 80).

9. Another historical, *Guha's Nail* (1952), set in medieval Kufa, was banned prior to July 23 for its depiction of resistance to tyrannical rule and screened after the military takeover.

10. The film's obscurity is underscored by the fact that it has not to this point been released on video.

11. Danielson (1991: 194), however, suggests that the problem originally arose due to competition between Umm Kulthum and arch-rival Muhammad Abd al-Wahhab for presidency of the musicians' union.

12. That Fathi Radwan, firebrand lawyer, former student activist, and Minister of National Guidance in late 1952 had conceived the original story for *Mustafa Kamil* no doubt played some role in its resurrection.

13. For an expanded version of this section, see Gordon 2001a.

14. Already engaged on two sets, Fatin Hamama, the female lead, found herself pressed into service for a third project. She recalls that filming ran into the early morning hours until she collapsed from exhaustion (Farid 1995a: 94–95).

15. The footage, which includes scenes of carpet bombing and naval battles, is vintage World War II. The background accompaniment is the finale to Mussorgsky's *Pictures at an Exhibition.*

16. The use of the post follows the historical record.

17. Egyptian units fighting in Palestine were woefully ill-equipped and ill-prepared for the ensuing combat. Munitions and armaments were in many cases neither up-to-date nor in good working order, and tragic accidents did occur due to equipment malfunctions. However, an army investigation of the specific charges revealed that although a high proportion of suspected rounds proved to be duds and the grenades often did explode prematurely, few of those armaments actually made it to the front. Likewise, some arms that backfired causing casualties were in fact not part of the suspected munitions lots.

18. Some of these sites had been opened to the paying public during the revolution's first year as museums or public gardens. Abdin Palace was opened as a museum in the spring of 1953. The gardens of Kubba, Montazah, and Ras al-Tin were opened for Sham al-Nassim and other special occasions.

19. Rosti, the son of Viennese nobility who had taken refuge in the Egyptian theater, was a pioneer of the emergent Egyptian cinema. A versatile stage and screen character player, his foreign mannerisms and distinctive accented elocution led to his casting as a duplicitous foreigner in a series of political propaganda films (or standard genre films that exploited the political situation) in the years immediately following the Free Officers coup.

20. Fayid (1999: 11), citing a personal communication with Ihsan Abd al-Quddus, suggests that Nasser reacted personally to rumors that his family had been depicted as impoverished. It is, however, hard to believe that Nasser would react so negatively to so obviously fictional, and likable, a family.

21. See for example, El Sadat (1957: 131–35, 158–59). Nagib's rejoinders ([Neguib]1955; 1975; 1984) are less than convincing in many respects.

22. The case went to trial in January 1951 with ten individuals—military, civilian, and one member of the royal family—indicted for illegal arms trafficking. The court handed down acquittals in March 1953; an appellate court upheld the initial ruling, save for LE 100 fines handed down against two junior officers. Nonetheless, the scandal generated intense animosity towards the palace, the high command, and affiliated pashas, precisely because the rumors, innuendoes, and traceable links rang so true.

23. Nasser refers here to the Free Officers sweep of elections to the board of the Officers Club in late 1951, a direct challenge to palace authority. Following this the palace ordered the elections annulled—the event is referred to in the film scenario—an act which precipitated a crisis atmosphere and sparked the officers to hasten their military operation.

24. The rapprochement between Ihsan Abd al-Quddus and the regime, as well as the long-term personal relationship between him and Anwar Sadat, no doubt helped pave the way toward the film's eventual release. After his release from prison, Ihsan refrained from addressing domestic politics and devoted greater energies toward producing fiction.

25. *Rayya and Sakina* featured stage stars Nagma Ibrahim and Zuzu Hamdi al-Hakim as the murderous sisters. Distributors, however, balked at the lack of a

major star, so Abu Sayf, who always attempted to foreground new talent, selected Anwar Wagdi to play the police lieutenant on the killers' tracks. To enhance the realism of *The Monster,* Abu Sayf interviewed police investigators who had been involved in busting the gang on which he based his story (al-Nahhas 1996: 74, 78).

26. The new black-red-white tricolor flag was adopted in 1958, so utilization of the old flag alone could not definitively place a film story in the pre-revolutionary era.

27. Sirhan gained the nickname for his numerous roles as "a courageous young man who avenges the wicked and unjust thanks to his endurance and physical force" (Ramzi 1995b: 280).

28. For a photo spread of the filming, see *al-Musawwar,* June 13, 1958.

29. The project had been initiated by director Izz al-Din Zulficar, who had been diagnosed with a terminal illness just as filming was set to commence. Zulficar gave the nod to Chahine (Fawwal 2001: 42).

30. Mazhar had a bit part as a British officer in Zulficar's *Port Said* and played the pasha's venal son in his 1957 epic *Return My Heart,* which will be treated below.

31. The script is credited to novelist Abd al-Rahman al-Sharqawi, the original story and dialogue to Yusuf al-Sibai. Naguib Mahfouz and directors Izz al-Din Zulficar and Muhammad Abd al-Gawwad are credited with script treatment.

32. He has tried to emphasize his humanist call for understanding between antagonists. Asked by Samir Farid (1993: 82) whether *Saladin* was state propaganda on behalf of Nasser's leadership of the Arab world, he replied: "I'll be straight with you. Perhaps we can say that the state, by financing the film, saw that as a goal. I believed strongly in Arab unity, and today I believe firmly in the need for such unity. But when I directed *Saladin the Victorious* I wanted to direct historical films and battles, and such things do not come cheaply. . . ." Also see Fawwal (2001: 160–63).

33. Al-Sharqawi (1896–1920) took to the hills after avenging the murder of his uncle. He combined social banditry with nationalism, robbing the rich to give to the poor, as well as sabotaging British trains. For oral traditions, see Larkin (1992).

34. Salih's 1961 drama *Heroes' Struggle* had been received to great critical acclaim and has been considered one of Egypt's best films (al-Hadiri 1984b; Ismail 1984). His scripted but never filmed rendition of Mahfouz's trilogy remains one of the great "what ifs" of Egyptian film history. For Abu Sayf's official version of the conflict with Salih, see *al-Musawwar,* February 2, 1966, pp. 39–40; for Salih's return to directing in the mid-sixties, see Chapter 6.

35. Tawfiq Salih, who intended to make a very different adaptation before the project was reassigned to al-Imam, grants the director this point (January 7, 2000). Armbrust (1995: 86) also notes that compared to other historicals, which are "notorious for their inattention to details of dress and set design," *Palace Walk* "acquitted itself rather well."

36. See "A Sense of Frustration," *Time,* September 20, 1965, p. 42. The article also notes riots in Damietta after the killing of a suspected smuggler by coast guard troops and the recent crackdown on the Muslim Brotherhood.

37. One of these was later excised, although not necessarily under censorial pressure.

38. Rasheed El-Enany (1993: 51) suggests that the problem regarding Mahgub rests with a writer who has not yet honed his social philosophy: "While he strongly

condemns the corrupt social system, he seems equally unwilling to exempt, on this account, the individual from the responsibility for his own fall. . . . The method of presentation would have us think that the individual would have fallen anyway regardless of the social condition. In later novels Mahfouz solved this problem through more balanced portrayals of his protagonists and tighter linkage between social injustice and the individual's fall."

39. For discussion of the novel, see Enany (1993: 51–53) and Moosa (1994: 54–69). Unfortunately literary treatments of Mahfouz universally ignore his relationship to the film industry, either as an original scenarist or source of literary adaptation. This despite the likelihood that far more people have come to "read" his classic print texts on screen than between book covers. There is one major published study of Mahfouz on film (al-Nahhas 1990), but the author, unfortunately, has little to say about *Cairo 1930.*

40. Muhammad Hasanayn Haykal's classic indictment of the intellectuals (1961).

41. Ibrahim had been arrested in 1961 after spoofing nationalization on stage. The audience reportedly roared, but police officials visited him after the show ("The Endless Road," *Time,* November 17, 1961, p. 28).

42. The meeting is sexy, too sexy for some critics (al-Nahhas 1990: 29).

THREE

Revolutionary Melodrama
Torch Songs and Other Tropes

I proclaim you Layla, wife of Anwar. I now believe that times have changed. I was wrong to cling to outmoded customs. We live in an age that does not recognize class distinctions. An age of freedom, of equality, of democracy. . . .

Daughter of Nobility, 1953

In a day, in a month, in a year,
Wounds heal and fade away.
The life span of my wound is longer than life.
Farewell happy days; farewell love, farewell dreams. . . .

Love Story, 1959

Interludes

As crowds of people pour into the streets of Port Said celebrating nationalization of the Suez Canal Company, Huda Sultan strides determinedly to the balcony. The music swirls into a martial rhythm and she sings, leading the masses in an anthem to an independent Egypt and its leader. It is the only number performed in the patriotic *Port Said.* Coming at the outset of the film, the song sets, rather than breaks, the narrative action. This is a defining moment of revolutionary melodrama in the early Nasser era, the merger of film art and the staged spectacle of political festival. Like other singers of the day, Huda Sultan recorded anthems extolling the goals of the new regime. She and others performed these songs at gala fetes marking the anniversary of the officers uprising, the expulsion of Farouk, and the proclamation of a republic. Many were soon forgotten. Others, like "God is Greatest" would resound for a generation until they too were replaced by the anthems of a newer, post-revolutionary era.

The political drama *With God on Our Side* contains no songs, but does feature three dance numbers, two belly dances and a pseudo-pharaonic ensemble performance, all of which occur in the royal presence. Only the second belly dance, performed in a swanky nightclub, figures directly into the narrative: through her sensual swaying the odalisque passes secret information on to dissidents in the audience. Each number, however, enhances the narrative power of the film, underscoring the profligacy of king and courtiers, pashas and parliamentarians. And yet the entertainment is Janus-faced, for the dances also fit well into existing conventions of melodramatic film narrative based on the common wisdom that a successful movie mandated musical interludes. The filmmakers actually captured this contradiction when, during the first number, they cut back to the junior officers at the front listening to the same music on the radio during a nighttime cease-fire. Vocally scornful of those partying back home while they battle on foreign soil, the future revolutionaries are nonetheless lulled by the evocative, familiar sounds. The film audience, likewise, cognitively understands the political intent of the musical narrative, while at the same time, presumably, enjoying—and expecting—the musical interludes.

Such interludes—and the underlying production sensibility—became a primary target of Egypt's new cinema. Entertainment had its place, but not, argued many critics, at the expense of serious, artistic, socially meaningful art. While not all Egyptian films featured a requisite song or dance number, a significant number did. With the advent of talkies, music and movies, singing and acting, often went hand in hand. In an essay penned in the mid-1960s, Galal al-Sharqawi, a recent graduate of the Cinema Institute who went on to become a major director (he directed his first film in 1965), calculated that 38 of the 106 features made between 1930 and 1939 "gave pride of place to singing" (El-Charkawi 1966: 87).

According to Viola Shafik, more than one-third of the 918 films produced between 1931 and 1961 featured songs, and often at least one dance, either a belly dance or folkloric choreography. Between 1944 and 1946, when film production began to increase dramatically, more than half the films featured such musical interludes (Shafik 1998: 103).[1] The number of musicals increased in the two years just prior to the Free Officers coup, and this trend, characterized by one writer as a "superabundance," continued until Suez (Ezzedine 1966: 48).

Musicals comprised a wide variety of film types. Early on, certain scenarists and musicians—Muhammad Abd al-Wahhab is especially important in this respect—worked musical numbers in as leitmotif to dramatic action (Shafik 1998: 109). Films in which the lead star played a singer or dancer proved extremely popular, as did the classic Hollywood backstage musical with a supporting cast of revue players (Dougherty 1998). In other films, in which either leading or supporting players are entertainers, the musical number is merely an expected break in the action. Sometimes the musical interlude is purely gratuitous. There are no songs or dance performances in Niyazi Mustafa's *The Prisoner of Abu Zaabal*, but in one scene Munira Sonbol, preening before a mirror, performs an impromptu private belly dance, with full score in the background.[2]

Not unlike their Hollywood counterparts, Egyptian producers well understood that music sold theater seats. It should not be surprising, therefore—nor essentialized to particular characteristics of Arab narrative or musical traditions—that the busiest and highest paid actors on the Nile could carry a tune, perhaps better than they could act. According to Shafik (1998: 103), more than forty-six different singers starred in feature films. The best of them, from a cinematic standpoint, proved extremely versatile and comfortable in front of a camera. Umm Kulthum, who acknowledged her own lack of experience, made only six films.[3] Others—Layla Murad, Farid al-Atrash, Naima Akif, Muhammad Fawzi, and Sabah—developed winning screen personas, playing in light romances or tear jerkers. After the mid-1950s the younger generation of stars began to hone their acting skills. Huda Sultan played both good wife and temptress, primarily in a string of B-films, and Shadia, who had become the leading singer-actress by the early fifties, emerged as a serious leading lady in some of the most important films—most serious drama, but also several key comedies—of the mid- to late sixties, films in which she did not sing.[4] Suad Husni mixed serious dramatic, comic, and musical comic roles from the start of her career. Abd al-Halim Hafiz, a fine comic in lighter films, and the epitome of the tortured lover in his heavier vehicles, developed a more mature style that he seemed poised to carry over into the 1970s before illness kept him away from the movie sets. Other singers—Fuad Muharram, Nagat, Warda, Adil Mamun—tried less successfully to parlay their voices into screen careers.

Even those directors least interested in musicals and most successful outside the genre found themselves compelled to utilize the primary talents of singers and dancers. Huda Sultan sang five numbers in *Boss Hasan* because Salah Abu Sayf needed to sell the picture to his producers (al-Nahhas 1996: 72).[5] If these numbers fit comfortably into the melodramatic tropes of an earlier era, Abu Sayf soon endeavored to direct more creative, even path-breaking musical numbers. The belly dance that precedes the murder of a young dancer in *Raya and Sakina* remains a master-stroke of suspense, heightened by the confluence of camera shots—quick cut close-ups, many at skewed angles, of victim's and killers' faces, a rhythmically swaying chandelier, a tea pot boiling over—and the rising pitch of the music. Abu Sayf also helped dance sensation Tahiya Carioca redefine herself as a dramatic actress in *A Woman's Youth* (*Shabab Imra'a* 1955) and *The Thug* (1958). Even so, at the height of his creative powers he found himself drafted by producer Ramsis Nagib to direct Farid al-Atrash in a sentimental romance. *Letter from a Missing Woman* (*Risala min imra'a maghula* 1963), an undistinguished work, was, Abu Sayf admitted, "the first and last time in my artistic life in which the star was chosen before the script" (al-Nahhas 1996: 144).

Melodrama

Well before the politics and political economy of the sixties, these movies became a focal point of cinematic criticism. The broad critique encompassed all film genres whose purpose, profit-driven, was to "provoke physical emotion which can be more readily aroused in a simple audience than can loftier emotions" (El-Charkawi 1966: 89–90). Al-Sharqawi's essay, published in an English-language anthology on

Arab cinema, reflects the critical ideology of the public sector as well as any. By the early fifties, the Egyptian film had become a hodgepodge, "theoretically designed to satisfy all tastes." He, and others, felt particular scorn for the melodrama:

> As in all melodramas, the author uses traditional means to interest and move an essentially working-class audience. Obviously, love always takes pride of place, spiced with base seduction, rape, adultery, prison, murder, suicide and madness, with a background of brooding for the sympathetic victim.[6] . . . Most of the scenarios can be summed up as follows: A young girl and a young man fall in love. One is rich, the other poor. The parents of the rich one oppose the match. Or the young man is a vile seducer. Result: the girl is seduced and has a baby, being the object of general opprobrium until, after many tribulations, things work out. The girl's innocence is recognized, the young people marry, and everyone is happy. The happy ending was still compulsory. . . . Other subjects crop up with wearisome frequency and each new season has its fashion. Whenever a film was successful, producers rushed to engage its authors for the purpose of writing other scenarios dealing with the same theme. These themes, with the horrifying situations already referred to, were well designed to wring tears from Egyptian audiences, who are particularly responsive to the sorrows of others. It was, after all, their own fate to endure misery in one way or another. In this fashion it was claimed that the box-office success of a film could be guaranteed.

Al-Sharqawi notes that the July revolution led to an "increased number of patriotic films," a small group of sixteen that he categorizes into two categories and five sub-categories (ibid.: 94–95).[7]

Yet, while championing the effort to dismantle conventional melodramatic, musical, and comedy tropes, al-Sharqawi, like many others before and after, views his mission through tightly fit blinders.

Those blinders, perhaps best encapsulated in his disdain for "traditional means," need to be stripped away in order to more fully grasp and reevaluate the degree to which the Egyptian cinema changed well before the institutional transformations of the 1960s. Only then can we look beyond the dozen or so purely "political" or "serious" works, to engage a far broader group of films that truly constitute a "revolutionary" corpus, not necessarily radical in style or message, but very much reflective of the social agenda propagated by the new regime and embraced by many of its subjects.

Private capital studio productions punctuated by traditional melodramatic tropes, these films addressed what al-Sharqawi defines as classic themes of social class, privilege, patriarchy, and outmoded traditions, but through new lenses. I do not suggest that from a cinematic perspective these films are in any way revolutionary, nor that they were necessarily intended to fuel either an artistic or cultural revolution. They look entirely conventional. Yet by openly challenging traditional politics and social constructs, by expressing hopes for a new Egypt, and by taking full advantage of the opportunities to bend, if not reshape official guidelines for cinematic discourse, the makers of these films helped to move the nation in bold new directions.

Class-Crossed Lovers[8]

What really constitutes social drama? One example—and it was categorized as such in the official *Panorama of Egyptian Cinema* published by the Ministry of Culture in 1983—is Mahmud Zulficar's *The Good Earth* (*al-Ard al-tayyiba* 1954). In this film, land reform saves a young heiress with progressive leanings from the legal maneuverings of her jealous relatives. Saadiya (Maryam Fakhr al-Din) is not a peasant, but as the product of an illicit affair was raised as one on her father's estate. Her secret, heartbroken father (Husayn Riyad) pampers her and in an early aside bemoans his inability to truly express paternal affection. When, after his untimely death, the pasha's will reveals her true status, she brings her peasant family, their flock, and a wandering circus troupe into the big house. The pasha's unfaithful wife (Zuzu Madi) and cousin (Abd al-Salam al-Nabulsi), secret lovers who had withheld his medicine during an episode, effectively murdering him (a la Bette Davis in *The Little Foxes*), now conspire to usurp her rights. When she refuses to grant them trusteeship, they persuade Ahmad, the wife's handsome but hedonistic brother (Kamal al-Shinawi), to pose as an itinerant photographer, win Saadiya's heart, and snap some socially incriminating evidence of her cavorting with her lessers. Saadiya stands to lose the farm, as well as her love—Ahmad has naturally fallen for her and sits uneasily with the prosecution—until the revolution, proclaimed in newspaper headlines, saves the day. The young lovers are happily reunited in an irrigation canal, a classic "wet ending."[9]

Until its dramatic denouement, *The Good Earth* represents the archetypical transitional pre-revolutionary social film, sitting astride two eras. In an opening scene clean, well-fed peasants sing the title song while they work (it is not the only musical number in the film, even though none of the stars sing). Saadiya's biological father is a humane master, racked by guilt at his inability to reveal to her the truth of their relationship. Her concern for the poor, here grounded in her upbringing, reflects reformist attitudes prevalent by the early 1950s. A conventional resolution—the lovers reunited, the peasants back at work for a benevolent, if less propertied elite—challenges no class boundaries. Nonetheless, by 1954, when *The Good Earth* hit the theaters, barriers to depictions of cross-class romance had come down as quickly and dramatically as official portraits of Farouk.

The cross-class romance theme, like the peasant of noble lineage theme, was hardly new to Egyptian films, but it was now expressed in terms both rawer and more optimistic. In the classic pre-revolutionary melodramas happy endings were usually predicated on a turn of heart in which the upper classes prove beneficent. When class lines are crossed the frame of reference is generally that of a modernizing and modern-looking middle class (Armbrust 1996: 94–115). Thus in *The White Rose* (*[al-Warda al-bayda']*, Muhammad Karim 1933), the middle class son marries up. In the pathbreaking realist drama *Determination,* the son of a popular quarter on the middle class track saves his sweetheart, the girl next door, from a lecherous, older, and clearly "old fashioned" suitor. Often, when class lines were romantically crossed the gap was not so great. Even in Ahmad Badrakhan's post-July 1952 scripting of the revolution, *With God on Our Side,* the problematic romance is between the pasha's daughter and her middle class cousin who might be her social equal, but for his father's foolhardy patriotism.

When the gap was wider, especially when it involved the "real" poor, however sanitized the depiction, romantic resolution tugged heartstrings and brought ease, not least because the upper orders show compassion for the lovers. Mistaken class identification usually paves the way for forbidden romance. In *Layla, Daughter of Poverty* (*[Layla, bint al-fuqara']*, Anwar Wagdi 1945) Anwar Wagdi plays the pasha's son who falls for Layla Murad, a peasant girl, mistaking her for a fellow blue-blood, then marries her anyway. When class lines are challenged in socially improper contexts, palliative shifts of fortune ensue. In another popular cliche, the pasha pursuing the chambermaid suddenly changes heart and turns paternal.

The musical *Bread and Salt* (*[al-Aysh wa al-milh]*, Husayn Fawzi 1949), is a classic rendition of this pre-revolutionary trope. Busbus (Naima Akif), a provincial girl newly arrived in the city, finds refuge in a working-class quarter. The salt-of-the-earth (thus the title) neighborhood denizens are all honest and decent, not least Sabir (Saad Abd al-Wahhab), a law school graduate who has, with the financial assistance of his friends, returned to the quarter to set up practice. He works under a placard that reads "Uplift, do not trample the truth," lectures his neighbors on civic duty—an explicit modernist critique of working class wiles—and more or less convinces them that their district should become a paragon of honesty.

Working class mores, whatever the shortcomings, contrast favorably to the upper class world of the cabaret, but the allure of the aristocracy nearly proves too great for all concerned. Against his better intuition, Sabir takes on the accounts of a local bey (Abbas Faris). Then Busbus and three friends (Hasan Fayiq, Hasan Kamil, and Mukhtar Husayn, a common slapstick trio), eager to up their income, pose as caterers for a fete held at the bey's country villa. In scenes reminiscent of The Three Stooges, they crash the party, parodying elite manners through their own charming vulgarity. The beautiful Busbus naturally draws the amorous attention of the bey, who endeavors to win her affection through promises of wealth, prompting a jealous Sabir to punch him in the nose. Fortunately, before things reach a crisis stage the bey relents and the social order is restored as a wedding procession for Busbus and Sabir fills the alley.

In *Amal* (Yusuf Maaluf 1952), a different mode of cross-class romantic resolution is utilized: the discovery that the poorer partner is really a blue-blood cast-off. Like Saadiya in *The Good Earth,* Amal (Shadia) is the secret love child of master and servant who is raised as a peasant on the family estate, unaware of her true lineage. In *The Good Earth* this particular problem is resolved relatively early on: the audience knows Saadiya's true status before she learns of it, and the crux of her problem, in any case, is not to prove her pedigree but to retain her inheritance. In the earlier, pre-revolutionary *Amal* the heroine's true status remains a mystery (except, perhaps, to well-attuned viewers) longer into the story. Here the culprit is not a weak-willed, socially constrained father, but Amal's villainous uncle (Farid Shawqi), who had stolen her inheritance and expelled her from the house when she was a baby. She, of course, has grown into a beautiful fallaha, and one day, riding a donkey and singing, she attracts the attention of the scion of a neighboring estate (Muhsin Sirhan), who happens to be engaged to Amal's cousin, the daughter of her evil uncle. By the time the convoluted plot has worked itself through—Amal winds up charged with theft and left by her uncle to die of asphyxiation in a cellar—her lineage has been revealed, her inheritance restored, and the path cleared for her to marry the young aristocrat without breaking any social taboos.

In the new cinema that emerged after the Free Officers coup the once paternal, perhaps guilt-racked pasha suddenly turned truly venal, and the salt-of-the-earth *ibn* or *bint al-balad* (native son/daughter) might actually marry up without the convenient discovery of lineage, and the privileged partner marry down with parental approval. Cross-class romance became a primary—if not the primary—plot convention of the new cinema in the years immediately following the officers' seizure of power, both in "serious" drama as well as musical comedy.

REVOLUTIONARY MELODIES

A year prior to the release of *The Good Earth,* Anwar Wagdi had directed, produced, and co-starred in a far more forthright call for severing of class distinctions. In *Daughter of Nobility* (1953), he plays the commoner who falls for the pasha's cloistered granddaughter. She is played by Layla Murad, Wagdi's frequent co-star in a long and immensely popular line of *Layla* movies and, until recently, his wife. Their last collaboration before his untimely death, the film is a clarion call to a new social order. Remarkably, in the *Panorama* (1983: 36), *Daughter of Nobility* is categorized simply as a "melody." [10]

For the new cinema, Wagdi is a good place to start. He rose to stardom on the basis of good looks and charisma, more a star than an actor. Initially a second male lead, he went on to achieve greater success with the *Layla* films, which he inherited in the mid-1940s from pioneer director Togo Mizrahi. In these and related works he successfully transitioned from playing "a frivolous aristocrat . . . hanging out with a spoiled crowd, most of whom wear riding outfits" into "the link . . . between rich and poor [classes]" (Ramzi 1997: 46). By the early 1950s Wagdi wrote, directed, produced and starred in his own vehicles. Increasingly he scripted himself as a commoner, often down on his luck. The essential humanism he evoked fit well with the spirit of enthusiasm that swept new-regime Egypt. In a last burst of filmmaking before his death in 1955, Wagdi produced three major films: *Daughter of Nobility,* in which he plays a dashing phone repairman who makes a fortuitous house call at the pasha's villa; *Dahab* (1953), in which he plays a Chaplinesque tramp who raises an elite foundling; and *Four Girls and an Officer* (1954), in which he plays the reform-minded supervisor of a girls reformatory.

Daughter of Nobility pits Layla (as in many other films, Murad plays under her own name) against her tyrannical, tradition-bound grandfather, Shawkat Pasha. As the story opens, the pasha prepares to leave on hajj, and the great house is in a tizzy. To compound the confusion, the telephone is out, but the primary buzz is anticipation—by "upstairs" and "downstairs" respectively—of a period of relative freedom. Layla's uncle, Tawfiq Bey, has arrived to chaperon his niece; he has visions of films, concert halls, and cabarets. Such expectations are soon quashed by Shawkat Pasha's insistence that Layla remain indoors for the entire duration of his absence. All her entertainment needs, he assures her, will be provided within the confines of the estate. When Tawfiq, the Pasha's brother, protests that the world has changed, he is reminded sternly that Layla's deceased mother had transgressed social boundaries with a commoner. His granddaughter's guardian, the pasha remains resolute: "Layla is a daughter of nobility and she will remain a daughter of nobility!"

The pasha, played with relish by Zaki Rustam, is a marvelous caricature of outmoded traditional elite society. A master of Arabic

Crossing class swords—Anwar Wagdi, Zaki Rustam, and Sulayman Nagib in *Daughter of Nobility.*

elocution, Rustam was the quintessential silver screen aristocrat, and parlayed this role in light comedy and heavy drama into some of the most significant screen roles of the early revolution. Here it is all good fun, as the pasha insists that "Layla will be raised as I was," and that it was "modernism" that led her mother astray. Beneath the cajoling and kisses is a steely determination, visible in his piercing eyes, as well as his immaculate dress and finely-curled mustache.

In the new social revolutionary era Shawkat Pasha and his ilk become more than whipping boys of the modernists. In a spirit of frivolity, Wagdi takes this film in bold new directions. Tawfiq Bey, Layla's sympathetic uncle, a self-proclaimed modernist, will help her subvert his brother's wishes, but until he makes a decisive stand he too becomes a foil. In an uproarious early scene, Wagdi takes advantage of new-found directorial liberties to poke fun at an aristocracy that had been stripped of both titles and acreage in a flurry of reformist legislation promulgated in the months after the Free Officers' seizure of power. The scene pits the pompous bey (Sulayman Nagib, a fine comic) against a cheeky telephone operator (the irrepressible Ismail Yasin), who takes the opportunity afforded by anonymity to pillory Egypt's doomed, now title-less elite:

> *Operator:* Good day, Effendi Sir, if you are an effendi.
> Or good day, Bey Sir, if you are a bey. . . .
> *Tawfiq Bey:* Excuse me, who is this?
> *Operator:* This is the phone company, Brother. . . .

Increasingly irritated, Tawfiq Bey turns imperious. When the operator demands he be addressed with respect, the bey responds: "Respect!? Yes, sir, I'll give you respect!" He pours a glass of water down the receiver, which spurts out over the lines into the operator's face. When the operator recovers, the bey informs him that he is Tawfiq Bey Singadar, the brother of Shawkat Pasha Singadar, listing grandfather and great-grandfather, and so on. The fictive lineage evokes all the faded glory of Egypt's Turco-Circassian elite. Unflapped, the operator retorts with a string of comical curses: "Ohhh, such a long name??!! What a crowd, damn you all!!" Furious, the bey demands to speak to a supervisor, and the operator naturally play acts the part, promising to flay the disobedient employee—until he notices his real supervisor standing over him, stammers abuse at himself and slaps his own face. The subaltern may not yet get the last word, but he has clearly found his voice.[11]

Naturally, in her grandfather's absence Layla meets and falls for a stranger. Family history repeating itself, he is just what Shawkat Pasha fears most: Anwar, played by director Wagdi, who has been sent along with the disobedient operator to repair the phone. Directed to the kitchen, the two encounter Layla, whom they mistake for a servant. A cross-class comedy of manners ensues. Before he ever learns Layla's true status, Anwar has fallen in love. The two go for a surreptitious motor-scooter ride, see a film, and Anwar proposes.

Unfortunately, the socially reactionary chief butler informs Tawfiq Bey that a relative has spotted Layla out on the town in the company of a strange man. Layla dutifully confesses that she has fallen in love and that her paramour works for the phone company. "Chairman of the board?" Tawfiq asks nervously. "A bit lower," she replies, on down the line until the truth be known. Tawfiq, revealing to his niece the secret of her birth, informs her that her inheritance, tied up in pious endowments (another realm of early Free Officer reform), rests on marrying with her grandfather's approval. But Layla remains steadfast. Sympathetic, her uncle takes her to visit Anwar, who still believes his intended is a scullery maid, and her uncle, dressed in peasant *gallabiya,* the cook. To complicate affairs, Tawfiq Bey falls for Anwar's cheeky sister (the madcap Zaynat Sidqi). A double wedding is held, but the party is spoiled by Shawkat Pasha's unexpected return, prompted by a tip from the ever loyal, and class-consciousless butler. A pained Wagdi is left alone on the dais, while Murad sings of her broken heart.

But this is no way to end a Wagdi-Murad romance (at least not a film romance). The pasha, through his solicitor, offers to buy out "Anwar Effendi," and sitting under a portrait of Farouk, the lawyer lectures Anwar on social propriety and sarcastically endows him with undeserved middle class status. Anwar goes to the villa to protest, but Shawkat Pasha, revealing his intent to disinherit Layla, a consequence that he suggests will lead her to reconsider her love for the commoner, persuades Anwar to renounce his marriage. A distraught Anwar agrees to play-act the deceitful lover, confessing to Layla that he is interested only in her riches. In the foyer, however, Tawfiq Bey berates the pasha. Renouncing family ties and wealth, he thumbs his nose at his brother and starts to undress. Caught up in the fracas, Shawkat Pasha's lawyer invokes Quranic verse and tenders his resignation. When Layla, too, threatens to walk away from home and fortune, Shawkat Pasha relents. He has had a sudden revelation:

> I proclaim you Layla, wife of Anwar. I now believe that times have changed. I was wrong to cling to outmoded customs. We live in an age that does not recognize class distinctions. An age of freedom, of equality, of democracy. . . .

The film ends in classic Wagdi fashion, with a reunited couple, a double wedding, ululation, and a burst of song.[12] A traditional resolution—the misguided aristocrat sees the light and turns benevolent? No, for in this story the benevolent turn upends, rather than reinforces, class lines.

In *Dahab,* classified a "presentation" in the *Panorama* (1983: 40),[13] Wagdi plays Wahid (his usual film epithet), a Chaplinesque minstrel who discovers a foundling outside the gates of a villa. This is *Daughter of Nobility* with a harsher edge. The baby is the maid's daughter by the master of the villa. The master (Sirag Munir) and his wife (Mimi Shakib) have ordered their niece (Magda) to drown the infant, but she places it curbside and waits until Wahid, hearing a cry, finds it. When the niece emerges from the shadows, Wahid tries to hand over the child, but comes away only with the niece's name, Dahab, which he will give to the baby. Cut ahead to an eight-year-old Dahab (Fayruz, Egypt's Shirley Temple), who accompanies Wahid as his musical sidekick. Hungry, they beg, unknowingly, at the same villa, where they are turned away, but not before a second encounter with the niece. A year later they are successful cabaret stars. Now Dahab's biological father, broken by gambling debts, asserts his rights. A secular court grants Wahid custodianship, but a religious court confers legal custody on her natural parent, a clear statement of secular reformism by the filmmaker. However, in a quick-cut finale all is resolved. Wahid is summoned by a suddenly repentant couple to talk Dahab down from the window ledge of a downtown high-rise. As reward he may reassume his parental duties. Social parentage wins out over biology.

The third film of this trio, *Four Girls and an Officer,* is equally transitional. No less a musical, no less comic, and in some ways less challenging to pre-coup paradigms than the prior two, this film has garnered attention in critical studies as a purveyor of positive images of junior military officers, and has traditionally been considered a "social film" (*Panorama* 1983: 40).[14] The story concerns a burgeoning romance between Wahid (Wagdi), the military director of a girl's reformatory, and the cheeky, undisciplined orphan Naima (Naima Akif). Wahid, who believes that compassion rather than martial discipline will best reach his charges, does daily battle with the corrupt headmistress (Nagma Ibrahim) whose iron-fisted rule of law only incites food fight and riot—in one case to song.[15]

A blossoming, albeit administratively improper, romance is cut short when Naima and her three cohorts (the child star Libliba and the song-and-dance twins Ragaa and Awatif) accidentally set their dorm room ablaze and escape out into the world. They sing for bread until an eccentric but rich man (Abd al-Warith Asr) takes them in. Seeing a striking resemblance between Naima and his neighbors' lost daughter, Huda, he persuades Naima to play act the part, coaching her in intimate details of family and home. Naima successfully convinces Huda's governess (Zaynat Sidqi), then the parents, who welcome all four girls into the family. But Naima pines for Wahid, who, unbeknownst to her, has been dismissed from the reformatory. To confound matters, he shows up at her homecoming party, unaware that Huda's mother (Amina Rizq) has a secret agenda, to arrange and announce his engagement to her daughter. A last flurry of confusion ensues when Wahid, outraged by his discovery of the girls' deception, prepares to take them back to the reformatory. Huda's mother now suddenly admits she saw through the ruse from the start, yet has come to love Naima as her daughter and will adopt her. By now Naima is out on the railroad tracks, but Wahid saves her and the day. How does this film rate as "social drama" over the two prior efforts?

More Than a Romance

The same year the theme of cross-class romance found its most dramatic representation in Youssef Chahine's *Struggle in the Valley (Sira' fi al-wadi* 1954, released as *The Blazing Sun).* Chahine's sixth feature is one of the first Egyptian films to depict rural life as less than idyllic. For Chahine this represented a dramatic shift from the romanticized countryside of his earlier *Nile Boy* (*Ibn al-Nil* 1951). In addition to a critical view of traditional notions of honor and vendetta (themes that will be explored in this and other films in Chapter 5), Chahine took his camera out of the studio and into the village to capture aspects of rural life, including specific rites of passage (in this case a marriage) with a quasi-ethnographic eye, a trend that would be followed by Salah Abu Sayf, Baracat, and other directors in succeeding years. It is also the first film to pair Omar Sharif, Egypt's new screen sensation in his film debut, with Fatin Hamama, the adorable child-star turned leading lady who would soon become Sharif's wife.[16] Here their romance crosses—and validates the crossing of—traditional class boundaries. She is Amal, the pasha's daughter, he Ahmad, the overseer's educated son, an agricultural engineer.

Class-crossed lovers—Fatin Hamama and Omar Sharif in *Struggle in the Valley.* Courtesy of Arab Film Distribution.

However cliche-ridden the film may appear to be, with *Struggle in the Valley* Chahine took Anwar Wagdi's challenge to romantic taboos a step further. In doing so, he insured that the comfortable plot resolutions of films like *The Good Earth* or *Daughter of Nobility,* however genuine the sentiments expressed, would forever be deemed old fashioned. When Amal, having graduated from boarding school, returns to the estate she finds her affection for Ahmad, her childhood playmate, rekindled, only now with romantic overtones. Ahmad, who instructs the peasants in modern farming techniques, shifts easily between gallabiya and western dress; Amal is resplendent in a sleeveless, knee-length summer dress and modern urban bobbed haircut. Hamama and Sharif's first filmic encounter, a roadside reunion cut short by the impatience of Amal's boorish cousin (Farid Shawqi in a rare, but memorable aristocratic turn) is electric. The cousin also has romantic designs on the pasha's daughter, but the melodrama really takes off when he and his uncle (Zaki Rustam in his next major role after *Daughter of Nobility*) conspire to ruin the season's crop, undoing all of Ahmad's work in order to teach him his place and prevent the crop from being sold to an outside bidder.

To mask their subterfuge they plot to sow discord between the peasants and local tribespeople. Ahmad's father, the estate overseer (Abd al-Warith Asr), is framed for the murder, by the pasha's nephew, of a tribal shaykh. Despite the illogic of the charge—the lack of motive, the close friendship between victim and purported killer—rigid rules of vendetta blind the shaykh's son, Sabir (Hamdi Ghayth), to the pasha's villainy, and he seeks vengeance against Ahmad, his childhood friend. Forced to defend himself from imminent attack, Ahmad is unable to do anything to save his father, whose execution mid-way through the film shocked audiences of the day, earning the film notoriety for its genre-bending audacity. In the end, of course, justice is meted out in melodramatic fashion. After a climactic slugfest between Omar Sharif and Farid Shawqi, filmed on location in Karnak Temple, with the revenge-bound Sabir on the prowl, a remorseful pasha arrives to confess his role in perpetrating the crisis. His nephew shoots him, then is apprehended by Sabir, who suddenly understands that he has been a pawn in a great aristocratic game. Order restored, then re-ordered, the pasha's daughter and overseer's son are allowed to walk off into the sunset on their own terms, without pre-revolutionary plot contrivance.

The point is, of course, that there are new plot contrivances at play. Revolutionary melodies like the Wagdi films and melodramas like Chahine's went hand-in-hand with a new emergent cinema of social realism. Realism in the Egyptian film industry, however "new," should always be understood within the context of studio production values and genre conventions. At the same time, tracing their lineage back to Kamal Salim *(Determination)* and Kamil al-Tilmissani *(Black Market),* the new realists sought to inject a degree of class consciousness into the industry that had heretofore been stifled. The director of *Black Market,* writes one critic (Ramzi 1995a: 148),

> does not classify the heroes of his film according to moral categories, but by social class, distinguishing between exploiter and exploited. But this does not

> mean that he fixes the traits of each character. A number are opportunists who take positions contrary to their [class] interests. Their acts follow in an autonomous manner, the fruit of the interaction between their interior and exterior world. These are the "real" characters that we see evolve throughout the film.

In *Black Market,* the exploited masses, personified by the modest, hard-working inhabitants of a popular quarter, suffer when the price of "bread and salt" skyrockets due to the malfeasance of local merchants (with Zaki Rustam as one of the worst). Produced in 1943 but shelved by censors until the end of the Second World War, the film bombed commercially and Kamil al-Tilmissani faced difficulties finding future backing for new projects.[17] The most significant work of new realism was Salah Abu Sayf's *Boss Hasan,* a collaborative effort by the director, lead star Farid Shawqi, and author Naguib Mahfouz, which opened to favorable reviews in June 1952, a month prior to the Free Officers coup.

In many respects a prototypical pre-revolutionary film, *Boss Hasan* managed to transcend melodramatic conventions (including the utilization of songs, as noted above) to achieve something new. Hasan (Farid Shawqi) is a skilled factory worker, well-liked and happily married, yet consumed by disenchantment. Returning home from the plant in an early scene, he playfully sneaks up on his wife (Huda Sultan), who sings contentedly about cooking *mulukhiya* (mallow, a quintessential Egyptian dish). The joyful return, however, quickly sours when Hasan sits upon a rickety chair, then discovers that the gas light has been cut off due to unpaid bills. Summoned shortly thereafter to do repairs at the Zamalek villa of Kawsar (Zuzu Madi), a rich widow who had spotted him at work, he devours the surroundings, instantly falls prey to her guiles, and soon abandons his family to become a kept man. When his wife and son finally trace him to his new home he disowns them. It is only after near tragedy strikes—during an argument while driving, Hasan and Kawsar run down his son, who has been forced to leave school for the factory—that Hasan returns to his senses. In a showdown with Kawsar and her new boyfriend (Rushdi Abaza) shots are fired, resulting in her death. Standing trial for murder and seemingly gallows-bound, Hasan is saved by the surprise confession of Kawsar's husband (Husayn Riyad), a shadowy character confined to a wheel chair who claims to have fired the fatal shots. Freed, Hasan and his wife ride off in a carriage to the strains of a final musical number.

What makes *Boss Hasan* transitional are not the melodramatic tropes, but the stark distinctions drawn between rich and poor. The loyal circle of neighborhood friends who raise funds for the boy's operation, all played by familiar sympathetic character actors (Mahmud Shkuku, Abd al-Warith Asr, Mary Munib, and al-Sayyid Badir), stand in stark contrast to the dandies who surround Kawsar, just as Huda Sultan, in her *milaya* and head scarf stands in contrast to the tightly-bodiced, elegantly coiffured and fashionably painted Zuzu Madi. Madi's outfits always expose her legs; the only shot of Sultan's legs are under the sewing machine table she sits at to support her and her son. More striking is the filmmaker's visual definition of physical boundaries that separate working class Bulaq from elite Zamalek. When Hasan crosses the old iron Abu al-Ela bridge to Gezira Island the soundtrack swirls with Gershwin's "The Man I Love." The streets are wide and tree-lined, the houses manicured. Yet, evil lurks behind the pretty facade—drinking, gambling, illicit sex—whereas real beauty is to be found in the communality and industriousness of Bulaq.

Bitterly torn between familial love and material desires, Hasan remains a sympathetic character. He renounces his family, and especially his son, at great pain. If he is ultimately not allowed to cross the Abu al-Ela bridge for good, the message is not the social conservatism of an upper stratum seeking to maintain rigid boundaries. Rather, Hasan's rise and fall underscores the ease by which the rich take advantage, then dispose of the poor. Among the best scenes are those in which Hasan, having donned the tuxedo and adopted elite manners, now thrown over, drinks too much and slips back into his protean proletarian deportment. It is an important moment in Farid Shawqi's acting career, his first starring role—in a part he conceived for himself—with clear antecedents of his emergent populist tough-guy persona (Armbrust 2000b).

In an urban context, the new realist films at once condemn the conditions of poverty while emphasizing its virtues. Certainly not in a Victorian sense, but neither with the ideological rigidity of socialist realism. There is an ambivalence at play, one best solved not by the abolition of poverty, however noble a goal, but rather by the allowance for lovers to move up and down the social scale, following their hearts and tugging at the heartstrings of film goers. Poverty which results from social inequity—always cinematically tied to villainous disregard for human life and spirit—is to be combated. Yet with the Free Officers revolution it is the virtuous poor, rather than the virtuous rich—they hardly exist anymore—who provide the moral compass for change.

The sentiment is to be found in the most entertaining of vehicles, such as Anwar Wagdi's *Dahab,* which the director labeled a "socialist" film (Abu Shadi 1999: 35). The good father is a wandering clown in hobo rags with a kind face and a heart of gold. When he and the younger Dahab make it, it is the result of having paid artistic and social dues. They connive an audition before an eccentric impresario (Ismail Yasin) and get the proverbial lucky break. Lest the virtues of poverty not be overly romanticized even in a comic romance, Wagdi in one earlier scene depicts street children fighting over a discarded apple, precisely the kind of urban poverty previously outlawed by the production code.

Other films already noted—*The Good Earth* and *Four Girls and an Officer*—depicted poor but industrious wandering performers. Atif Salim's *Deprivation* (*al-Hirman* 1953), the story of an abused runaway child (Fayruz), brought a harsher realism to a melodramatic formula. Bunduq (Hazelnut, a street waif's nickname) is not of the abject poor; her mother (Zuzu Madi) is an actress, her father (Imad Hamdi) an industrial engineer. Because her mother's career precludes maternal obligations, her parents separate, her father taking custody. He is a doting, conscientious single parent, but Bunduq has a penchant for mischief. When she playfully pulls a switch on a visit to his factory, he is injured. Assuming the worst, she flees to Cairo, where she is taken in by a poor family as a servant. There she is overworked and beaten by the mistress of the house (Zaynat Sidqi in a very rare villainous role), until she escapes. In the end, mother and father reunite to successfully find her. Resolution may satisfy audience expectations, but the violent encounters between Zaynat Sidqi and Fayruz are far more intense than was the norm in the early fifties.

Other masterful heavies would follow. Izz al-Din Zulficar's adaptation of Yusuf al-Sibai's epic novel *Return My Heart* is the most famous. Sibai's epic revolves around the forbidden relationship between Ali (Shukri Sirhan), son of the estate gardener (Husayn Riyad), and Angie (Maryam Fakhr al-Din), the pasha's beautiful daughter. Standing in their way, personifications of social evil, are her father, who denigrates his peasants, even loyal servants like Ali's father, as animals, and her brother Alaa (Ahmad Mazhar in his first major role), a sadist who first appears (in identical fashion to Farid Shawqi in *Struggle in the Valley*) shooting a helpless animal from the manor balcony with a hunting rifle. Angie, not unlike Chahine's Amal, is reluctant to cast aside family or wealth, but finds herself dangerously attracted to an educated, modern son of a servant who works the estate.

Despite similar melodramatic tropes, the fundamental differences between *Struggle in the Valley* and *Return My Heart* are of scale and narrative approach. By highlighting the lengths to which a morally bankrupt aristocracy will go to preserve privilege—deliberately ruining a crop, then manipulating tribal tradition and peasant ignorance—Chahine's localized tale clearly embodies vital manifestations of the new artistic freedoms of the unfolding revolution. Zulficar, working from Sibai's best-seller, presents a sweeping historical romance, one that unfolds amidst the great events of the late liberal era: the Palestine War, Black Saturday, the Free Officers Coup, and land reform. The social oppression that forbids a romance between an heiress and a gardener's son—even (or especially) after he graduates from the military academy—is invoked repeatedly in tandem with the political tyranny of Egypt's ruling class. The plot is heavy-handed at times. After the pasha violently rebukes Ali's father for pleading his son's romantic interest in Angie, the gardener loses his ability to speak. His tongue returns to him suddenly, near the film's finale when, on the morning of the Free Officers coup, he finds himself chanting revolutionary slogans from his balcony.

At its most essential, *Return My Heart* spoke directly to the dream of a less stratified class structure. Ali and Angie are reunited after many years when he returns to the villa, now a revolutionary official, delegated after land reform (September 1952) to expropriate the family's suddenly illegal wealth. He approaches the manor, like Charles Ryder returning to Brideshead, carrying with him memories of a past life that seems dream-like. The pasha has fled abroad, leaving Alaa and Angie, virtual shut-ins, to maintain the estate. Still in love with Ali, yet jealously guarding her inherited privilege, Angie first appears cold, yet she and Ali quickly rekindle their flame and leave the big house together. When Alaa tries to stop them, firing again from the balcony, he wounds Ali but is killed in the return fire. In the finale, Ali, the son of the soil, now part of the new ruling structure, recuperates at home with his family (his father again speaking) and bride-to-be, the liberated aristocrat, by his side.

Return My Heart is Egypt's *Gone with the Wind,* a wide-screen, color encapsulation of the crucible of modern Egypt—with a political spin. Zulficar's adaptation of the popular epic novel became the quintessential movie rendition of the revolution, and is recalled as such by Egyptians who grew up in the sixties and watched it annually on television in late July.[18] The Wagdi musicals and the dramas directed by Chahine, Zulficar, Salah Abu Sayf, and others represent twin paths toward the same goal, as well as twin peaks of achievement. Yet the films of the "social realists" continue to garner respect in the serious critical literature, while Wagdi's films, as well as those of other melodramatists, are consigned to the lower depths as "melodies" or "presentations." Certainly not all melodramas, comedies, or musicals—and I reprise these categories guardedly—should be viewed for political or cultural revolutionary tropes. Sometimes a romance is just a romance. The two decades after July 1952 produced scores of them, many fine—and genuinely entertaining—films. Many continue to depict a never-never-land of studio manners, stage spectacle, backstage shenanigans, parlor games, and bedroom farces; others revolve around macho heroes, Farid Shawqi, then Rushdi Abaza, who thwart evil and restore tarnished honor.

However, before we too easily consign them to the margins they warrant critical re-viewing. Intentionally or otherwise, many of these films visually represent the dramatic social and cultural transformations propagated and inspired by Nasserism and its dreams of a new, progressive, independent Egypt. As with historicals or biopics that mask present political commentary behind period costume and insignia, we need to learn to view melodrama and musical comedy between the lines and beyond the gags, tunes, and choreographies.

NIGHTINGALE OF THE REVOLUTION

No discussion of musicals, revolutionary anthems, cross-class romance, or the virtuousness of material suffering can be complete without consideration of Abd al-Halim Hafiz, the "Brown Nightingale" *(al-Andalib al-asmar)*. More than any other figure, either singer or film star—and he was both—Abd al-Halim embodies the Nasser revolution, capturing the spirit of an enthusiastic, forward-looking, youthful nation in his music, whether love songs or nationalist anthems, and his screen performances, whether comic or tragic, and whether the fresh, sweet face of his early films, or the creased, battered visage of his final works. Neither his films nor his vast array of songs can be separated from the era in which they were performed. When Egyptians recall the Nightingale—and it is his death, not that of Nasser or even Umm Kulthum, that is marked annually on the calendar as a public event—it is with all the bittersweet nostalgia for a golden era that has long since passed, "our sweet days," as in the title of one of his earliest films.[19]

He was born Abd al-Halim Ali Ismail Shibana on June 20, 1929 in the West Delta town of al-Halawat. Orphaned at a young age, he and his three siblings were raised by an uncle in Zagazig. At sixteen, he followed an older brother, Ismail, to the music academy in Cairo, where he specialized in stage music and the oboe. In music school he met Kamal al-Tawil and Muhammad al-Mugi, budding superstar composers and lifelong friends who would be among his primary collaborators in succeeding years. To make ends meet he taught in a girls' primary school. Summers were spent with his musical cohort at the Tawil family beach house in Alexandria.[20] In a scene replete with cinematic cliches, Abd al-Halim Shibana first took the microphone to sing when the vocalist scheduled for a radio session failed to show. He was urged forward by Tawil, the song's composer, who had long tried to convince him to focus on vocals (al-Imrusi 1994: 65–68). Soon after, renamed Abd al-Halim Hafiz—he wanted to distinguish himself from his brother, Ismail Shibana, who had already embarked on a successful singing career—he cut his first headline recording.[21]

Hard as it is to believe in retrospect (as hard as it is to believe in all the film scenarios where he struggles for recognition), Abd al-Halim's new-found career as a crooner foundered. The hagiographies highlight his self-doubt, thoughts of bowing out, sentiments which are no doubt credible. Reading between the lines a somewhat different character also emerges—however vindicated by posterity—a stubborn perfectionist with a clear sense of artistic self. Abd al-Halim would not take the easy route by singing old standards the old way. He bombed during a ten-night run in Alexandria. It was a week after the Free Officers coup, but the beach crowd was obviously not ready for an artistic revolution (al-Imrusi 1994: 54–64).

His career took off the following year. In November 1952, according to his published, probably ghost-written memoirs, he was summoned to the headquarters of the military junta, where Nasser spoke to the importance of art in building a new society and anointed him the voice of the new era (Hafiz 1977: 148–49).[22] Eight months later he performed at a concert honoring the abolition of the monarchy. There, and again the following month, at the first annual Revolution Day gala, Yusuf Wahbi introduced Abd al-Halim to the nation as the new star to usher in the birth of the republic (al-Imrusi 1994: 73). Astutely image-conscious, Abd al-Halim had declined an invitation to open the latter show, preferring to wait until the audience grew more attentive (Hasanayn 1995: 31). The Nightingale never looked back. In 1955 Muhammad Abd al-Wahhab, who would be a life-long patron, signed him to a two-year recording contract that included production of two films.

Three years after the Free Officers coup, a year before Suez, Abd al-Halim Hafiz had established himself as the most promising and prominent singer of his generation. His reputation as the bard of the revolution was solidified by his collaboration with the best nationalist lyricists and composers (Hasanayn 1995: 93–127). Everyone sang nationalist anthems in the heady first years of the revolution. When she heard news of the Free Officers success, so the story goes, Umm Kulthum immediately commissioned a song (Danielson 1997: 161). Leading composers and lyricists competed to capture the spirit of the times, but Abd al-Halim's anthems were in a league of their own. By the onset of the socialist decrees, Egyptians awaited eagerly his annual collaboration with Salah Jahin (lyrics) and Kamal al-Tawil (music). He continued to insist on headlining nationalist galas, not fearful of ruffling feathers of even the powerful Umm Kulthum. The "Star of the East" *(Kawkab al-sharq)* would sing at Revolution Day fetes, but his was the awaited thematic highlight (al-Imrusi 1994: 287–88). When, one year (1964), she tried to bump him from prime time, he refused to appear onstage until leading members of the revolutionary command interceded to restore his positioning.

In her mannerisms and fashion consciousness, the great lady—also a child of the countryside—evoked a sense of earthy propriety and modesty. By contrast, Abd al-Halim Hafiz personified a nation of smiles as well as tears, hand slaps, practical jokes, triumphs over adversity and, ultimately, ever-present mortality. His was the quintessential Egyptian story: the poor orphan whose talent eclipsed all others, but who still needed the melodramatic lucky break; the cultural icon who was finally brought low by an insidious disease that devoured him from inside as he struggled to record one more song, perform one more concert, film one more movie. Abd al-Halim is the true son of the soil, not, like so many other performers (although not Umm Kulthum), the progeny of urban, cosmopolitan Cairo or Alexandria, and his ailment, bilharzia, was rooted right in the rich, muddy waters of the Delta.

His life, for all his star power, remained clouded in mystery, and in death he has become canonized. The anniversary of his passing, March 30, 1977, is occasion for a month long media-fest. His films screen on television, the radio plays even more songs than usual, and the print media churns out special tribute editions. With the exception of a few recycled tabloid exposés, primarily rekindling rumors of secret marriages to Shadia in the fifties and Suad Husni in the early sixties (Amr 1995), the tone is hagiographic. For a brief period early on, some thought he feigned, or at least played up his illness to outdo another chronically ailing singer star, Farid al-Atrash. We might never be able to touch the real Brown Nightingale, except perhaps by scratching between the lines of hagiography. What remains is the voice, the image, and above all the screen persona, so seemingly natural that it is hard to believe otherwise.

Abd al-Halim Hafiz made sixteen films between 1955 and 1969 (al-Malak and Sa'd 1977). His first three films screened in 1955. In *Our Sweet Days* (*[Ayyamna al-hilwa]*, Hilmi Halim 1955) he played second male lead—to Omar Sharif and in tandem with Ahmad Ramzi—for the first and only time.[23] The remaining films were all his, including *Girls and Summer* (*[al-Banat wa al-sayf]*, Fatin Abd al-Wahhab 1960), in which he appeared in only one of three single-act segments.[24] He completed a string of eleven movies between 1956 and 1962. A five year absence was then broken by *The People's Idol* (*[Ma'budat al-gamahir]*, Hilmi Rafla 1967), which was followed a year later by *Father's Up a Tree* (*[Abi fawq al-shagara]*, Husayn Kamal 1968). There were other planned projects, including a non-musical role to be directed by Kamal al-Shaykh, but poor health intervened (Kamal al-Shaykh, January 23, 1996).[25]

The films are all romantic, some lighter, some more somber, most featuring four to six songs. With only several exceptions, Abd al-Halim played essentially the same role: a sensitive youth struggling to achieve some combination of financial and romantic success, fame and fortune beyond his social means. The female objects of desire—and Abd al-Halim played against virtually all the leading screen beauties of his day[26]—are unobtainable due to their higher social class (Amal Farid in *Nights of Love* [*(Layali al-hubb)*, Hilmi Rafla 1955]; Lubna Abd al-Aziz in *The Empty Pillow* [*(al-Wisada al-khaliya)*, Salah Abu Sayf 1957]; Maryam Fakhr al-Din in *Love Story* [*(Hikayat hubb)*, Hilmi Halim 1959]; Zubayda Tharwat in *A Day in My Life* [*(Yawm min umri)*, Atif Salim 1961]), a pure-hearted willingness to yield to a less deserving sister (Magda in *Today's Girls* [*(Banat al-yawm)*, Henry Baracat 1957]), or misguided aspirations to do better than the gentle, unassuming boy on the next balcony (Zizi al-Badrawi in *Girls and Summer*). Whether a struggling student, artist, journalist, or school teacher, he usually lives at home or shares quarters with a flatmate or two. Occasionally he broke the pattern: in *Song of Devotion* (*[Lahn al-wafa']*, Ibrahim Imara 1955) he and his uncle are wealthy musicians; in *Today's Girls* he shares a flat in upscale Maadi and can afford membership at the club; in *Girls and Summer* his family summers in Alexandria; in *My Prince Charming* (*[Fata ahlami]*, Hilmi Rafla 1957), his only commercial disappointment, he plays a playboy. Wherever he fits in a real sociological hierarchy, he is always a figure for mass identification in clear contradistinction with his social betters. His often marginal existence is underscored by scenes in which he borrows—sometimes without asking—suitable courting clothes from a flatmate, eats beans from a pot cooked over a kerosene primus stove, washes his own clothes in a metal basin, slips out past landlords to avoid rent queries, and gets around by bicycle. He played the loveable trickster as well as the forlorn victim, often a combination of the two. Personal ambition, however, is always tempered by compassion. His triumphs are always the victory of social justice and propriety over narrow-minded social conservatism and excess.

His films, derivative of earlier movies that celebrated middle and lower class virtues, are not ideologically forthright revolutionary epics like *Struggle in the Valley* or *Return My Heart.* They draw upon pre-revolutionary melodramatic tropes, but carry them a step further to meet the clarion call for a new era. His first two films served as introductions. *Song of Devotion,* in which he shared top billing with Shadia, is a light backstage romance.[27] In *Our Sweet Days* three financially strapped students sharing a flat vie for the affection of the beautiful boarder downstairs (Fatin Hamama). But it is Omar Sharif who gets her, shattering the friendship until her fatal illness brings the three friends back together.

While both films reveal Abd al-Halim's ease before the cameras and portend his film persona, it is in his third film, *Nights of Love,* in which he received his first top billing, that his character reaches full fruition. In the romantic comedy, a loose spin-off of *The Man in the White Suit,* he plays Ahmad, a clerical employee in a textile firm who develops an indestructible fabric, but finds credit bestowed upon a superior. When he musters courage to go to the boss's home to complain, he inadvertently crashes a costume ball where, in an outrageous parody of upper and middle class manners, he is taken for a wealthy scion dressed as an employee. This because of his straight-lined suit and *tarbush* (fez). Bemused party-goers stick a pencil behind each ear and tilt his horned-rim glasses forward, and before he knows what has hit him, Ahmad has won the prize for best costume and been smitten by Samia (Amal Farid), the boss's daughter, who poses as a domestic, while her cheeky servant (Widad Hamdi) wears a lady's *yashmak* (Turkish veil). By the time Ahmad realizes his romantic predicament, he finds himself competing with Samia's rich cousin. In the end, naturally, he is both recognized as the true genius and betrothed to the boss's daughter.

The formula quickly multiplied in future roles. In *Love Story,* which is loosely autobiographical because of the hero's life-threatening malady, Abd al-Halim again falls for the debutante (Maryam Fakhr al-Din). Ahmad lives with his blind mother (Firdaws Muhammad) and younger brother in a small apartment, and works as a school teacher to make ends meet (also autobiographical). He supplements his income and fulfills his artistic muse by performing at private parties. At one such event, he falls for Nadia. His performance, however, is a disaster, and he leaves downhearted, walking moodily along the Alexandria corniche. Suddenly Nadia pulls up in a sedan. She joins him in the moonlight as he sings "A Day, a Month, a Year" (lyrics by Mursi Gamil Aziz, music by Kamal al-Tawil), a ballad of unrequited love:

> In a day, in a month, in a year
> Wounds heal and fade away.
> The life span of my wound is longer than life itself.
> Farewell happy days, farewell love, farewell dreams.
> My love, I see you from afar,
> As if we were on a sleepless path alone
> And every step away from you is night,
> My suffering, my memory, a new wound.
> My love, I see you in my soul, I see you in my heart, in my love I see you.
> I get peace from your words, the laughter on your lips.
> I see you and the night of separation, from afar, a single wing
> On the wounded is longing . . . he knows the end of his wound.
> In a day, in a month, in a year
> Wounds heal and fade away.
> The life span of my wound is longer than life itself.
> Farewell happy days, farewell love, farewell dreams. . . .

From this moment onward, Ahmad and Nadia battle class-based social constraints, then, after he becomes successful, the sudden discovery of congenital heart trouble. At a gala performance Ahmad collapses. When he discovers the severity of his case—Nadia already knows because her father (Mahmud al-Maligi) happens to be Ahmad's physician—he breaks their engagement.[28] Suddenly Nadia's father proposes a trip to London for experimental surgery. The initial prognosis is good, but rumors of failure escalate. Panicked, Nadia decides to fly to London. At the airport she sees him descending the stairs of a newly arrived flight—he has been miraculously cured—and runs to him for a tarmac embrace.

In the lighter, Capra-esque *A Day in My Life,* Abd al-Halim plays Salah, a tabloid reporter assigned to cover the airport arrival of another Nadia, this one a millionaire's daughter (Zubayda Tharwat), fresh back from five years finishing in Europe. Accompanying him is his photographer roommate, Yunis (Abd al-Salam al-Nabulsi, a frequent co-star in his lighter vehicles). When their car breaks down, they flag a bus home. Sitting by them is Nadia, who has decided to elude father, step-mother, and fiance. He unaware of her identity, she ignorant of his professional assignment, Salah and Nadia fall in love. When Nadia does discover—and misconstrue—the circumstances of their initial encounter she acquiesces to her earlier arranged engagement to a cousin. Again, resolution comes swiftly, with the truth revealed, parental concession to a less than society page romance, and an airport reconciliation.

Abd al-Halim played this classic character for the last time in his penultimate work, *The People's Idol,* a reworking of *A Star is Born* with the gender roles reversed (although the "idol" in the title refers not to the male novice but to the female mentor). Released in 1967 after a five-year screen absence, the result primarily of his poor health, the film features an older actor, his youthful face lined prematurely, as well as a plumper, but still ravishing Shadia. Yet, as if time has stood still, the two reenact all the key symbols of his earlier work, including their collaboration in two films, *Song of Devotion* and *Dalila* (Muhammad Karim 1956). In *The People's Idol,* Abd al-Halim again plays a struggling artist, this time an actor, who lives alone in a flat in medieval Cairo that he rents from a doting, cheeky landlady (Zaynat Sidqi, reprising the part she played in *Our Sweet Days*). He gets by on credit extended by an alley of supportive neighbors (the buddy character here is played by Fuad al-Muhandis, the leading comic star of the 1960s). Every day he leaves the alley on bicycle for a downtown theater, where he plays a supporting role and pines for Suhayr, the female lead. When his part calls for a romantic interlude on stage he panics, but off stage he successfully woos, then loses her as his star, as singer rather than actor, eclipses hers. While he moves into a villa, Suhayr falls into drink and depression. Finally they are reunited at a party, and after a cold spell he wins her back with song.

If there is one enduring screen image of Abd al-Halim in this film it is him riding a bicycle, singing, through the not-yet crowded streets of Cairo. The bicycle has been a key cinematic symbol of the upright commoner. In *Bread and Salt* the young neighborhood lawyer gets around on a bicycle. Anwar Wagdi and Ismail Yasin pedal side by side, at times arm in arm, on their way to fix the pasha's phone in *Daughter of Nobility*. In *The Prisoner of Abu Zaabal*, Muhsin Sirhan pedals around Port Said on a bike to which he pays loving attention, and it is in the handlebars of his cycle that Mahmud al-Maligi has his thugs plant the incriminating narcotics.

Rich boys have cars, rich girls drivers; poor boys take public transportation and ride bikes.[29] Abd al-Halim is often painfully aware that not having access to a vehicle leaves him at a competitive disadvantage. In *The Empty Pillow* he misses Lubna Abd al-Aziz on their daily walk, then sees her drive off in her fiance's convertible. In *Love Story* he takes a ride home from Maryam Fakhr al-Din in her sedan, but later frets that he cannot meet her out at the Pyramids on his bicycle. In *The People's Idol* he takes Shadia for a spin on his handlebars, while they sing a duet. Wildly in love, he rides home from the theater singing as he pedals through the city, enters the alley, interacts playfully with kiosk vendors and café denizens, then climbs the stairs to his lonely flat. The scene contrasts sharply with Shadia's later unannounced arrival in a chauffeured limousine.

Abd al-Halim's last film, *Father's Up a Tree,* seemed to portend a shifting persona for a more cynical, ambiguous era. Although clearly too old for the role, the Nightingale again played a student. In the beginning Adil and his classmates cavort on the beach during summer vacation. When he and Amal (Mervat Amin) find themselves alone, he tries to kiss her but is rebuffed, despite his invocation of free love. Frustrated, Adil leaves Egypt for Beirut, where he takes up with a voluptuous cabaret dancer (Nadia Lutfi). Unaware of his specific whereabouts, his father (Imad Hamdi) flies to Lebanon to bring him home. The father, however, soon falls for Beirut's libertine charms. In a powerfully emotive ending, father and son tearfully confront each other in a cabaret, then walk out arm in arm as the dancer looks on, heartbroken. Exiting, Adil encounters Amal—his friends have

Abd al-Halim Hafiz and Nadia Lutfi in the explosive—and immensely popular—*Father's Up a Tree.*

changed. "I've also changed, Adil," she replies. The final scene depicts them back on the Alexandria beach, running then embracing and kissing numerous times, silhouetted by the setting sun.

Father's Up a Tree may not be Abd al-Halim's greatest film, but it stands apart from the corpus for both its tone and its impact. The film was a smash success, playing for fifty-two straight weeks at the downtown Diana Theater and setting unprecedented attendance records. In popular parlance the Diana became the "Cinema *Abi fawq al-shagara"* (Magdi Abd al-Rahman, April 12, 1996), and the nearby bus stop was also nicknamed (al-Imrusi 1994: 113). The re-pairing of Abd al-Halim with both Nadia Lutfi and Imad Hamdi lent the film a particular resonance. Both had co-starred with him in *The Sins* (*[al-Khitaya],* Hasan al-Imam 1962), his last film in the early sixties, before his five year hiatus from the screen, and his most intense film to date. Lutfi had played his love interest, Hamdi his disapproving father. The dirty secret behind the father's disdain for his eldest son is that Abd al-Halim is an illegitimate child, and the slap Hamdi administers near the film's ending—so different from the usual fare for either actor—undoubtedly still resonated with many who viewed the new film, which again pitted father versus son, only this time less as opposites than dark soulmates. In *Father's Up a Tree,* father and son return home together, but neither is fully condemned—and Adil has somehow convinced his girlfriend to be freer. The film bristles with sexuality, not least for its famous "ninety-nine kisses" (including twelve at the conclusion). The blatant sexuality drew condemnatory sermons from mosque pulpits, which in turn drew larger crowds to the Diana.[30]

Not quite a romance, certainly not a melodrama in the conventional sense, *Father's Up a Tree* speaks, intentionally or otherwise, to the dislocations of Egypt after June 1967. Traditional sexual propriety is questioned. How should good girls and boys behave in the new Egypt? Egypt is abandoned for more alluring—and freer—shores. Parents disappoint, and children seem condemned to repeat history. Good girls reconsider long-held ideas about sexual propriety. The certainties of the early revolution, the optimism of Abd al-Halim's earlier works are dashed. And the Nightingale himself is ailing, without much hope for recovery. In an oft-told chapter in the hagiography, director Husayn Kamal presses Abd al-Halim to shoot the long opening beach scene bare-chested, but the star resists forcefully. When the director insists, Abd al-Halim takes him into his dressing room, where he removes his shirt to reveal the numerous surgical scars. Kamal breaks down in tears, then the two resume the shoot with the star clothed (al-Imrusi 1995: 121). It is a poignant off-camera moment that speaks volumes about the particular artistry of cinema. The aging, afflicted star is once more youthful, cavorting on the beach, frustrated not by his inability to shake a parasitical ailment, but by his failure to win a kiss on the very beaches that had so often been the scenes of romantic triumph.[31]

Movies for the Masses

For Husayn Kamal, too, there is an ambivalent moral. After directing two literate, critically acclaimed films, *The Impossible* (*al-Mustahil* 1965) and *The Postman* (*al-Bustagi* 1968), the young director finally achieved popular success with a sexually titillating musical. But Kamal only got the assignment after the star managed to persuade his wary backers to overcome initial hesitations about so unorthodox a selection. Muhammad Abd al-Wahhab and Magdi al-Imrusi were concerned about Abd al-Halim's health, in part due to problems encountered during the filming of *The People's Idol,* a project that took four years to complete and went way over budget (it did, however, turn a profit; al-Imrusi 1995: 114–15). But al-Imrusi recalls expressing his particular concern over Kamal's "artistic" reputation directly to the young director:

> I told him, "Mr. Husayn, I saw *The Impossible* and *The Postman.* They were of the highest artistic quality." I stressed the word *artistic.* "You understand my point, Mr. Husayn. The critics and magazines wrote about these films, but each lasted one week in the theaters! Mr. Husayn, I believe in the place of fine artistry in the cinema, but I believe more in art that the critics and audience both like! You'll direct Abd al-Halim, and Abd al-Halim means popular. Whoever fails to respect the pleasure of the public, will not succeed. I believe that good work is first and foremost what the public likes. Because you're working, above all, to please the public" (ibid.: 115).

Kamal insisted he was ready for the challenge, and reminded his interlocutor that should the film fail, the director not the star would be held responsible, whereas any success would accrue fully to the star. He has ever after had to endure the scorn of taste-conscious critics who accuse him of "yielding to commercial pressures" and "threaten[ing] to revive in full force the worst traditions of the Egyptian cinema—songs, dances, and vapid melodrama" (Baker 1974: 412).

After the peak years of the early to mid-1950s, the proportion of movies that "gave pride of place to singing" receded. Musical interludes did not vanish, but the old-fashioned backstage musical fell out of fashion. Farid al-Atrash and a newly blonde Sabah still made films not very different from theirs of a decade earlier, but without the creative energy. A new generation of singers emerged on the big screen, but none carried the following or produced the string of hits that their predecessors had. Shadia's acting career broadened, as Abd al-Halim's cinema output diminished. Historically set dramas, such as the Mahfouz novels filmed by Hasan al-Imam, still featured a belly dance or three; otherwise the folkloric choreographies of Mahmud Ridda began to predominate. For a more mod audience there was a newer style of pop music that worked its way on screen: Suad Husni and the "Limelight Trio" (Samir Ghannam, George Sayyidhum, and al-Dayf Ahmad) as a mop-topped rock-and-roll quartet in *Crazy Kids ([Shabab magnun giddan],* Niyazi Mustafa 1967). Husni, while a talented song-and-dance performer, cultivated from the outset a much more diversified set of roles. Abd al-Halim, whose acting career receded in the sixties—not for lack or popularity, but for lack of physical stamina—reinvigorated the musical, first with *The People's Idol,* a classic remake of his earlier corpus, then with *Father's Up a Tree,* a greater spectacle in all respects and, as director Kamal has insisted, not a conventional musical. And yet, Kamal admits that his interest in the project stemmed, at least in part, from a desire to "accept the challenge" of making a popular film (Farid 1993: 113).

For a director, and a public sector Cinema Institute product, whose earlier work had been decidedly unconventional, the turn to commercialism may be couched in terms of selling out or surrendering to market pressures, the sinister forces indicated by his colleague Galal al-Sharqawi earlier in the decade. Turning the populist call of the revolution on its head, Kamal responds that he would rather see his name on the marquee of a popular theater in middle and working class Shubra than at the Cinema Club or Film Center (ibid.). If he told Magdi al-Imrusi what he had to do in order to land the Abd al-Halim film, in one respect he is still correct. His most artistic, "experimental" films may have wowed the critics, but it is his commercial films—*Father's Up a Tree, Empire of M's* (*Imbaraturiyat mim* 1972), and others—that filled the theaters. Abd al-Halim's final film has even achieved cult status. Young men flock to lower-class neighborhood cinemas when it screens to recite the lines and sing along as the film plays (Armbrust 1998). Although one particular musical number, during which Abd al-Halim and Nadia Lutfi cavort in the Lebanese hills, is often shown on television, the film itself is never broadcast, adding to its mystique.

THE CROONER AS REVOLUTIONARY ICON

With Israeli bombs falling around Cairo in June 1967, Gamal Abdel Nasser reportedly ordered the radio to play Abd al-Halim's nationalist anthems in order to rally the population.[32] After the war, unlike Umm Kulthum, who took to the international stage to raise funds and boost morale (Danielson 1997: 184–86), the Nightingale swore he would sing no more political songs. He later relented, but the next decades never produced anything to match the Nasser-era anthems.[33] After Nasser's death these songs were banned from the radio; they remained unavailable until after Sadat's assassination, when the Mubarak government allowed their re-release on cassette, the first collections narrated by Galal Muawad (Qandil 1995). Even to harsh critics of the Nasserist legacy these remain the songs that fired their youth.

For anyone who lived the Nasser years, the Brown Nightingale cannot be thought of except in holistic terms. His corpus of songs and movies can be divided and cataloged by type (short versus long songs, love songs versus political anthems, tragic versus comic films, with *Father's Up a Tree* in its own unique category). But as a popular icon, in all his manifestations—crooner, patriot, romantic, clown, sufferer—he is inextricably linked to the spirit of the era. And because his screen persona so clearly matched—and fed—popular perceptions of his own ongoing struggles in and with life, struggles to which many can still relate, and because those films continue to spark laughter and tears, this has been his most lasting legacy. The lyrics to a torch song like "A Day, A Month, A Year" may be read—or heard—simply as beautiful words accompanied by a haunting tune. But many, versed in cinema and its lore, will be able to place it, if not to a particular film, scene, or starlet, at least within a broad set of cinematic icons, of which Abd al-Halim is one of the most sacred. The Nightingale of the Revolution is the quintessential sentimental poor boy, held back by want and affliction, who, after the requisite dark night of the soul—during which he always sings the saddest tune of the soundtrack—makes it, conquers illness, gets the rich girl, and lives happily ever after as the curtain falls and the audience applauds.

Notes

1. Sixty-two films screened between 1940 and 1943; that number rose to 119 for the period 1944–1946, with fifty-two films screening in 1946 alone.

2. The scene is brief, less than two minutes, and ends abruptly when Stefan Rosti, her jealous lover, interrupts her.

3. Despite her lack of experience, she demanded and received an "astounding" level of artistic control over the productions, including full participatory rights in all production matters and final say on song selection (Danielson 1997: 89).

4. Shadia made seven films between 1947 and 1960, Sabah thirty-nine between 1945 and 1960, Huda Sultan thirty-three between 1950 and 1960, Layla Murad twenty-four between 1938 and 1954, Farid al-Atrash twenty-three between 1946 and 1958 (Ezeddine 1966: 4).

5. Mahmud Shkuku also sang one number. Abu Sayf later admitted including the numbers "in order to guarantee the film's commercial success. . . . Time has its requisites, and in the forties or fifties a film without music was impossible."

6. Of the fifty-three films produced during the 1945–46 season, al-Sharqawi identifies "9 girls seduced, 2 rapes, 3 cases of adultery, 9 murders, 3 suicides, 2 attempted suicides, 2 cases of madness."

7. Al-Sharqawi denotes two categories, films "inspired by actual historical events" and films "criticizing the old regime." The historicals are subdivided as follows: a) anti-colonial films, including *Down with Imperialism, Mustafa Kamil, Kilometer 99,* and *A Man in Our House;* b) two Palestine War films, *Land of Peace* and *The Dark Girl of Sinai;* c) three Suez War films, *The Prisoner of Abu Zaabal, Port Said,* and *Blazing Love;* d) two films about the "contemporary revolution," *With God on Our Side* and *Return my Heart;* e) one film about Algeria, *Jamila.* The films critical of the old regime are divided into a) those that depict exploitation of the peasantry: *Struggle in the Valley* and *Our Green Earth;* and b) anti-monopoly films: *The Thug* and *The Silent One.*

8. Parts of the following section were originally published in Gordon (2001b).

9. I first heard this categorization from Livia Alexander, which she used in her paper, "*Ismailiya Raih Gai:* Reviving the Musical Tradition in Egyptian Cinema," presented at the Middle East Studies Association, December 1998.

10. Categorizations are not provided in the Arabic listing, only in the English and French section. "Melody" could presumably be more properly rendered as "musical."

11. A snippet of this scene may be accessed on the CD-ROM, "Isma'il Yasin fi al-kumbyutur."

12. In real life their fairy-tale romance collapsed amidst Murad's frustrations at artistic constraints imposed on her by Wagdi. The final straw may well have been her discovery that he had obtained legal control of her finances, leaving her with nothing.

13. Again, no Arabic is provided. Presumably the word would be *"isti'rad,"* which should be rendered as "musical review." The song-and-dance numbers performed

by Wagdi and Fayruz, in one scene along with Ismail Yasin, mark the difference between this film and *Daughter of Nobility,* in which only Layla Murad sings.

14. "Social" films are those that are seen by critics to forefront social issues, however melodramatic the tropes employed. The point, of course, is that the designation is inconsistent and appears highly capricious.

15. A year earlier Nagma Ibrahim played her greatest film role, Raya in Salah Abu Sayf's *Raya and Sakina.* Here she turns her Dickensesque look to wonderful comic purpose.

16. Michel Chalhoub, multi-lingual, athletic (a polo player), and strikingly handsome, had been pressed to take a screen test by Chahine, a fellow "old Victorian." Re-christened Omar Sharif, the rest is film history. Hamama, a child star since the age of twelve (her first film appearance was in 1940), was already being touted as the leading lady of her generation. *Struggle in the Valley* was the first of their six collaborations, all but one as romantic co-stars, before Sharif left for Hollywood in the early 1960s.

17. Samir Farid (February 7, 1996) considers al-Tilmissani a true intellectual and the "only real political director in Egypt." He made a handful of other films, including a popular adaptation of Numan Ashur's drama *The People Below,* which he also scripted. Thereafter, according to Farid, al-Tilmissani was "hounded out of the industry." He went to Lebanon, where he wrote films for the singer Fayruz, but without his name attached, and died there in 1972. See his stinging critique of the industry in *Ruz al-Yusuf* (al-Tilmissani 1955).

18. Egyptians in their forties and fifties recall the annual television event the way many age mates in the United States might recall the annual broadcast of *The Wizard of Oz.*

19. And the title of a recently published appreciation (Hasanayn 1995).

20. Kamal al-Tawil came from an elite family with Wafdist connections. His uncle, Abd al-Fattah al-Tawil Pasha, had served in the last Wafd government. Although this uncle became a victim of the revolution, Kamal became one of its greatest musical champions, scoring the most important nationalist anthems performed by his friend, Abd al-Halim Hafiz.

21. The song, "Encounter" ([Liqa']; lyrics by Salah Abd al-Sabur, music by Kamal al-Tawil), was not a success.

22. The story may be apocryphal, but Danielson (1997: 166–67) notes Nasser's similar personal involvement in soliciting the support of Umm Kulthum.

23. Fatin Hamama received top billing. Sharif was second, and Ramzi, in his first appearance, was listed among the supporting players. Abd al-Halim received special billing as a featured player. The film, his first, is often listed second because it opened four days after *Song of Devotion* in March 1955.

24. He starred with Zizi al-Badrawi. The male leads in the other two segments were Kamal al-Shinawi (with Maryam Fakhr al-Din, directed by Izz al-Din Zulficar) and Husayn Riyad (with Samira Ahmad, directed by Salah Abu Sayf).

25. The veteran director does not recall the substance of the project, only that Abd al-Halim very much wanted to break away from his musical format.

26. Abd al-Halim's female co-stars were Shadia (3 films), Fatin Hamama (2 films), Amal Farid, Ayman, Magda, Lubna Abd al-Aziz, Mona Badr, Sabah, Maryam Fakhr al-Din, Zizi al-Badrawi, Zubayda Thawrat, and Nadia Lutfi (2 films).

27. Shadia reportedly complained when his name was to appear before hers. See *Ruz al-Yusuf,* January 17, 1955. Her name topped his in both film credits and advertisements.

28. This perception mirrors popular understandings of Abd al-Halim's failure to ever marry.

29. In Abd al-Halim films good girls may also take public transportation (Fatin Hamama in *Our Sweet Days*) or ride bikes (Magda in *Today's Girls* and Nadia Lutfi in *The Sins.* There were an estimated 21,000 bicycles in Cairo in 1952 (*Egyptian Gazette,* August 5, 1952).

30. Recalling a far different society, Magdi al-Imrusi (1995: 121) describes Muhammad Abd al-Wahhab's response to concerns over the sermons: "Idiot, go pay him to continue! The people listen, then they leave the mosque to go see the film. Watch . . . as long as he speaks like this, I guarantee the film will keep running!"

31. For later scenes when he did appear bare-chested, Abd al-Halim underwent extensive sessions with a make-up artist to cosmetically cover his scars.

32. According to al-Imrusi, Nasser ordered radio stations to broadcast "Welcome, Battle" (Ya ahalan bil-mu'arik) every half hour. See Ahmad al-Naggar, "Abd al-Nasir talab min Haykal idha'at ughniyat 'ya ahalan bil-mu'arik' kull nusf sa'a," *al-Ahrar,* January 16, 1995.

33. After the 1973 October War, "God is Greatest," the anthem of Suez, was revived for schoolyard assemblies. The Mubarak era has produced its share of nationalist pop songs, but most are restricted to televised filler spots in between programs.

FOUR

Free to be "Bad"
The Revolution's New Woman Onscreen

I feel liberated from everything. From Abbasiya, tradition, marriage, and from the need for anyone to provide for me. I'm just like you now.

I'm Free, 1959

A girl is just like a boy!

The Open Door, 1963

Ladies' Man

Crusading journalist, social reformer, political gadfly, and the most widely read author of his time, Ihsan Abd al-Quddus (1919–1991) was, above all, a ladies' man. On the walls of the family apartment hang a series of sketched testimonials. In one, he sits nearly naked, cross-legged, pen to paper, with an ink bottle to the side—an unmistakable take on the famous statuette of the pharaonic scribe whose figure became the symbol of the national book organization. "The Egyptian writer who has roused a slumbering people and taught it the words *freedom, individual,* and *revolution. . . .*"[1] In another, he is a young man on the run, his pen dripping ink, each drop resembling a leading old-regime politician. From his left arm dangles a woman, bare-shouldered in a knee-length tightly-fitted dress. In yet a third sketch his pen is linked to a series of hearts.

A ladies' man. Despite the caricatures—and some of the film characters that surely were modeled on him—he was not a Casanova. He may have occasionally penned himself as such, and the figure of the available bachelor writer, a popular cinema motif, did become linked to his image. A handsome man with a gentle face, he may well have fluttered the hearts of female confidantes. But above all he captured them on paper, in short stories and novels that were the most widely read works of fiction in the Arab world, and which burst onto the screen in some of the most popular, beloved, and fondly remembered films of the Nasser era.

His pedigree pointed him toward both print and motion picture media. His father, Muhammad Abd al-Quddus, had abandoned an engineering career for the stage, and played character parts in eight films. His mother, Fatima al-Yusif, left the stage in 1925 to found *Ruz al-Yusuf* (after her stage name), still the most influential journal of arts and politics in the country. Ihsan took his law degree from Cairo University, then, like his parents, switched careers, joining the journal as staff writer and working his way up to editor-in-chief. He gained prominence as a political essayist in the late 1940s, just as the movie industry took off and the political order came crashing down. Still in his twenties, he became a leading voice of liberal discontent with the established order. When he called for the British ambassador's removal in 1945, he wound up in prison for a fortnight. When he cried out against the defective weapons given Egyptian soldiers in Palestine, he faced physical harassment, but gained the ears of young rebels who soon became Free Officers. After July 23 he stood with the mutineers, but when he later urged them to step aside and restore civilian rule in 1954, he again served time. In 1955 he made his peace with the regime, trumpeting the broad outlines of a progressive social ideology and pan-Arab aspirations. At the same time, perhaps chastened, perhaps drawn by a different muse, he traded the pen of political punditry to write fiction. Now the ink would drop hearts rather than pashas' heads.

Ihsan was never a master craftsman of narrative or prose. Native and non-native students of modern Arabic literature have virtually ignored him (although many of us first encounter him in intermediate language courses). He was, however, unparalleled in circulation. It is easy to see why, notes one sceptic. His works "have appealed to successive generations of adolescents and young adults faced with the task of reconciling traditional mores with the forces of change in the post-revolutionary Arab societies. This appeal has been intensified by Abd al-Quddus's choice of style and lexicon, both of which made few demands on the reader" (Allen 1982: 95–96). His stories do not analyze relations between social classes, nor do they provide insight into the life of the urban or rural poor. He rarely spoke to or about the heartland. Rather, he spoke to the youth of a modernizing middle class who struggled to free themselves of social and parental constraints, to adapt and adopt changing social and gender roles, and above all to experience and understand the notion of romantic love. "You taught us to write of love, to live and breathe, learn from, separate from, sleep on, and greet the morning with love," wrote a female colleague in eulogy (Madiha Izzat in al-Quwaysni 1991: 239). If he did not teach them how to make love, he certainly gave voice to their deep desires. In Naguib Mahfouz novels, lovers steal kisses (and sometimes more) on rooftops or in darkened stairwells; in Ihsan's stories they pet brazenly in the back seats of convertibles, arrange trysts in plushly furnished bachelor pads, and dance the night away—with a variety of partners—to the sounds of flowing whiskey and rhythm and blues.

Men read his stories, but he was, above all, a woman's writer. His salon was his laboratory. Not the fashionable bachelor pad of popular cinematic imagination, but an office in the family's enormous Zamalek apartment, where he lived with his wife and two young boys, and where the door was always open to any woman, friend or stranger, with a story to tell about dashed dreams and frustrated ambitions (Muhammad and Ahmad Abd al-Quddus, December 15, 1995). As a consequence, the female characters he created—however one may criticize them as the product of a male pen, even perhaps male fantasies—were far more complexly drawn than any who had been heretofore crafted. His most popular have been characterized, at least by film critics, as "bad" *(sharir)*. By this they generally mean women who have taken, or endeavor to take, control of their lives, no longer simply the weak-willed victims of their fairer sex. Fatin Hamama, who made a major leap of artistic faith when she agreed to play

Nadia, the tortured teenage hero of *I Can't Sleep,* has described the transformation from classic "good" to the "bad" girl:

> During the forties and most of the fifties she was generally a helpless girl. At that age I played roles that were given me. I had no concern with the ways of the cinema. Now from a more prominent position I try to get more involved. In the late fifties the working girl began to emerge, she became educated and worked, and had personality. So the writers began to write about her (Farid 1995a: 69).

In translating these roles from printed page to film, she and others brought to the screen a "new woman," one who

> reflects what our contemporary society has achieved thanks to our links to the civilized world around us, which has opened its life to us. She is the daughter of this new society with all that it has granted her: culture, education, freedom, the liberties of an open world far from the world of chains and obstacles. She is the new woman who has found herself, achieved her being, asserted her personality, and left behind the world of femininity (Yusuf Khalif in al-Quwaysni 1991: 257).

Ask any middle class reading and film-going woman who was in her teens or twenties during the Nasser era what movies she recalls as most impacting her life; she is bound to include *I Can't Sleep, I'm Free, Where's My Life, Don't Put Out the Sun, The Empty Pillow,* and a host of other adaptations.

Between 1952 and 1970, a small group of Egyptian filmmakers brought major adaptations of ten Ihsan Abd al-Quddus novels to the big screen, along with three sets of one-acts based on his short stories. Two of the novel adaptations became musicals starring Abd al-Halim Hafiz: *The Empty Pillow* and the blockbuster *Father's Up a Tree.* The rest are straight dramas without musical interludes. Of the ten, five feature women as the main character. These films afforded a select group of actresses some of their most memorable roles: Magda (*Where's*

My Life? [Ayna 'umri], Ahmad Diya al-Din 1956), Fatin Hamama (*I Can't Sleep [La anam],* Salah Abu Sayf 1957) and *Don't Put Out the Sun* (*[La tutfi' al-shams],* Salah Abu Sayf 1961), Lubna Abd al-Aziz (*I'm Free [Ana hurra],* Salah Abu Sayf 1958), and Nadia Lutfi (*The Dark Glasses [al-Naddara al-sawda'],* Hussam al-Din Mustafa 1963).[2]

Ihsan's gaze focused squarely on the rooted upper middle class, his own world of the club, Alexandria beach vacations, automobiles, college educations, and professional careers. This is an important consideration when gauging the image of Egypt that his own work brought to film screens. When Salah Abu Sayf, already ensconced in popular and critical imagination as the filmmaker of the streets, directed four Abd al-Quddus adaptations between 1957 and 1960 he felt pressed to redefine social realism within the salon. Critic and interlocutor Hashim al-Nahhas (1996) calls this Abu Sayf's period of working "outside the neighborhood." The director never abandoned that working class world entirely, but his vision as a filmmaker broadened, and the Abd al-Quddus adaptations represent a significant element of that broadening.

Ihsan's stories are lushly romantic tales of broken hearts and shattered love affairs. The endings often appear conventional, reinforcing rather than toppling traditional conservative gender roles. When they did rattle the foundations of that order, they might be changed for the screen adaptation in order to suit dramatic or social conventions. Yet, each in its own way seethes with social, and occasionally political, ferment that reflects the revolutionary spirit of Nasser's Egypt. Ihsan's primary female characters are, in one respect or another, all rebels. They may suffer for it, and they may even wind up in a seemingly subservient position they swore they would never occupy. They may be misguided—even "bad"—but they always capture their readers'/viewers' sympathies precisely because of their rebellious streak, and because even if they are not convinced of what they stand for, what they stand against is surely wrong. If life's resolutions sometimes disappoint, or seem somewhat conventional even by the days' standards, it is not the destination, but the rebellious route that is important.

What Price Freedom?

Where's My Life? (Magda)

Ihsan's women all chafe under outmoded social and familial pressures, and long desperately for an escape hatch. None more so than Aliya, the teenage heroine of *Where's My Life?* As portrayed by Magda, the youthful, ever-suffering starlet of the fifties and sixties, Aliya appears destined for disaster. When she learns she is to be married to an elderly uncle, the teen's first response is to put on her best dress and parade down to school to thumb her nose at her suddenly former teacher and principal. Uncle Aziz (Zaki Rustam) has been the family benefactor since Aliya's father died, plying the teenager with gifts, bailing her out of trouble at school, and sustaining the family accounts. When, upon Aliya's sixteenth birthday, he now proposes marriage, her mother (Amina Rizq), who expected to be asked herself, cannot refuse. The nanny (Firdaws Muhammad) weeps, but the mother steels herself for her daughter's sudden transformation from exuberant adolescent to caged wife. Giddy with her suddenly grown-up status and liberation from school, Aliya never realizes, until she finds herself confined in her jealous husband's house, then moved out to his country estate and kept under the watchful eyes of his two spinster sisters, that her new life will not be what she dreams.

Ahmad Dia al-Din's film adaptation rests primarily on the star turns of his players. Magda, resplendent in her early scenes with her long, flowing hair, button nose, and breathless voice, transforms herself from self-absorbed princess into pathetic victim, a wronged teenager suddenly turned woman. Then, after her husband dies and she returns to her mother's house, she turns recklessly flirtatious. Zaki Rustam first appears the kindly bachelor uncle, yet his sinister eyes and wry smile reveal early signs of improper designs. On his wedding night he playfully chases Aliya around the house in his bathrobe—she still calling him "Uncle"—then allows her to sleep alone, untouched, when she collapses on the bed. But when her girlfriends invade the house the next day before his sexual desires have been fulfilled, his frustrations begin to reveal a brutal nature. Any lingering sympathy will be dashed by scenes in which he first locks away, then beats Aliya for her expressions of adolescent independence.[3] Amina Rizq, already carving out her niche as the ever-suffering mother, here carries a sad burden of resigned complicity as a powerless, ultimately negligent parent who allows her instincts to be overruled by financial considerations and outmoded social conventions. Finally there is Yahya Shahin as Doctor Khalid, the ambivalent male hero of the film, who tries and eventually perseveres in guiding Aliya toward the straight and narrow after she has returned to her mother's house, bruised but unchastened.

Refusing to play the widow—as her mother has obviously done for years—Aliya pays no heed to her precarious social position. She goes out in provocative sleeveless polka dot outfits, drawing the attention of desirous young men who follow her on their bicycles and show up at her doorstep with sweets. Doctor Khalid, who has followed her back from the country, assuming the role of proper suitor and male guardian, endeavors to make her understand that she can no longer associate with unmarried boys, but she spurns both his advice and his protestations of affection. "I'll live for myself," she asserts, reminding him of his earlier obedience to social norms: when she had taken refuge with him he had felt compelled to return her to her husband despite marks of physical abuse.[4] Adil (Ahmad Ramzi), a charming law student, appears a likeable enough suitor until informed of her social status. Provoked by older married friends, jealous of his innocent turn from their alcohol-splashed party routine, he makes improper advances, then physically assaults her. On both occasions Doctor Khalid intervenes, and Aliya finally takes refuge in his arms. At the end of one of Abd al-Quddus's most titillating, but least reform-minded film adaptations, the wayward young woman discovers her place in the traditional embrace of a husband who is slightly older but with honorable designs.

I CAN'T SLEEP (FATIN HAMAMA)

If Aliya is a "bad" girl in the cultural scheme of things, she is an angel compared to Nadia Lutfi, the troubled teenager wrestling with demons that keep her up nights and threaten to bring disaster upon those she loves in *I Can't Sleep.* Nadia, too, is in some respects a victim of social and cultural mores; yet she is far more pro-active in embarking upon questionable behavior. Fatin Hamama may have easily played Aliya (although the role is all Magda); she had to be persuaded to play Nadia (al-Nahhas 1996: 104).

I Can't Sleep marked a double departure for Salah Abu Sayf. His first venture into the troubled world of the middle class (on its own terms, not compared unfavorably to the alley), it was also a rare, and early, venture in color production.[5] A prologue to the film depicts young Nadia being raised by a doting father (Yahya Shahin) after her parents' divorce, then at boarding school. When Nadia, now sixteen, returns home to find her father newly re-married and very much in love, she connives to poison a happy household. Normal hurt feelings co-mingle with Freudian jealousy as she successfully engineers a rupture, not only between her father and his wife, Safiya (Maryam Fakhr al-Din), but also between father and brother (Omar Sharif), who is wrongfully accused as Safiya's lover. Suddenly alone with her father, yet saddened by his unhappiness and nagged by guilt, she introduces him to a school friend, the brassy Kawsar (Hind Rustam). Then, right after the wedding she discovers that Kawsar has only married for money, and has a boyfriend (Rushdi Abaza) on the side. When Nadia threatens to reveal Kawsar's infidelity, she finds herself outplayed, suddenly engaged, with her father's naive approval, to the boyfriend. In the climactic scene, she flees her wedding ceremony, running up to her room, where she confesses to her father. After he leaves to confront the pretenders, a fallen candle sets Nadia's wedding dress aflame. She lives, but will remain an invalid in the care of her father and uncle, having sacrificed her chance for true, independent love.

Again, the text can be viewed/read as bending, yet reinforcing traditional social roles. The "bad" girl is clearly and horribly punished for her anti-social behavior. This view is underscored by an important and provocative sub-plot. After returning to her father's house at the outset of the film, a rebellious, sexually confused Nadia seeks the counsel of a romance writer, a middle-aged bachelor (Imad Hamdi). Soon afterwards, the two embark on an affair, but the relationship ultimately comes to an end when the writer becomes engaged to Nadia's former step-mother. In true melodramatic fashion, Nadia discovers this when she visits Safiya to confess her role in ruining the prior marriage. Instead of cleansing her conscience, Nadia's once seemingly liberating relationship is abruptly thrown back in her face, and she now feels betrayed by yet another man. As a plot vehicle, the discovery helps steel her determination to break out of her cycle of lies. As a moral, it only widens the web of deceit into which good and bad women find themselves snared.

As a film role, however, the part of Nadia remains seminal. For an actress with the impeccable screen reputation of Fatin Hamama, a child star turned romantic lead, Nadia Lutfi provided a consummate challenge. Off screen she was already into her second marriage, having divorced director Izz al-Din Zulficar and embarked upon a fairy-tale romance with Omar Sharif (her uncle in this film). Her past roles, however, as the victimized girl of upstanding virtue afflicted by terminal illness or duplicitous relatives, now gave way to a heroine with a self-destructive streak and uninhibited sexuality. It was a role that Hamama felt uncomfortable assuming, yet it made her a more accomplished actress.

I'M FREE (LUBNA ABD AL-AZIZ)

Adapted from Ihsan Abd al-Quddus's most famous novel, *I'm Free* catapulted a new actress to stardom. Lubna Abd al-Aziz had scored her first role alongside Abd al-Halim Hafiz in Salah Abu Sayf's prior film, a musical adaptation of Abd al-Quddus's *The Empty Pillow.* In that film she had served primarily as the object of desire in a story about unrequited first love. Recurring images of her face upon Abd al-Halim's pillow and the coming together of two hands in secretive sidewalk meetings are her most important contributions to the film. With *I'm Free* she transformed her artistic persona into beauty with an attitude, exactly as Ihsan wrote Amina, his rebellious, cheeky heroine.

Until it embellishes and then subverts the author's racy ending, the film, scripted by Naguib Mahfouz, is a fairly faithful adaptation. From the opening shots of Amina flirting coyly with neighborhood school boys from her balcony—something "proper" Abbasiya girls did not do—through her scandalous decision to avoid marriage and pursue a university degree, Lubna Abd al-Aziz embodies the teenage girl who knows she is the prettiest in the neighborhood and has learned to flaunt it. She lives with her paternal aunt and uncle because her parents, who divorced when she was an infant, each desired their own independence. Aunt (Zuzu Nabil) and uncle (Husayn Riyad), once abusive overlords, now appear increasingly confounded by a niece who defies adult authority and responds to physical and verbal attack with bemused, silent nonchalance. When Amina rejects the proposal of a suitor in order to attend the American University in Cairo, her aunt and uncle deliver her up to her loveable, irreverent father (Muhammad Abd al-Quddus, Ihsan's real-life father), who agrees she will now be more help than bother, and allows her exactly what she has demanded throughout, her freedom.

But freedom to what end? Amina graduates from AUC and takes a job working for a foreign corporation (in the novel she takes a boyfriend at college, but they drift apart after graduation; this is all missing in the film). One day, spontaneously, she phones Abbas (Shukri Sirhan), the book-wormish neighborhood boy who had always intrigued her. Now a journalist with strong anti-monarchical credentials, he is both surprised and delighted. Their reminiscences soon turn philosophical.

> *Amina:* In any case, all that was long, long ago. It seems to me that a hundred years have passed since we were living on Ganzouri [Street]. It also seems years that I've been struggling to get where I am now.
>
> *Abbas:* And where are you?
>
> *Amina:* I've got freedom—that freedom that Abbasiya considered immoral. I'm free now, and I don't think I lack morals.
>
> *Abbas:* And I don't think you're free!
>
> *Amina:* How do you mean not free? I feel liberated from everything. From Abbasiya, tradition, marriage, and from the need for anyone to provide for me. I'm just like you now. You have a degree and so do I. You have a job and so do I. You earn a salary and so do I. I'll bet I even earn more than you. What else do I need to be free?
>
> *Abbas:* You're still not really free. . . . Don't be angry. Please let me ask you one question: why do you want to be free?
>
> *Amina:* Oh, so I need a reason now?!
>
> *Abbas:* Freedom is a means, not an end. . . .

Over time, Abbas convinces Amina that she should dedicate herself to a political cause: national liberation and revolution. After several visits punctuated by similar spirited interchanges, they recognize the depth of their mutual feelings for each other, leave the office and wind up at his flat, embracing and cooking lunch together.

Ihsan Abd al-Quddus ended his story on an ironic, if mildly scandalous note. Amina surrenders much of her soul to Abbas, moving in with him, waiting on him at times in ways that made her recoil with memories of her aunt's servitude, and supporting his politics. Yet she pointedly never marries him and does not surrender her career. The screen version adopts a more socially and politically schizophrenic finale, a more conventional male-female relationship with a touch of revolutionary propaganda thrown in for good measure. In the movie Amina continues to print and circulate anti-regime manifestoes after Ahmad's arrest (he is never arrested in the novel). Finally, she, too, is nabbed (Farouk's picture looms large at her interrogation). In prison, under the watchful eye of the warden, and witnessed by her father and suddenly benevolent uncle, Amina and Ahmad are married. Before the long walk back to her cell block that ends the film, Amina declares that she is finally free. Abbas has noted the date: July 21, 1952, two days prior to the Free Officers rising, Egypt's salvation, and the release of (most) political prisoners.

DON'T PUT OUT THE SUN (FATIN HAMAMA)

After bringing Amina to life with such fresh-faced spunk, Lubna Abd al-Aziz went on to become a major star as romantic and comic-romantic lead in the following decade.[6] For his two succeeding Abd al-Quddus adaptations, Salah Abu Sayf turned back to Fatin Hamama to play the leads. In *The Blocked Path* (*al-Tariq al-masdud* 1958) he cast Hamama as a more traditionally sympathetic fragile character trapped between an illicit affair with a romance writer (Ahmad Mazhar) and later a well-meaning, but socially constrained rich peasant son (Shukri Sirhan). In *Don't Put Out the Sun,* a more typical "bad" girl role, Hamama again played a teenager having an affair with an older man, played again by Imad Hamdi. This time, to make matters naughtier, he is a married man, her piano teacher. When his wife begins to suspect that the home lessons are taking an improper turn, Fathi takes Layla to a vacant flat, empty save for a piano, and gives her a key. The relationship is clearly manipulative, and doomed to failure. Fathi draws promises from the smitten teen that she will never marry, while providing her the fiction of a stable relationship grounded in their own secret hideaway. Pressured by his wife and confronted with social convention, he will later yield, breaking Layla's heart in the process. Yet, the romantic coupling of Imad Hamdi and Fatin Hamama, frequent co-stars in a long series of tear-jerkers, insures that however misguided or wrong their affair is—a relationship with a married man always destroys a household, Layla's mother (Aqila Ratib) tells her—this one will be read as tragic love.

Fathi will eventually break Layla's heart in cruel fashion. When her widowed mother is informed by Fathi's wife of the situation, she tries to counsel, then grounds her daughter. Layla protests that her mother does not understand "true" love, and later sneaks out, searching for Fathi, then waiting for him at their flat. Fathi eventually arrives, having been informed that she has run away. Apologetic, still smitten, yet firm, he insists she return home. Layla's torment is quickly compounded by a family decision—taken by her mother, her maternal uncle, and her oldest brother, Ahmad (Shukri Sirhan)—that she marry. The arranged marriage quickly breaks down. The wedding is somber; alone with her new husband Layla tries, but cannot resist his sexual advances. Shortly thereafter, she flees her husband and returns home. When his physical abuse later becomes apparent to the family they secure her divorce.

"True" love rooted in proper relationships is at the essence of the story, and for Layla the impropriety cuts both ways. Like other adaptations of Abd al-Quddus stories, this film begins with an aphorism taken from the novel's opening: "Life is based in principles; search for your principles . . . find your life. Ihsan." Each of her siblings, all growing up in a household without a patriarch, likewise search for romantic fulfillment. With the exception of the materialist-minded Mamduh (Ahmad Ramzi), who dies in a motorcycle accident after an argument with his older brother, all will succeed, even, ultimately, Layla. Her sisters eventually succumb to persistent suitors, and her eldest brother, torn between familial responsibilities, his own emotional insecurity, and, later, guilt for his brother's death, will finally propose to Shahira (Nadia Lutfi), the upstanding beauty who has been courting him from the outset. Layla's road is rougher. Still pining for the unattainable, she pursues Fathi; spurned by her former lover who for the first time exhibits deep sentiment toward his wife, she swallows a bottle of pills.

The road to redemption and romance runs through Suez. Ahmad, still fearful of romantic commitment and torn by guilt, volunteers to join the guerillas in the Canal zone. At camp he meets and befriends Mahmud, the suitor of his sister Nabila (Layla Fawzi). When he returns home, slightly wounded, he gives his blessing to Nabila's engagement, finally presents Shahira to his family, and, in the process introduces Layla to his friend Midhat, to whom she becomes instantly attracted. Brothers in arms become brothers-in-law on the domestic front, and the "bad" girl, punished both properly (emotional devastation) and improperly (arranged marriage) for her social transgressions, starts a new life, as do her siblings, rooted in love relationships that are at once ethical and romantic.

THE DARK GLASSES (NADIA LUTFI)

Ihsan Abd al-Quddus's import as a cultural icon for the era is evinced by the penned aphorisms that open many of his films, always signed "Ihsan," first name only. No other writer of equal or greater stature—Taha Husayn, Naguib Mahfouz, Yusuf Idris—would be known or cited in such familiar terms. Equally, if not more so, is the resonance of characters. In a remarkable case of literature/film begetting stardom, the young actress who played Shahira in *Don't Put Out the Sun*—a "good" girl through and through—took her stage name from the quintessential Abd al-Quddus "bad" girl. At the urging of producer Ramsis Nagib, Paula Shafiq became Nadia Lutfi. *Don't Put Out the Sun* was her ninth film, but she stood on the verge of stardom. A year later, in 1962, she played opposite Abd al-Halim Hafiz in *The Sins,* a role that was primarily cosmetic, not unlike Lubna Abd al-Aziz's in *The Empty Pillow.* Soon after, however, art really intersected with life when Nadia Lutfi the actress portrayed the character who is perhaps the most memorable of Abd al-Quddus's "bad" girls to grace the big screen.

The Dark Glasses took the "bad" girl to new depths, making her redemption all the more powerful. Maddy, short for Madiha, is Amina from *I'm Free* with a hidden, dark side, symbolized by the sunglasses she wears in public, even when indoors. Her screen entrance recalls Amina's, legs and lower torso shot from behind, but whereas Amina wore a calf-length dress and gazed down at the neighborhood boys from her balcony, Maddy sports tight pants and struts amongst the boys, poolside at the club. Before the camera shows her face, she stops and spills a pitcher of water on three lounging young men, then skips off. Such is Maddy: carefree, flirtatious, sensual, a hard drinker and, in the film's most celebrated scene, a hard dancer. That night she meets Umar (Ahmad Mazhar), a solitary figure sitting quietly off to the side while she and her crowd play spin the bottle. A conscientious factory manager with frustrated ambitions to write, and a bachelor, he takes her to his apartment and introduces her to his "friends," the authors on his wall of books. They include Western and Arabic classicists: Balzac, Shaw, Shakespeare, Chekhov, Taha Husayn, Abbas al-Aqqad, and Ahmad Shawqi. Umar is clearly interested, but rebuffs Maddy's efforts to seduce him, protesting his conviction in a more deep-rooted love.

Maddy and Umar then engage in a battle of wills that ultimately validates his deeper emotions, but only after she turns the tables on him. Repulsed by her friends, even by their perky nicknames (Susu, Fifi, etc.), he insists upon calling her Madiha. In the late night hours, unbeknownst to Maddy, he drafts a novel titled "The Dark Glasses," for which she is the inspiration and in which her sunglasses symbolize a mask worn to conceal her inner self. During their courtship he wrests her away from her indolent circle and tries to impart a sense of social consciousness, taking her to visit Mustafa, a good-hearted laborer whose arm has been crushed in a factory accident. Initially put off, Maddy soon proves an adept student. When Umar leaves for Germany to study new industrial techniques (he returns far more enthusiastic about European labor reform than new technology), she closets herself in her room, reading, shunning her friends, and ignoring the concerned queries of her parents, who also lead a dissolute life of drinking and gambling. When she goes out it is to visit Mustafa, first in the hospital, later at his modest apartment. Her weakening willpower, however, is captured in fits of restless tossing and turning in bed, somewhat reminiscent of Nadia in *I Can't Sleep,* here punctuated by the pounding rhythm of African drums.[7] When she awakens, the romantic lilt associated with Umar returns, but eventually the drumming prevails. Much to Umar's dismay, when he returns, unannounced and flowers in hand, he finds her back at the pool cavorting with her old chums. Maddy, who had succumbed to loneliness, runs after him, only to find her apologies rebuffed.

Suddenly hero and heroine reverse roles. Seduced by promotion, then an appointment to the board of directors, as well as by the attentions of the boss's brassy daughter, Umar abandons his social conscience for the corporate ladder. But Maddy pursues him relentlessly. In the climactic scene she waits for him at home, adding copious notes to his manuscript, which she discovers lying unfinished on the desk in his study. When he returns intoxicated, with the boss's daughter on his arm, Maddy confronts him. In a prior scene, Mustafa had visited her at home, enduring the humiliation of her parents and their guests, to inform her of Umar's sudden turn-about, his indifference to working conditions at the plant and promotion of labor-saving machinery that will result in mass layoffs. Now Maddy confronts him with the repercussions of his new-found careerism and hands him her dark glasses, for his own use. The following day he offers his resignation to the board of directors, finds Maddy at their usual Nile-side rendezvous, and, to a musical flourish, snaps the glasses in half.

Nadia Lutfi went on to play her share of good girls, but she is best known, after Maddy, as Riri, the good-hearted whore in the adaptation of Naguib Mahfouz's *Autumn Quail,* then as the corrupting dancer in *Father's Up a Tree,* based on another Ihsan Abd al-Quddus story. In the latter case she does not really play one of Ihsan's "bad" girls, for her part is secondary in a film in which the main characters are men gone astray. *Father's Up a Tree* is, in this sense, different from the other Abd al-Quddus stories discussed above. Bad girl, without male parental supervision, repents and finds shelter in the arms of a strong, progressive, even fatherly man. However conventional the plot resolutions or flagrant the male fantasies—common charges levelled against such scenarios—these were films for, about, and loved especially by, women. *Father's Up a Tree* is more a man's movie, and the ongoing television ban that restricts its screenings to cut-price theaters in poorer neighborhoods that women do not generally attend (Armbrust 1998) has reinforced its positioning as such, even while enhancing its allure to women.

At the same time, the film's decidedly late sixties, post-1967 aura reflects a changed positioning for the classic Ihsan character. If there is a "bad" girl, it is not the gold-hearted whore played by Nadia Lutfi, but Adil's age-mate girlfriend, Amal, played by Mervat Amin, who initially resists his efforts at sexual exploration, but in the end agrees to "change." Her transition from good/sexually reluctant to bad/sexually permissive girl marks an interesting transformation. Ihsan may still rein in his males; the swinging bachelors always seem to settle down and the wayward married men return home to restore domestic tranquility. It is his women, ever challenging, if hardly ever toppling, social mores who remain the most intriguing, and decidedly more liberated characters, whatever the emotional cost and however conventional the resolution of their predicaments.

A Woman's Voice

Ihsan Abd al-Quddus was not the only author to see his new women brought to the screen. Henry Baracat's 1963 adaptation of Latifa al-Zayyat's novel *The Open Door* provides interesting comparison to the Abd al-Quddus portrayals, particularly those brought to the screen by Salah Abu Sayf. Baracat, in contrast to the master realist, is the great romantic director of the era. Like so many contemporaries, he claimed artistic lineage from Kamal Salim's 1939 *Determination.* Yet, Baracat's artistic signature was "poetry and emotion" (Farid 1993: 41–42), punctuated by lush soundtracks and, often, musical numbers. He favored Fatin Hamama over all other stars; he used her often and she played in some of his best, most popular films.[8]

In *The Open Door,* a fairly faithful adaptation of the woman-authored coming of age novel, she plays another Layla, a young woman with a desire for freedom no less powerful than that of Ihsan's Amina in *I'm Free.* The film opens with an anti-colonial demonstration by female high school students, activity alluded to but never depicted outright in the novel. After Layla speaks, the students, all dressed in matching uniforms, carry her on their shoulders chanting "Long live Egypt." Home, however, is a different story. While mother and brother Mahmud watch helplessly, her father beats her with a slipper, chasing her into her room. When Mahmud tries to comfort her, gently suggesting that she has indeed transcended proper social roles, Layla

Almost kissing cousins—Fatin Hamama and Hasan Yusuf in *The Open Door.*

again explodes: "You also tell me I'm wrong?! A girl is just like a boy!"

The only one who can console her is her cousin Isam (Hasan Yusuf), who lives upstairs. "You're my little sister," he tells her playfully, stroking her cheek, but their eyes now reveal newly emergent feelings. Interrupted by Layla's mother, Isam runs upstairs to a crescendo of strings, holding his chest; Layla presses her face to her mirror, hangs head and chest over the balcony in a swoon, then dances around her room. That night each lies awake in bed.

Isam, however, ultimately disappoints her. When, much to their father's dismay, Mahmud announces that he has volunteered to join the freedom fighters in the Canal zone, Isam promises to accompany him, but under maternal pressure (he lives in yet another fatherless household), quickly relents. The next morning Layla sees her brother off with patriotic pride, while Isam, still in his pajamas, lingers in the background. She retains special affection for her cousin, but flirts at parties, arousing his jealousy. They continually make up until she discovers that Isam has been playing around with the maid. Concurrently she meets Mahmud's guerrilla buddy Husayn (Salih

Salim, a handsome ex-footballer who never achieved stardom), who has accompanied her brother home on leave.

Her faith in men shattered, Layla goes onto the roof, only to observe downtown Cairo burning in the distance. It is January 26, 1952, Black Saturday. "Everything beautiful has ended," she sighs. Her brother's comrade tries to reassure her: "This isn't the end. We'll work out the ending—you and me and Mahmud, and all those who love Egypt." She is touched by his sincerity and has clearly been smitten, but coming so soon after the shock of Isam's betrayal, the emotional timing is bad. Later, after Mahmud and Husayn have been arrested, then freed after July 23, brother, sister, and buddy hang out together, but Layla still resists Husayn's very proper advances, insisting that "there's no such thing as love" and that she is "not tied to anyone." In the summer of 1956, with Husayn studying in Germany and she a Cairo University coed, Layla becomes engaged to her charismatic literature professor (Mahmud Mursi). At their engagement party, however, the professor betrays wandering eyes, then confides that he is attracted not to her free spirit, but to her obedience. "There is no such thing as love," he informs her, "only desire."

The film scenario then conflates the final chapters of the novel in order to punctuate the romantic finale. In the book, Layla secures a teaching assignment in Port Said, with her father's grudging consent (her fiancé believes she will only be gone several weeks until a transfer back to Cairo is arranged), but she stays "for months" (al-Zayyat 2000: 325). There, disobeying parental orders, she visits her newly-married brother at his home, where she spends time with and finally falls for Husayn. And she lives through the bombardment and street fighting of the Suez war. In the movie her broken engagement to Dr. Fuad (his name has been changed from Ramzi) is more precipitate, and melodramatic. Layla never leaves home and Mahmud and Husayn, still commissioned soldiers, are back in Cairo when the war erupts. During a blackout she encounters Husayn on the stairs. They cower, then embrace, and he beseeches her to accompany him to the front—for the nation, the people. The climax occurs at the train station (in the novel the train station figures into the story when she heads off on her teaching assignment), from which Husayn and Mahmud will depart for the front, while Layla, Fuad, and her parents will evacuate Cairo. Observing the disembarkation of refugees from the Canal zone,

Layla decides to leave instead with the soldiers. When Fuad tries to restrain her, she hands him back his engagement ring. "All my life I've been afraid," she asserts, then runs to catch the departing train.

Baracat's style is lush. His film opens with a romantic flourish as Layla and Isam discover their mutual affection, then builds toward the final crescendo as Layla flies down the rail platform and is swept onto the train and into her lover's arms. Rejecting her own cynical predilections, she opts in the end to affirm both love and freedom of choice. The professor becomes her foil, for it is his denunciation of true love that sparks her resurgent emotionalism. It is thematically important that like Isam and her father, and unlike both her brother and Husayn, Fuad cares little for the national question. He thus comes to symbolize both the authoritarian social patriarchy of her father and the political tyranny of the old regime.[9] Husayn offers her an alternative. He speaks with guarded optimism as Cairo burns in January 1952, then in October 1956, with bombs raining down on the city, implores her to follow him for "something bigger than us."

CROSS-DRESSING IN A MAN'S WORLD

What happens when the new woman becomes a career woman? In *I'm Free,* Amina discovers that work in the corporate world is not all that liberating. She earns a salary and climbs the office ladder, but harsh realities eventually overtake her:

> She returned to her office and determined to spend the day in hard work. Somehow she could accomplish nothing and for the first time her room seemed narrow and restricted, its walls almost suffocating her. She put out her hand to ring for a cup of coffee in the hope that it might lift her depression. Suddenly she remembered that company regulations forbade coffee during working hours. She remembered, too, that private telephone calls were also forbidden. In fact, all outside calls were supposed to be registered in a separate book, if made during working hours. For the first time she winced when she recollected that company

> rules forbade her going into a fellow employee's office except on business (Abdel Qoddous 1978: 205–6).

The film captures these thoughts with a swirl of signs in front of her eyes—in English—telling her what is allowed and forbidden. Still, she stays at it. What will happen when she gets promoted to an executive position?

The question became increasingly relevant throughout the Nasser era. Women who entered university in ever growing numbers emerged with skills that put them in competition for technical and administrative posts.[10] In 1961, 0.9 percent of the female labor force in Egypt held executive, administrative, or managerial positions. By 1976 that percentage had increased only to 1.7, but popular cultural representations—film, literature, caricature—point to the social liberationist aspirations of Nasserist Egypt and the societal tensions therein. In a short comic scene in the otherwise weepy *Love Story* (1959), the Abd al-Halim Hafiz character, having scored artistic success, is asked about women's rights during an impromptu encounter with a roving radio correspondent. When he speaks on behalf of female aspirations, surely serious, but also image-conscious, he endears himself further to his upper-class love interest, who happens to be listening. It is an ambivalent moment, gently male-chauvinistic even though well-intentioned. In the following decade, with the sexual revolution in full swing, women began to assert themselves onscreen, and movies reflected even more the resultant societal ambivalence.

Cross-dressing in Egyptian film has a venerable tradition within a broader comedy-of-errors corpus. Both men and women impersonated each other, usually for romantic ends, but, as in Hollywood, men did so more often and for greater comic effect. Under the influence of Milton Berle as much as local custom, Ismail Yasin had performed in drag in the fifties (see especially *Madam Hanafi [al-Anisa Hanafi]*, Fatin Abd al-Wahhab 1954). Abd al-Munim Ibrahim followed suit when he became a comic lead *(Madam Sugar [Sukkar Hanim]*, al-Sayyid Badir 1960, a loose remake of *Some Like it Hot)*, as did others like Muhammad Awad (*Widow Wanted [Matlub armala]*, Isa Karama 1966).[11] By the early sixties it was time for women to again cross-dress, now to confound both male sexual and gendered predilections.

In *For Men Only* (*[Lil rigal faqat]*, Hussam al-Din Mustafa 1964), Nadia Lutfi and Suad Husni played two eminently talented but professionally frustrated chemical engineers working for a petroleum company who pose as men in order to gain on-site access to the oil field. The two women are certain that if they are allowed to abandon the laboratory for the drills they will be able to pinpoint the still-elusive underground repositories. Company policy stands in their way until opportunity strikes in the persons of two new, effeminate engineers who are assigned to the home office. Assuming the new employees' identities, speaking in gruff tones, sporting matching wigs, mustaches, and horn-rimmed glasses, the girlish Salwa (Husni) and more demure Ilham (Lutfi) pass as somewhat effeminate, but unquestioned males in the gender-segregated world of the oil workers.[12]

Professional rebels, but still proper, socially conservative young women, their own sexual timidity places them in a series of precarious positions. Each is initially assigned to room with an attractive male co-worker: Salwa with the precocious, sexually-starved Fawzi (Hasan Yusuf), and Ilham with the morose, romantically cynical Ahmad (Ihab Nafii). After an awkward night sleeping in clothes and costumes, with Salwa romantically approached by Fawzi, who in a trance-like state envisions her (and other employees before this) as a woman, the newcomers persuade their roommates to allow them to share quarters. Then in the company club, where the men pair up to dance, Salwa again finds herself in Fawzi's awkward semi-conscious embrace. Salwa, more than Ilham, finds the masquerade mentally trying, and threatens to retreat to Cairo. Neither really enjoys the lack of city amenities, but they persevere. Real trouble sets in when the two imposters gratefully shed their disguises for a week-long beach vacation in Suez. There, posing as sisters of the men whom they are impersonating, they "meet," date, and fall for Fawzi and Ahmad. In the end, after the requisite number of close calls, true identities are revealed—initially to their lovers, later, after being caught embracing in costume, publically. Romantic vows are exchanged and, according to the women's calculations, oil discovered. In the flush of true love, the unmasking, and the gush of black gold the cardinal question, whether Salwa and Ilham stay on site, retreat to the company's Cairo headquarters, or to the matrimonial kitchen, is never resolved.

While Egyptian law expressly forbids discrimination in hiring on the basis of gender, ingrained attitudes, particularly "the extreme discomfort felt by most Egyptian men regarding being seen to be supervised by a woman," persist (Sullivan 1986: 133). The conundrum was addressed in uproarious fashion in the screwball comedy hit *My Wife is General Director* (*[Mrati mudir amm],* Fatin Abd al-Wahhab 1966) featuring Shadia and Salah Zulficar, at the time real-life husband and wife. Based on a script by celebrated playwright and scenarist Saad al-Din Wahba, the film chronicles the battle of the sexes, on domestic and professional fronts, when a husband finds himself working under his wife in a government office. Produced with all the panache of an early-sixties Hollywood bedroom farce, it lampoons gender stereotypes, male chauvinism, and the general absurdity of office working relations. Ismat (Shadia)—a name that can be either male or female—and Husayn (Zulficar) are a slightly irreverent couple, well-off enough to afford a spacious split-level suburban home, but not to keep up a reliably working automobile. The movie's coda revolves around their morning ritual of jump-starting "Yasmine" by rolling her downhill with a helpful push from the *boab* (dookeeper). This is a team effort, until Ismat's promotion, after which she is rewarded with a company car and driver. Husayn cannot accompany her because she has been assigned as director in the office in which he works, and the couple, facing the awkward situation of a husband seen to be taking work orders from his wife, decides to keep their relationship a secret from his colleagues, who are now, suddenly, also her subordinates.

The office is a madcap setting staffed by six men (including Husayn) and a saucy secretary. Unaware they are to be supervised by a woman, they prepare to greet their new director. Abu al-Khayr (Tawfiq al-Daqn in a rare comic role) recites a welcoming praise poem, naturally in male declension. He, like all the others—including a highly neurotic Adil Imam in a very early role—is dumbstruck when Ismat, who they initially take for a visitor, finally reveals that she is their new boss, shakes hands all around and assumes her rightful place behind the director's desk. None is more stunned than Abd al-Qawi (Shafiq Nur al-Din), her gangly, hunch-shouldered, carefully preened deputy. Rosary in a tightly clenched fist, the pious zealot runs to pray after shaking hands with his new boss. Before doing so, he orders Hanafi, the office gofer, to fetch his slippers, which are always kept handy in a cardboard filing folder. Abd al-Qawi, who bases his obsession with ritual cleanliness on Ibn Hanbal, one of the four foundational medieval Islamic jurists, clearly has both sandaled feet in the Middle Ages. Other snippets show him summoning Hanafi in an urgent tone or heading for the restroom, sandaled and pant legs rolled up. Soon Hanafi learns to come without summons. Yet, like all others involved, Abd al-Qawi will come to reassess deep-rooted assumptions about gender in the new era.

More than running her department, Ismat's mission is to convince her staff that she is properly ensconced in a "man's" world. Her task is compounded by Husayn's increasing frustration at the predicament in which they find themselves as a result of their charade. From the outset he is privy to speculative office chatter about the new director's age, looks, and social life. At work all is business, although she flirts with him when her office door is closed. At home they laugh about their colleagues and try to maintain a modern marriage.

Gender roles, however, will only bend so far. At home Ismat fetches a sewing kit to fix a loose button on her husband's jacket. At work feminine nesting instincts emerge as she rearranges sloppy desks. Initially she is the overly-sensitive partner. When she discovers that a vanity mirror has been installed in the company car that carries her to work, she demands its removal. In another mirror scene, this time at home preparing for bed, she imagines herself in a Turkish pasha's curled mustache. Eventually, however, the greater burden strikes the underling husband. To meet her demanding, efficiency-based time schedule he resists his wife's entreaties that he come to bed, staying up late, and eventually passing out at his home drafting table. When, at work the following day, she expresses her displeasure with the unfinished project, Abu al-Khayr intercedes on Husayn's behalf, explaining that he suffers from a domineering wife. Eventually, husband and wife are caught sharing a sandwich in the director's office, and the driver reports seeing Husayn sneak out of "her" house one morning. When he arrives to find the office abuzz with gossip, he throws down his identity card and reveals their secret.

As the social comedy turns more screwball the domestic sphere becomes a battleground. Husayn turns increasingly sultry while Ismat, suddenly a darling of the media, gives interviews and is invited to speak at Cairo University. At this gathering Husayn is queried by correspondents for a women's journal about his favorite foods. Irritated, he makes a scene and leaves alone. Then, wandering along the Nile banks, he encounters a fisherman and wife working together, he casting nets while she rows, the model of cooperative matrimony. Husayn returns home to find Ismat knitting, dinner on the stove, but otherwise ignoring him. "I want a wife and a friend," he now protests, apologizing.

In the penultimate scene, Ismat, having been transferred, bids farewell to her now devoutly loyal staff. All are crestfallen, not least Abd al-Qawi, who cautiously extends a handshake, then, relegating his beads to his forearm, grasps her hand warmly with both of his. Hanafi appears with the sandals, only to be told "it's no use." What about Ibn Hanbal? Abu Hanifa (another foundational jurist) says otherwise, the convert announces, sending the sandals flying with a sweep of his arm! Abd al-Qawi has clearly crossed the bridge into the twentieth century. Ismat's new posting, however, appears destined to be a second round in the battle to convince a threatened, male-dominated professional sphere that women have duly arrived. Then, as she commences with the uncomfortable first handshakes, in bursts Husayn, his secretly-arranged transfer approved, to introduce himself and announce "My wife is general director."

Fashion and Freedom: Summer Girls and Campus Coeds

For Men Only and *My Wife is General Director* challenge, if lightly, gendered roles in the work place of a new, modern, industrializing society. But what of the new, modern, westernizing society that in many ways reflected the youth rebellion of the sixties? The very Islamic facade, traditional and neo-traditional, that has characterized Egypt since the mid-1970s has for many, particularly foreign outsiders, reified notions of an unchanging oriental society, the very antithesis of the modernist thrust of most of the twentieth century. Egyptians certainly know better, and are reminded constantly through the rebroadcast of old movies just how closely their own society, at least in the cosmopolitan urban centers, mirrored the fashions, sounds, and beats of the broader generation-gapped world. Occasionally a fifty-something columnist will remind readers that record players in the home also played Elvis along with Abd al-Halim and that in the sixties "a silent army of Beatlemaniacs slowly grew" (Shebl 1996).

Egyptian movies had portrayed the allure, and at times the lurking dangers, of summer beach culture in a more mobile, sexually permissive age. *Girls and Summer,* based upon a trilogy of Ihsan Abd al-Quddus stories, highlighted the darker side of young unchaperoned men with access to beach cabanas, while *Father's Up a Tree* challenged young women to cavort a bit more freely. Somewhere, too, there was room for the pure innocence of summertime fun on the beach, a la Elvis, or Frankie and Annette. The beach movie would not be the first or last genre appropriated by Egypt's Hollywood, coopted brazenly, given a local stamp, and screened to popular adoration. In one film that has been broadcast often on television in recent years, a young woman's aspirations to sing rock-and-roll produced another cross-gendered, cross-dressed comedy.

In *Crazy Kids,* a free-spirited group of young women do "battle" with a group of muscle-bound guys at a Mediterranean resort. Hamdi, the club owner's son and biggest hunk of all, played by Ahmad Ramzi with great self-parody, is rebuffed by the most independent-minded of the women. Madiha (Suad Husni) is far more interested in jamming with The Crazies *(al-Maganin),* a pop-rock quartet played by the Limelight Trio along with Samir Sabri, the budding entertainment king, who here plays their pretentious, hip-talking fourth member, Ismat. In his absence—and it is not clear whether with or without the knowledge of the other band members—Madiha dons a mop-top wig and false goatee to pose as Ismat (again, as in *My Wife is General Director,* the androgynous name is utilized to cover cross-dressing, whether symbolic or real). A cross-gendered comedy of errors ensues. As male rock star, Madiha attracts all the girls, especially Hamdi's younger sister, who falls hard. Hamdi, accustomed to being the center of female attention, challenges and thumps his sudden rival in a comically played boxing match. Complicating matters, his father (Amin al-Hinaydi), a laughable nouveau riche with peasant tastes, announces that he will take Madiha as his second bride, a successful ploy to make his inattentive wife (Mimi Shakib) jealous.

Plot is far less important than style, in a film that borrows heavily in its zany chase scenes and especially in the editing of musical numbers from Richard Lester's Beatle movies, *A Hard Day's Night* and *Help!* The Crazies sing Arabized British-Invasion pop, including the title track and a variation of "Can't Buy Me Love."[13] The frenetic finale, a madcap chase around and through a vacant beach house, is played to a quasi-psychedelic pop score, at one point interrupted by the James Bond movie theme. When order finally prevails, after a plethora of comic punches and knocks over heads, Madiha's imposture is revealed. Casino owner and wife are reunited, their son and Madiha properly engaged. When "Ismat's" fans and suitors realize that he is she they all faint away.

As fashion mirrored music and both mirrored changing social mores, films and picture magazines reveal creeping hem lines and longer bangs, for men and women alike, as well as changing notions, however confused or ambivalent, of courtship, romance, and brazen sexuality. Sixties youth culture is featured prominently in the fashions sported by new, modern women who frequently graced the covers of popular weekly picture magazines, especially during the summer months when sun dresses and bathing suits revealed generous amounts of uncovered skin. The scarved, milaya-clad fallaha remained a key, although never monolithic, symbol of the nation, even for female imagings (Baron 1997; Dougherty 2000). Beauty and acting always went hand-in-hand, male and female film stars both mirroring and establishing popular conceptualizations of glamor and sexuality, fashion and physique. Movie starlets in the early 1950s films and fan magazines appeared most often in a boldly patterned summer dress, sleeveless and cut just below the knee. As actresses they generally remained pristine beauties, even as their screen roles began to exude a more smoldering sexuality. By the late fifties, if fashions did not change radically, the way dresses were worn—and captured by the camera—certainly did. Magda and Lubna Abd al-Aziz wore their summer dresses with an attitude in *Where's My Life* and *I'm Free,* and Nadia Lutfi nearly slid out of hers in *The Dark Glasses.* Fatin Hamama, who, despite her "bad" roles never exuded sexuality in quite the same manner, eventually dropped a shoulder strap when she ran along the sea shore in Saad Arafa's 1965 psychological drama, *The Confession (al-Itiraf).*

Shoulders are one thing, legs another. The gam shot had been a long-standing convention. Zuzu Madi's crossed legs in *Boss Hasan* suggested unseemly sexual power, and Hind Rustam used hers to similar effect as the seductive Galila in Badrakhan's biopic, *Sayyid Darwish.* Yet with Rustam, Egypt's Marilyn Monroe, the camera reorients itself away from legs and shoulders to breasts and buttocks.

Art meshes with reality—Nadia Lutfi as Maddy, the ultimate "bad" girl, in *The Dark Glasses.*

When Nadia first introduces Kawsar to her unhappy father in *I Can't Sleep,* Rustam wears the usual summer dress, albeit one that accentuates her more ample figure. When she moves in with the Lutfis, the first camera shot is of her backside, highlighted by high-waisted, tightly-fit trousers, shaking as she dances to Latin pop. Nadia may be "bad," but she is never depicted in such an exhibitionary mode. However, Maddy, played by Nadia's real-life namesake, is also shot first from behind in tight pants.

By the late sixties fashions had again changed. The young women portrayed in *Crazy Kids* or *Father's Up a Tree* sport mini-skirts, short shorts, and tank-tops, their hair flowing longer or, increasingly commonly, bobbed to match universal chic mode. The ultimate fashion statement was Suad Husni's Zouzou in the smash musical hit *Watch Out for Zouzou ([Khalli balik min Zuzu],* Hasan al-Imam 1972). The story of a poor girl who hides her social origins and becomes the darling of the university student body, *Watch Out for*

Zouzou is a "logical extension" of the modernist ethos prevalent in Egyptian films since the 1930s (Armbrust 1996: 117) in which the "schizophrenia induced by the uneasy coexistence of conflicting cultural heritages"—here the upwardly mobile, modern world of the co-educational university and the inert, oriental world of the gender-divided wedding festival or popular quarter cabaret—is "symbolically healed" (ibid.: 123).

At the outset Zouzou appears the paragon of popularity. In the opening scene, out on the track, she sports running shorts and tank top. Later, she dons a radiant red vinyl short-sleeved mini-dress and black tights, and proceeds to take her place as champion of the students' "positive" movement. With her progressive colleagues she challenges the sneers of Umran, leader of the rival "straight path," a satirically crafted representative of religious conservatism, who questions her forthright behavior. "An intense, unsmiling young man, wearing a long-sleeved shirt and narrow black tie (all the other college boys wear bright-colored, short-sleeved shirts open at the neck)," Umran "speaks a near-classical variant of Arabic, and is ever on the lookout for a chance to declaim publicly" (Armbrust 1996: 118). Hardly an accurate visual representation of a budding Islamist, he far more closely approximates the indecently upright and sexually uptight Abd al-Qawi in *My Wife is General Director.*

It is not Umran, however, but Zouzou's female rival for the affections of the dashing drama professor, Dr. Said (Husayn Fahmi), who exposes her, disrupting the harmony of the student body. When Said's jealous cousin discovers Zouzou's secret, she invites her mother and band to perform at a party that Zouzou attends as her professor's date. There the performers are ridiculed as old fashioned and vulgar. Humiliated, but ever loyal to her roots and family, Zouzou ties a scarf around her waist and dances in her mother's place.[14] Thus revealing her secret, she throws the party into havoc, scaring off her date, and threatening her standing with her schoolmates. The scene, considered by many the last great belly dance in Egyptian film history, is encoded with filmic symbolism because Zouzou's over-the-hill mother, who dances only briefly, is played affectingly by Tahiya Carioca, a cinema dance queen of the '40s and '50s.

If the expose occurs in a private setting, the showdown is out in the open, on campus. There, Zouzou counters Umran's renewed challenge. No longer able to hide her vulgar roots, she now speaks forthrightly to a new egalitarian Egypt. If she is to be blamed for anything, she argues, it is for having focused on her past—her background—and losing sight of her—all Egypt's—future. Umran, won over by a plea to common sense and a progressive, forward-looking vision of a united nation, apologizes. He and Zouzou shake hands, he still somewhat uncomfortably. To the theme song, the united students dance a grand choreographed finale in the garden, after which Zouzou and Said embrace, their ensuing kiss long even by *Father's Up a Tree* standards.

Zouzou has never been a "bad" girl. That is her mother's nightmare fantasy after she appears ready to renounce school for the dance hall. As Armbrust notes (1996: 123), the campus world of *Zouzou* is also a fantasy, albeit a positive one, of "mini-skirted students singing in public gardens." The song-and-dance is obviously fantasy, but the costuming is not. Photographs of Egyptian campuses from the late sixties and early seventies depict the increasingly informal attire of ever longer-haired men and shorter-skirted women. Of course, as Armbrust notes, student life at this time—if any—was hardly care-free. The light-hearted politics of *Zouzou* at once point to and veil the upsurge of dissident political activity on campus following the 1967 defeat. If *Watch Out for Zouzou* is indeed a political film, as many contend, its message is highly ambivalent. It exhorts students to "get back to your classes" once the immediate crisis is resolved, a message that may well be "dangerously close to propaganda" (ibid.: 125); concurrently it celebrates the struggle against a backward, divisive, narrow-minded, religiously-inspired vision that was far less easily contained on campus than on screen.

By the mid-seventies long hair began receding as beards grew longer, and short skirts gave way to a wide variety of increasingly popular "Islamic" dress. As a forward-looking society found itself rent by competing visions of progress and modernity, with religion leading one of the charges, the state, rather than confront vernacular ideologies like Islamism on screen, backed away (Abu-Lughod 1993). Zouzou's victory was for a new, forward-looking, less class-bound Egypt in which educated women, whatever their background—and however limited their actual opportunities—might, and increasingly did, express their desires for "freedom" in ways that were less likely to be condemned as bad. But that new Egypt would soon never be the same. Zouzou and her "positive" comrades packed in audiences at movie theaters. Theirs may have been the clarion call of the day, but it was not the call of the future.

NOTES

1. The caricature and testimonial, penned by the famous cartoonist-poet-lyricist Salah Jahin, is dated August 24, 1955.

2. Lubna Abd al-Aziz also co-starred with Abd al-Halim Hafiz in *The Empty Pillow.* Nadia Lutfi had a secondary role in *Don't Put Out the Sun* and co-starred with Abd al-Halim in the later *Father's Up a Tree.*

3. Abd al-Quddus's explicit point is that Aliya, despite her new status, remains a teenager who has no business being married.

4. On an earlier occasion, mistaking her for an eligible daughter, Khalid had asked Aziz (her husband) for her hand, then, embarrassed, beat a hasty retreat.

5. The film is usually listed in the filmography after *The Empty Pillow,* also released in 1957. Abu Sayf, however, completed shooting *I Can't Sleep* in 1956. The color production delayed the film's release.

6. Her two most notable comic roles were in *Oh, Eve!* (1962), an adaptation of *The Taming of the Shrew,* and *Bride of the Nile* (1963), both opposite Rushdi Abaza.

7. This was not an uncommon motif in 1960s cinema. A similar dramatic usage occurs in Husayn Kamal's *The Impossible.*

8. She, in turn, has spoken of a "deep friendship. . . . When we work together there is a strange understanding between us" (Farid 1995a: 80).

9. In the novel Isam, a successful Cairo doctor (whereas Mahmud is consigned to the Canal zone), regains reader sympathy when he is posted to Port Said, then killed in battle. In his last spoken words, however, in a prior episode, attempting to comfort Layla, he tells her that she need not accompany him to the front: "You're a woman, no one will blame you, this isn't your place after all" (al-Zayyat 2000: 347). In the film, he, Fuad, and Layla's father are all slightly overdrawn as apathetic to the nationalist cause.

10. The number of women enrolled in university rose from 4,729 in 1953 to 24,490 by 1965. The number of men over this period rose from 49,366 to 104,975 (*14 Years of the Revolution* [Cairo: Ministry of National Guidance, n.d.], pp. 15, 16, 46).

11. For a discussion of homosexual coding in such films, see Garay Menicucci (1998). A recent comedy, *Ambulance 55* (Magdi al-Hawwari 2001) that features a male character in drag hearkens back, according to one reviewer, to the "slapstick comedy of Ismail Yassin" (Amina Elbendary, "Two guys and a girl," *al-Ahram Weekly,* 27 September-3 October 2001, www.ahram.org.eg/weekly/2001/553).

12. Ironically, the two male engineers whose identities they assume are both far more effeminate than "they" are as play-acted by the two young women.

13. There is a snippet of the title track on the CD-ROM "Cinderella al-shasha al-Arabiya" (MetaMedia 1999).

14. For a clip of the dance sequence, see the CD-ROM "Cinderella al-shasha al-Arabiya."

FIVE

New Peasants, Old Ways
Tradition and Nation in Nasserist Films

Where's Hanadi, Mom?
By the will of God, my daughter. . . .
By the will of God, or of my uncle, Mom? Does God will evil?

The Call of the Curlew, 1959

This was the life of your father and his father before him. He wanted you to know the secret of the treasure-trove, but if he was alive now he would want you dead.

The Mummy, 1975

Juxtapositions

The heat beats down upon an Egyptian village. Pack animals process through the dusty streets. Prostrate on the ground, catching a bit of shade from a revolving water wheel, a weary peasant is lulled to sleep by the steady, ceaseless rhythmic creaking of the ancient wooden gears. Cut to a group of more energetic, muscular laborers deliberately picking at the earth to a different, powerful beat. Their work is interrupted by the arrival of a blind cleric, who, passing deliberately, almost frenetically through the muddied village byways, stops to thrust out a wanting hand. Though blind and touched by God, his face evokes neither kindness nor wisdom. An elderly laborer thrusts some money in his hand; receiving no response he looks upward, his gentle, creased face evoking a plea to the heavens—less, one feels, for the afflicted cleric than for the suffering peasants caught in a cruel cycle of exploitation.

Suddenly a convoy of vehicles appears bearing grim-faced, suited officials, a kindly officer, and a truck load of staid soldiers. The peasants look up, confused. Close-ups of their eyes bespeak a mistrust of authority, even though in this case (as is clear from the officer's insignia) it is revolutionary authority. As younger officials begin marking off the land a panicked cry reaches the village. A peasant jumps up from his repast, upsetting the table, and joins a mob running toward the fields. Emotionless soldiers hold back the throng while officials try to persuade the villagers that the government has their best interest, the best interest of the nation, in mind. The village children smile at the officer and the crisis appears momentarily to have passed. Then, precipitately, a second explosion of emotion, a cacophony of shouted protest, an effort to charge the field. The mood having shifted from placidity to panic, from pride to parody, the credits roll, framing each of the main characters as they struggle to give voice to their fears of a changing physical and social landscape.

The film is *The Rains Dried Up* (*[Gafat al-amtar],* Sayyid Isa 1968), a movie largely forgotten except by film historians who recall it as one of several works promoting the virtues of work in a forward-looking, socialist society. Trumpeted at the time of production as a new film about the new peasant, the movie, from the challenging juxtapositions that mark its opening, conveys a particular problematic of modernizing, post-colonial, Nasserist Egypt: the imaging of "tradition"—manners and customs, folk beliefs, popular religious expression—in the rural heartland. Particularly as embodied by peasants, tribespeople, and, in a broader sphere that takes us from the countryside to provincial capitals and the urban center of Cairo, men of religion. Exploited (peasants/tribespeople), or the instruments of their own degradation? Exploiters (men of religion) or agents of accommodation and culturally rooted revolutionary social transformation? If such questions persist unanswered, at least the Nasser era cinema attempted to address them in forthright, new fashion.

The Inscrutable Peasantry

Thirteen years after land reform, the Nasserist state added a new holiday to the calendar. Peasant Day *(Id al-fallah)* honored the modern sons and daughters of the soil. The "new" peasant, proclaimed a popular magazine, no longer fell prey to ignorance, poverty, or the abuses of a discredited and displaced feudal order. New peasants reflected the aims and achievements of a revolutionary socialist state. Enlightenment and freedom had triumphed over ignorance and exploitation. "Land reform did not only liberate the fallah; it also freed the fallaha," trumpeted the article. "The peasant woman, who once could not leave her home save for two occasions, the day of her marriage and the day of her death, has begun to work, to study reading and writing. House work has become the business of agriculture."[1]

Revolutionary iconography always included images of proud, strong agricultural workers tilling the soil, reclaiming the desert, working around the clock alongside massive construction machinery in a concerted effort to raise a new high dam at Aswan and construct protective barriers before the seasonal flood waters rushed downstream from the south. However, the revolutionary self-satisfaction belied deeper concerns. Four months before Peasant Day the tone had been more cautionary than celebratory:

> The experiment of resettling workers and freeing them from the imprisonment of exploitation is a pioneering humane experiment in keeping with the heart of the socialist revolutionary individual, Gamal Abdel Nasser, and it occupied many in thought and action. Then it became reality in our society when it was applied in Daqhaliya Province. As the experiment expanded it encountered problems, errors—and opposition. It is the responsibility of every bureau of the state today to support this new experiment, to protect it from the problems of feudalism and enmity.[2]

Land reclamation projects, trumpeted in the first years of the revolution and not initiated until a decade later, had become embroiled in corruption, inefficiency, and bureaucratic wrangling. Migrant laborers, once the bottom of the labor force, had begun to out-earn resident farm laborers, whose wages did not keep pace (Toth 1999: 99–132).

The peasant had been a prominent national signifier from the early days of Egyptian national expression. Mahmud Mukhtar's monumental statue of "Egypt Awakening," completed in 1928 and placed astride Cairo's central rail station, became a widely emulated model of national imagination (Baron 1997: 114).[3] A fallaha gazing outward represents the nation. One hand resting on a rising sphinx, the other lifting her veil, she is at once rooted to ancient grandeur and an embodiment of progress and modernity. In popular iconography Egypt always stood betwixt and between city and country, modernity and tradition. The middle class urban man or woman with all the western trappings of progress proved an equally malleable popular symbol, whether in literature or caricature, or onscreen. Yet, as in other modernizing colonial, then post-colonial societies, these urbanized modern icons could not match the "affective power of the peasant" as a "symbolic site" (Swedenburg 1990: 18–19) for shaping romantic national imaginings.

Yet in Egypt, as in other new-old societies, the contradictions of representing the peasantry were manifold. Those who sought to utilize the fallah (and fallaha) as national symbols found themselves confronted by a "fractured image" (Brown 1990: 1–22). Was the peasant truly a symbol of national liberation or of stubborn constancy, of rebellious activism or obsequious passivity? Could the peasant, at once ignorant and inscrutable, truly embody an awakening and arising nation? Could the peasant be liberated—and activated—in order to help build the new Egypt? Bringing "progress" to the least modern sector of society proved difficult in both practical and ideological terms. The very rootedness of peasant life that made it so attractive proved the most frustrating hurdle to overcome. Public health initiatives ran headlong into traditional folk cures, public education into conservative visions of childhood and gender roles. Even well-intentioned government initiatives to expand arable acreage might appear to be extensions of pre-revolutionary works projects, always viewed as punitive by those dragooned, as well as by those now writing the history of peasant exploitation.

More than any other sector of society, the peasant cuts to the heart of post-colonial self-identity. Poor, downtrodden, exploited, abused. Proud, resolute, physically powerful, thick-skinned. Indigenous, rooted, preservers of tradition. But also inscrutable, close-minded, superstitious, patriarchal and, above all, ignorant (ibid.: 61–71). Making the physical quality of life better for peasants represented one set of problems, truly bringing them into the modern era intellectually and culturally a far greater conundrum. What happens to the symbolic power of rootedness, and the iconographic stylistic so important to artistic metaphor, when the fallaha finally does cast off her veil (and ultimately her milaya), or when the fallah abandons, as some hoped, his gallabiya?[4]

In films, as in literature, the peasant posed a grand problematic, particularly in the Nasser era when "social realism" set out to depict and obviate rural ills.[5] "The film depicts the ignorance under which the peasantry lived during the period . . . and how the rich exploited this ignorance in order to attain their greedy ends." So wrote one critic (Ismail 1984) about Tawfiq Salih's *Heroes' Struggle* (*Sira' al-abtal* 1961). "A life ruled by fear, ignorance, poverty, disease"; but how to make the peasant a hero in his/her own ultimate deconstruction? Filmmakers, no less than other artists and intellectuals, grappled with the multiple natures and images of Egypt's indigenous rural sons and daughters—as well as their fathers and mothers. In the pre-revolutionary era, despite a growing call to address issues of agrarian reform, peasants, like desert nomads, had primarily represented a romantic "other." Poverty, the bane of most peasants, remained strictly off limits. Films more comfortably parodied or romanticized, rather than ethnographically or critically depicted, rural culture. Anwar Wagdi could court Layla Murad, a most unconvincing fallaha, in light romances. But serious literary works by progressive authors such as Taha Husayn, himself a proud refugee from rural ignorance, could never see their way to the screen.

With the arrival of a "new era" led by individuals committed to social justice and socio-economic re-alignment, the peasantry emerged on screen out of rural bliss. The path toward progress, however, proved winding and torturous. Suddenly cast as unfortunate victims of the feudal system and their own backwardness, then caught in the vortex of change imposed from above, it would only be toward the end of the Nasser era that peasants, along with tribespeople and other keepers of "tradition," emerged into their own as full participants in the new society, capable of helping chart their own course, no longer under the heavy hand of the whip, now working hand-in-hand with those outsiders trying desperately to help them improve their lot, and the national lot.

VENDETTAS

Those outsiders included filmmakers whose work, mixed with metaphors of romantic admiration, pity, and healthy doses of scorn, contributed to a social discourse on modernity that embraced a countryside that cried out for progress. These filmmakers, whether Youssef Chahine, graduate of the elite Victoria College, or Salah Abu Sayf, child of working class Bulaq, all framed and shot rural life through the lenses of the city. None appears to have been more torn by contradictory impulses than Chahine, who first attained prominence as a director chronicling the life of Egypt's rural and urban lower classes.

Nile Boy, filmed and screened prior to the July coup, reveals a romantic spot for the countryside that the urbanite director rarely depicted in his city tales. Hamidu (Shukri Sirhan), first seen as a young boy watching the trains pass by, has an insatiable curiosity to see what is at the end of the rails.[6] When he is forced to marry Zubayda (Fatin Hamama) after she becomes pregnant, his feelings of confinement intensify. In a musical montage following the wedding, he labors in the fields to a plaintive rural tune that is interrupted several times by faster rhythmic music that evokes rushing trains, the path out to a wider world. When such pressures build, he leaves, but Zubayda follows him, and when she falls onto the tracks of an oncoming train he saves her and professes his love.

Married and content for the first time, Hamidu's world is again overturned when Zubayda, after delivering a son, falls into shock. Presuming that she has died, Hamidu runs from the village and hops a lorry ride to the city. There he is enticed into a seedy world of gambling, drinking, and drug running. Chahine cross-cuts rural and urban images, juxtaposing purity and pollution. While Hamidu watches a belly dance in a drunken stupor, his older brother (Yahya Shahin) and fellow peasants joyfully sing a folk tune aboard a fellucca en route

Manipulating rural obscurantism—Farid Shawqi disguised as a peasant in *Struggle in the Valley.* Courtesy of Arab Film Distribution.

to Cairo. Ibrahim has come to find his brother, but by the time he arrives Hamidu has landed in jail, so Ibrahim returns home, where he dutifully provides for Zubayda and her son. Tradition here serves as social glue. In prison, Hamidu encounters a chaplain from his village. He had visited the cleric when he first arrived in Cairo, but had been put off by the man's nostalgia for rural life. Now, implored to put aside thoughts of revenge and return home, he listens. Released from prison, Hamidu catches the first train back to the countryside, arriving, in true melodramatic fashion, just in time to save his son from the flood waters that have suddenly overcome the village, and to be happily reunited with his wife.

With *Struggle in the Valley,* his next film, Chahine's romantic vision of the countryside gave way to more sober musings. The film starts with striking, romantic rural images, Omar Sharif looking skyward and peasants working the sugar cane to heavy-toned chanting. As the action commences, Ahmad (Sharif), the estate overseer's son who has become an agricultural engineer, supervises the peasants in new farming techniques. His reunion with Amal (Fatin Hamama), the pasha's daughter who is newly arrived from finishing school, is cut short by her boorish cousin (Farid Shawqi). They meet soon afterwards at a peasant wedding. Ahmad, who first appeared in western dress, here wears a gallabiya and turban. Amal, in a low-cut summer dress with a peasant skullcap (given her by Ahmad years ago) on her head, passes easily between separate male and female celebrations, greeting all the guests, then enters the bride's chamber, where she removes a delicate pair of earrings from her ears and presents them as a gift. Afterwards, she and Ahmad sit and reminisce by a water wheel. Filmed on location outside Luxor, without allusion to heat or dust, the film evokes a nostalgia—for the characters' childhood playfulness as well as a romanticized countryside.

All will of course quickly become undone as the pasha and his nephew provoke a tribal vendetta that is only resolved after the death of two innocents and the suddenly repentant aristocrat. In the end, the vengeance-seeking son of the murdered shaykh recognizes that he has been duped. Whether he will be willing to reexamine his instinctual response to manufactured evidence is another story. The set-up is far too easy, requiring only that the pasha's nephew don peasant garb, shoot the shaykh with the overseer's shotgun, and plant the weapon to incriminate him. Still, as Ahmad and Amal walk off into the sunset, it seems far more certain that class boundaries will fall than that the peasantry will cognitively fathom the extent to which they are imprisoned—and manipulated—by reactionary cultural mores.

Proof is to be found in the recurrence of similar tropes in later films. *Bahiya* (Ramsis Nagib 1960), scripted by the famed author Yusuf al-Sibai, features a similar plot contrivance. Here peasant lovers are separated by a blood feud instigated by another venal pasha working in collaboration with an insidious local shaykh (Husayn Riyad in a rare villainous role). As Shaykh Abd al-Rahman bemoans the collapse of amity between friendly clans, he instigates the murder of Bahiya's father, leaving a trail that points toward the slain man's best friend, the father of her childhood soul mate, now her romantic interest, Yasin (Rushdi Abaza). An only child, Bahiya (Lubna Abd al-Aziz) accepts male responsibility and pledges vengeance. Before fingers point in his father's direction, Yasin begs her to forsake the vendetta.

Distressed by their growing distance, he leaves for the army; when he returns he finds his father murdered and fingers pointing toward his lover. The two meet once more at their special rendezvous spot, but unable to reach accommodation, find themselves leaders of antagonistic factions. Eventually the true culprit is uncovered. Shaykh Abd al-Rahman's motivation is his long-standing lust for Bahiya's mother, and now for Bahiya. She is saved from his clutches by the timely arrival of Yasin, who fights off the shaykh's henchman and apprehends the villain in the climactic scene.

The vendetta and related cliches also figure prominently in a Farid Shawqi vehicle from the same period. In *Blood on the Nile* (*[Dima' ala al-Nil]*, Niyazi Mustafa 1961) the Shawqi character returns to his Nile village from military service only to walk into the middle of a blood feud that he is powerless to stop. Initially, peace seems attainable through the good offices of the local National Union representative.[7] But as events unfold he is unwittingly drawn into a spiraling cycle of violence, inadvertently plays a role in an antagonist's accidental death, and gets involved in a thorny relationship with the slain man's widow (Hind Rustam), with whom he eventually falls in love. In the end he and his new-found love sail away, rebels against their respective kin and all their related cultural baggage.

Portrayed by the likes of Rushdi Abaza, Omar Sharif, Farid Shawqi, and Lubna Abd al-Aziz, these peasants and villagers are attractive romantic leads. The pre-revolutionary political and social order is generally culpable for sparking the violence; only in *Blood on the Nile* does a revolutionary regime seek to mediate rather than inflame passions. And only in one case, that of Bahiya, the woman, does hero or heroine dutifully embrace the vendetta. Dramatic license, however, insists the violence escalate and draw them all into the fray in order to underscore the futility of the blood feud in constructing a progressive society.

Sinners and Saints

If the vendetta constituted a primary target of modernizers, no less powerful were critiques of traditional understandings of honor and shame, and the appropriate penalties to be paid, particularly by "wayward" girls. If Ihsan Abd al-Quddus became the champion of a new morality for the urban middle and upper classes, others took on the countryside. Taha Husayn, blinded at youth by village folk potions, wrote eloquently about the female burden of embodying male honor in his lyrical novel *The Call of the Curlew* (*Du'a al-karawan* 1934), which was adapted by Baracat and brought to the screen to great acclaim in 1959.

In many respects, Baracat's powerful adaptation followed the novel closely, but heightened the dramatic action in ways that at once played to the director's lushly romantic style and intensified the social power of Husayn's message. The film recounts the story of Amna (Fatin Hamama), a poor village girl working as a servant in the house of the young agricultural engineer (Ahmad Mazhar) who is responsible for the honor killing of her older sister, Hanadi (Zahra al-Ila) by her maternal uncle, Jabir (Abd al-Alim Khattab). As the film begins, Amna has returned to the scene of her sister's dishonor to torment the engineer by flirting with him, but never succumbing to him.

Like the novel, the film flashes back to reveal the origins of Amna's animus toward her unsuspecting master. Although backed by a typically lush Baracat score, the rural world he depicts is devoid of any romantic tableaux. In the opening scene Amna, her sister, and mother (Amina Rizq) are expelled from their village upon the murder of their father/husband, a disreputable character who paid the price for an adulterous dalliance. The women take refuge in a town where the two daughters (also the mother in the novel) find work as live-in servants, Amna for the district commissioner, Hanadi for a young, city-bred engineer. Amna becomes a confidant of the commissioner's daughter, Khadiga (Ragaa al-Gadawi), learns to read, to speak a bit of French, and to play the piano. Then one day her mother informs her they must all leave immediately, without notice. Only on their journey homeward does Amna learn that Hanadi, who is uncharacteristically morose, has been seduced by her employer. Enroute, they are joined by their uncle, who, in a flash, murders Hanadi and buries her secretly alongside the road.

Back in their village Amna awakens from delirium and asks her mother insistently about her sister's fate. Her words, scripted from a novel that contains little dialogue, capture the author's outrage at the honor killing:

Amna: Where's Hanadi, Mom?
Zahra (mother): By the will of God, my daughter. . . .
Amna: By the will of God, or of my uncle, Mom? Does God will evil?
Zahra: Your uncle deceived me. He promised to provide protection, but he had planned to commit this evil.
Amna: And you planned it with him! You both killed her!

Jabir, whose name has been changed from Nasir in the novel, slaps Amna down, then gruffly calls her mother into the next room, where he hands her an allowance and squares their alibi, that Hanadi fell ill and died. When Amna flees back to the commissioner's house she is welcomed without question. All is well until Khadiga becomes engaged to the engineer. Summoning her courage, Amna confides her sister's story to the mistress of the house, who breaks the engagement and packs Khadiga off to find a suitor in Cairo. Amna then moves into the engineer's house and undertakes to exact revenge by stealing his heart.

The melodramatic tendencies that have often kept from Baracat the accolades bestowed upon his leading contemporaries, here served the director well. Fatin Hamama's performance is central, and Baracat's favorite leading lady moves adeptly from frightened fallaha to scheming seductress, then slowly falls in love with the engineer. Ahmad Mazhar also shifts subtly from unhappy, sexually aggressive, self-centered cad to repentant, sexually frustrated, sympathetic paramour, transformed by an encounter with the potential for true love. A fully rewritten ending served to enhance the film's power (Sayf 1984: 56–58). In Husayn's novel, Amna reveals her secret to the engineer when he informs her, hoping to discover her true emotions, that he has been transferred to Cairo. Stunned by her revelation, the engineer insists that they remain bound by mutual love and suffering, and Amna agrees to leave with him.

In Baracat's version the climactic encounter is more powerful and the ending tragic. There is no transfer; Amna and the engineer have kissed during a picnic by the Nile. Terrified of her changing emotions, Amna flees to the house and shuts herself in her room.

When the engineer professes his love, she reveals to him the consequences of his peccadillo:

> She died because of you. My uncle killed her. She was a victim, and you're the one who caused it all—and you still live free! You never thought about her. You never asked where she had gone, or what she is doing. You live, while the earth that holds her is more kind to her than you. But why should you think of her? Hanadi is a servant. Her life is cheap and her honor has no value.

The engineer retreats. A distance shot frames each sitting disconsolate in separate rooms, Amna on her bed, the engineer by the dining room table.

Another invented sub-plot draws the film to its tragic conclusion. As Amna proceeds to leave the house for the last time, her uncle Jabir lurks in the bushes, his shotgun cocked. The engineer again professes his love, asserting that he has changed, and would now die without her. "Hanadi will always be between us," Amna replies resolutely. Heading for the gate, she spots her uncle and runs back into her lover's arms. He spins her around just in time to take Jabir's shot in the back, collapses, and dies with a smile on his face. Amna falls to her knees distraught, as Jabir, apprehended, is led into the courtyard.

Taha Husayn's text, complain many critics, is a flawed, if beautifully lyrical narrative.[8] In addition to a fundamental flaw in the story's premise, the unlikely expulsion of "three helpless women" from their village, Amna is "far too articulate, too sophisticated for a girl of her circumstances" (Badawi 1993: 125). She reflects "a superiority on the part of the writer. . . . The explanation is perhaps that Taha Husayn was sent away from home to study when he was too young to fully understand the way of life of people in the provinces although he does not realize this and writes as a straightforward outsider. . . ." (Hilary Kilpatrick in Allen 1987: 151–52). If the novel indeed "lacks a great deal of 'realism of presentation,'" it can be argued that "the author here is primarily concerned with presenting an ethical and social message: he intends to make people aware of the crimes committed in the name of honor, and wishes perhaps to indicate that love should take the place of revenge" (Hamdi Sakkut in Allen 1987: 150).

If Taha Husayn opted for a happy ending in which Amna, like him, escapes the ignorance of rural life, Baracat, in his own inimitable fashion, molded a more powerful, affecting story. In keeping with his cinematic voice, his adaptation is more romantic, and ends on a note of melodramatic redemption. Audiences loved *The Call of the Curlew;* at the same time critics recognized that Baracat had taken his artistry to a new level, presenting a film in which solid acting and "lithe, economical camera movement" dominated without the usual musical interludes and swirling scores (Sayf 1984: 58).[9] Perhaps emboldened by this reception, the director returned once more to the countryside, to explore the problematic of traditional attitudes in striking, yet ultimately alienating fashion. This despite another star turn by his—and Egypt's—favorite leading lady.

Baracat's 1965 adaptation of *The Sin* (*al-Haram;* translated as *The Sinners,* 1984), a 1959 Yusuf Idris novel, depicts the harsh lives of migrant workers, their exploitation by the owners of large estates (the time is just prior to the July Revolution), and the discrimination against them by resident peasants. Told via flashback, the film concerns the investigation into the murder of a newborn child whose abandoned body is discovered on estate grounds. As the estate manager, Fikri Effendi (Zaki Rustam in his penultimate and last great role), dutifully carries out his investigation, village residents quickly condemn the migrants—"It must be those people," proclaims Fikri Effendi without any evidence—as a way to deflect their own inward search for a recent out-of-wedlock birth mother. Soon the culprit is discovered in the migrant camp. She is Aziza (Fatin Hamama), a young woman in a feverish, mentally unstable state. As Aziza is carried from the fields back to the migrant camp, relieved townsfolk jeer. Later, however, they turn curious, and ultimately feel sympathy for the victim, which prompts a reevaluation of their relationship to their seasonal, landless neighbors.

Aziza's story is an individual tragedy played out against a larger cultural backdrop that is rooted in traditional conceptualizations of familial and communal honor and shame. In her feverish state, she recalls her marriage to Abd Allah (Abd Allah Ghayth) and their happy, if difficult, life as they raise a family of four children, all of whom they take on their migratory rounds.[10] When Abd Allah falls ill and is confined to bed, she finds spare work in their home village. One day, when she sneaks out into the local fields to dig surreptitiously for potatoes, she is raped by a foreman and becomes pregnant. Failing to induce a miscarriage, she binds herself tightly to conceal her condition; then, as her delivery date nears she rejoins the migrant camp, where she hopes to deliver her child in secret.[11] As her physical condition deteriorates, sympathetic laborers, not suspecting her true condition, build her a protective shelter alongside the fields and cover for her work.

One night, as the migrant laborers dance and sing, she flees the encampment to give birth. The festivities drown out the baby's cries, but when the sound wanes she tries desperately to hush it. Passing out with her hand over its mouth, she inadvertently smothers the infant. When she revives, she abandons the corpse and flees back to the encampment, where she grows increasingly ill. After she has been revealed as the child's mother, she is tended with pitying curiosity by both villagers and fellow migrants. She seems to recover momentarily, then runs to the scene of her crime, where she collapses and dies. Her body is transported by night back to her village.

Critics marveled at Baracat's most unconventional adaptation of the richly psychological story, praising the cast, scenarist Saad al-Din Wahba, and, not least, the director himself (al-Hadiri 1984a: 43–47; al-Salamuni 1984: 48–49). Baracat had fully abandoned his trademark style and presented a truly "realist" film. He shot no scenes on sound stages. The soundtrack utilized only peasant pipes, drums, and chants. Baracat, of course, utilized his favorite actress—"realism" is understood to be within bounds of the star system—but in this film Hamama suffers physical and emotional anguish in all but a few brief scenes, those depicting her happy marriage. The ensemble acting, rare for a Baracat film, expanded the story, as Idris had written it, beyond Aziza's tale to encompass two societies thrust together in tragedy. For audiences, however, the film proved too harsh, too realistic. Despite a redemptive ending, the public simply did not go, and Baracat's undisputed masterpiece quickly closed.

The Sin is therefore a problematic film. It remains a stunning, critically acclaimed adaptation of an important work of fiction.[12] It brought to the screen a changing perspective of peasant woes and wiles. Idris, also a son of the village, wrote less scornfully than Taha

Husayn of rural culture, focusing rather on social and economic conditions in which nomads and peasants found themselves trapped. Baracat's depiction of the coming together of the two communities carries an understated power. "We're just like you, only we don't have land to cultivate," one migrant tells a new-found acquaintance. So does the film's allusion to the potential moral and political strength of worker solidarity. When Aziza dies, the field laborers look skyward. The foreman, somewhat cautiously, tries to force them back to work, but the labor contractor breaks his switch and the peasants walk off the field to pay respects to their "sister." In a final striking image, when the truck bearing Aziza's body pulls away, villagers line their rooftops to silently bid her farewell. A voice-over explains that the tree under which she died will become a fertility shrine. The petty elite of the village—the manager, the estate clerk, and others—have become more humane by this juncture.

Moving Mountains

Fashioning a new peasant went hand in hand with constructing a new Egypt. If the ideological and cultural construction of Nasserism commenced rapidly, the actual physical endeavor took somewhat longer. Plans for the Aswan High Dam, reclamation of the "Liberation Province" in the western Delta, and television were in place by 1955. Regional politics and conflicts sidetracked nearly all these projects. When finally undertaken in the early 1960s, they each fell under the panoply of the state's newly proclaimed commitment to Arab Socialism. "You and me, he and she, it's our duty to build Socialism," as Abd al-Halim Hafiz sang in his 1960 anthem "The People's Responsibility" (Mas'uliyat al-sha'b; lyrics by Salah Jahin, music by Kamal al-Tawil).

On screen, the socialist work ethic continued to collide with the fundamental mistrust of peasant world view. Fractured visual and textual images persisted even in new films that celebrated the virtues of physical labor. History still provided the costuming with which to clothe contemporary problems. All but one of the films discussed below are set in pre-revolutionary eras, eras in which the peasant, beaten down by oppressive regimes, had yet to "arrive." Nonetheless, the ultimate message conveyed by these films is that the peasant remains as much a part of the problem as of any solution.

The Mountain (*[al-Gabal]*, Khalil Shawqi 1965) encapsulates all the ambivalence of revolutionary socialism. Adapted from a Fathi Ghannam story, the film opens to striking images of hardy, muscular men pick-axing away at the hard rock and tunneling deep into the mountainside on the west bank of the Nile, across from Luxor. Such images have led some critics to categorize the film as a positive representation of labor. According to Duriya Sharaf al-Din (1992: 102),

> *The Mountain* . . . accentuates in clear fashion the idea of the elevated value of [physical] labor as the sole path to attain worth, or in the case of the resource in this film, the treasure. Here the men's forearms are the means; anything other than work is a deceptive, false means that leads only to a deep chasm of ruin/loss and futility. The inhabitants of the mountain discover that their mountain does not hold buried treasure, rather that they are the ones who own this wealth through their toil.

For all the positive images of labor, there are, however, a plethora of negative representations that make the film a much more complex ideological exposition. In a brief biographical sketch of the director, critic and film historian Kamal Ramzi (1995b: 258) describes *The Mountain* more directly as a film that "denounces the ancestral traditions of a mountain tribe that refuses modernity."

The primary plot involves efforts by a reformist architectural engineer (Umar al-Hariri) to move the peasants down off the mountain into new housing. This story is clearly rooted in Hassan Fathy's famous, failed efforts to create an "architecture for the poor" at Gourna in the second half of the 1940s (Fathy 1973). At the film's outset, the tribal chief (Abd al-Warith Asr in a rare negative role), a stern personification of unyielding adherence to the past, speaks out against relocation. The engineer, a respected but mistrusted outsider, rides up the mountainside to debate him, despite warnings from his native friend, Husayn (Salah Qabil). Husayn is the classic wavering traditionalist, caught between two worlds. Intuitively scornful of his own tribal world, he trusts the engineer, but ultimately finds the modern world equally, if not more tarnished than the world that he seeks to leave behind.

The struggle to modernize the peasants proves futile. As in Fathy's account, the primary culprits prove to be "peasant obscurantism and bureaucratic hostility" (1973: 149ff). The architect recalls the "tangled and thorny undergrowth of petty obstruction, conspiracy, inefficiency . . . the daily pinpricks" (ibid.: 150) as most demoralizing. While his critique of official obstinacy is compelling, his view of the peasantry—especially after acts of sabotage directed against his project—betrays the frustration of a well-intentioned outsider:

> . . . in doing this they were directly hurting themselves, for they were all earning good money as laborers in the village, and the new houses were, even financially, better than their old ones which, for the most part built on government land, were virtually worthless. There is a proverb which says: "If you know the reason, surprise will stop," and here there was more than one reason. First, the patriarchal system is very strong, and everybody obeys the heads of families, who, in Gourna, were tomb robbers. They were both feared and respected by the people, and they used their power to preserve their trade. They had no intention of giving up their nice, profitable, squalid houses in the cemetery with treasure waiting to be mined under their floors, to move to a new, hygienic, beautiful village away from the tombs. Second, the Gournis are all closely interrelated, and no one would fail to support a family chief in any enterprise. Third, a kind of shame had prompted them, the shame of being considered cowards for not taking part in the sabotage (ibid.: 176).

True to form, the tribal chief in *The Mountain* does order the village's destruction, although by fire rather than by cutting dikes as in Fathy's account. Falling to his knees amidst the burning structures, the engineer pleads, cries, and ultimately curses the tribespeople. The scene cuts quickly to his antagonist's smiling face; the victor celebrates his triumph with a nighttime party, a visually and aurally intense scene, replete with music and ceremonial stick dancing.

Eventually, the progressive Husayn (a character type who has no counterpart in Fathy's account) leads a contingent down to rebuild the village. The project's rebirth, however, is again sabotaged, this time by the arrival from Cairo of a royal princess (Layla Fawzi) and her retinue, patrons of the project who care little for its reformist agenda and see it rather as a playground for a facade of beneficence.[13] When she had first arrived, after the fire, the princess had demanded the arsonists be punished, but been dissuaded by the engineer's insistence that "They are not criminals; they just don't understand." When she returns to inspect the rebuilt village, the peasants look on, enticed but embarrassed, as the urbanites throw their own nighttime party, drinking heavily and dancing amorously to recordings of western pop music. "I'm like you, Husayn," the engineer protests, sensing the degree to which his native ally is wavering. "I want to throw her out, kill her. Give us a chance . . . tomorrow. . . ."

The morrow only further confounds the locals. The princess hosts an outdoor gala that features folkloric performances of dance and horsemanship. Before this, however—and in obvious contradiction to the architect's efforts to promote a traditional aesthetic—her soldiers provide the new homeowners with western-style clothing, literally throwing the garments at their feet. When the tribal chief comes forward to greet the princess he denounces the housing and is arrested, sparking a riot. Husayn now returns to the mountain. When the dispirited engineer confronts the princess, blaming her and her companions for all the troubles, she retreats to her car, then runs him down in the deserted village square.

Back on the mountain, a second plot unfolds: the search for pharaonic antiquities, the lifeblood of the tribespeople. The seemingly virtuous physical labor, filmed with such power, is directed not at tilling or restoring the soil, but at uncovering buried treasure to sell to foreigners who steal Egypt's patrimony for their own benefit. Husayn's father, who discovers hieroglyphs in a deep mountain passage, reveals his find to the *khawagaya* (Zuzu Madi), the foreign woman who owns property on the west bank. Then, followed in a surreal scene by his youngest daughter (Magda al-Khatib), who, sweating profusely, crawls after him as if against a river's current, he descends deep into the mountain and begins to attack the tomb wall. Amidst a crescendo of noise and music, he turns, wide-eyed, notices his daughter and strikes her with his pick, then returns to his maniacal task. As he breaks through the partition, sand suddenly pours into the chamber, burying him alongside his already dead victim.

Caught between worlds, Husayn forsakes the beautiful fallaha (Samira Ahmad) with whom he had dreamed of sharing a new home in the valley, to share the bed of the rich foreign lady. It is the tribal chief who ultimately convinces him that the *khawagaya* is not "one of us," and he leaves her. In the startling finale, the two new allies enter the passageway to excavate the site where his father perished. To a swirl of space-age and classical music they wade through a rising fog, then begin striking the walls, their blows synchronized. As they break through the wall, the camera angle shifts to capture them from inside the uncovered, empty chamber. Screaming "Father!" Husayn drops his lantern. The film ends with a sudden shot of the mountain, the repeated echoes of his cry resounding through the valley. Ill-begotten, rather than virtuous labor is thus depicted as a maddening, self-destructive passion, one that produces only stagnation and death, the obliteration of mind, body, and family.

Lacking a major male or female lead,[14] a strong romantic theme or clear resolution, it is not surprising that *The Mountain* failed to capture popular acclaim. It remains a film of academic interest, cited often by Egyptian film historians—I think mistakenly—as a classic socialist-era depiction of labor and, more appropriately, as an early public sector project that sought to inject a greater degree of literary artistry into the industry. After this debut, director Khalil Shawqi, who got his start in the new television industry, made only three further films (one of which sat on the censor's shelf for eight years) before returning to the little screen (Ramzi 1995b: 258). In retrospect his most regarded film should be primarily remembered for its exploration of the witting and unwitting role played by peasants and tribal peoples in the foreign exploitation of Egyptian historical treasures. This theme was treated more directly by Shadi Abd al-Salam in his masterful film *The Mummy (al-Mumiya'*; released in English as *The Night of Counting the Years)*, completed in 1969, but not screened publicly until 1975.

A strikingly beautiful, multilayered work of great visual and emotional power, Shadi's film remains a paragon in Egyptian cinema history due both to its artistry and subject matter. Championed as a film that charted "a completely new course, a different methodology and rhythm" (al-Salamuni 1996: 122), the film has in many respects never been equaled.[15] The dialogue, scripted for city and country dwellers alike in formal written Arabic, is sparse. The soundtrack consists primarily of the wind and strains of modern, atonal strings (Daud 1996). Although Shadi intended to shoot in black-and-white, and imagined his sets and costumes accordingly, Cinema Institute officials, concerned with distribution potential, insisted he film in color. Accordingly, he and art director Salah Marii reversed certain color schemes (for example dressing the tribespeople in black rather than white). Fortunately, Shadi was permitted to hold the ground on his plan to utilize little known or unknown faces in his major roles. This allowed him to "drill his actors to reveal inner conflict without exaggerated performance and without efforts to play heavily on viewer emotion" (Abd al-Rahman 1996: 228).

Set in 1881 and based loosely on actual historical events (Colla 2000: 113–14), *The Mummy* recounts the struggle by Egyptian and Western Orientalists to stem the flow of pharaonic treasures from the Valley of the Kings and Queens onto the international market some sixty years before Hassan Fathy tried to move the tribespeople off the mountain. The film opens in a darkened chamber in the Egyptian Museum, where Gaston Maspero, director of antiquities, dispatches a young Egyptian archaeologist, Ahmad Kamal (Muhammad Khayri) to Upper Egypt. There, working with local military authorities who have failed to mount an effective blockade, he will seek out an insider to reveal the site of the hidden tombs. His trip coincides with the death of the tribal shaykh, whose stark burial is depicted on a windblown mountain side. Immediately thereafter, the shaykh's brother and another elder initiate his two sons into the secret of the tribe's existence. Wanis (Ahmad Marii) and his elder brother (Ahmad Higazi) look on in horror as their uncle slices through a mummy wrapping and forcefully removes a large Horus-eye amulet. Later, when the elder brother protests this desecration to the elders, his paternal uncle replies sarcastically, "Those whom you call 'the dead' are nothing but dust and wood from a thousand years ago. No one knows them, neither fathers nor sons." This is followed by an unveiled threat:

> This was the life of your father and his father before him. He hoped that you would learn the secret of the treasure-trove. But if he was alive today he would wish you dead.

Shortly thereafter, unbeknownst to Wanis, his older brother is murdered, his body thrown into the Nile rapids.

Wanis quickly learns more of his tribe's dealings with the shady antiquities merchant, Ayyub (Shafiq Nur al-Din), and his on-site go-between, the obsequious Murad (Muhammad Nabih), who also runs a prostitution ring. His world collapsing, Wanis becomes infatuated with the trappings of the archaeologist. He wanders the ruins with a "stranger," a peasant who has been trained in excavation (and who wears white, in contrast to the tribal black). Still not knowing his brother's fate, Wanis confronts Ayyub, tries to take back the Horus charm, and is beaten senseless. Murad, sensing upheaval and trying to cut his own losses, informs Wanis of his brother's death and proposes an alliance against tribe and merchant. Instead, Wanis approaches the archaeologist's boat to speak to the authorities.

Shadi's ambivalent ending rivals Khalil Shawqi's, only his is more mournful. In the last scene the archaeologist descends into the burial chamber to supervise the removal of the mummies. The tribespeople look on, bewildered. Their leaders cower behind the rocks, unbowed, awaiting a better day to do battle. The ship pulls slowly away from the dock. As the screenplay describes:

> Wanis runs along the bank forsaken, disregarded, lost; he is crying, his hands on face. He looks behind him to his destiny, as tears flow from his eyes. He looks back to his destiny, towards the voice, then runs further from the village, and the mountain—just as his brother did, just as the stranger did, further away. The steamer—and all aboard it—floats further away, like a pearl in the light of dawn, as the image freezes.

A final frame contains a quote from the Book of the Dead: "Rise up, you will not die. You were called by your own name and resurrected" (Abd al-Salam 1996: 287).

The Mummy, as longtime Shadi associate Magdi Abd al-Rahman has written (1996: 220–30), is a tale that spans three eras. The action is set in 1881, the year before the foreign occupation of Egypt. As such, the film speaks to the country's thwarted desires to assert political autonomy in a modernizing context. The archaeological record, dating to the New Kingdom, constitutes a second era, linked to the film's "present" by Maspero's opening recitation from *The Book of the Dead,* Shadi's textual nod to the nationalist theme of Egypt awakening from slumber (Colla 2000: 114–19). Finally there is the chronicle of the film's origins, the patronage of culture minister Tharwat Ukasha and of Italian director Roberto Rossellini, then the torturous road to the screen, six years after completion.[16]

The Mummy took so long from print to release for a variety of reasons. Some were financial, the result of a complex interplay between a film that had been shot, at government insistence, in color, thus at great cost, and the post-1967 war austerity economy. But morale seems to have played as much a part as money. As Elliott Colla has suggested (2000: 111–12, 136–37), the national mood following the June defeat, then the "distractions" of Sadat's liberalization also influenced both the film's final formulation and eventually its lack of public attention. Colla's reading of the "doubled framing ritual of burial"—the early scene of the shaykh's funeral and the final repatriation of the pharaonic mummies—suggests a "tension between the nationalist, redemptive surface of the film," scripted prior to June 1967, and the "sense of ambivalence and national melancholia just underneath," the product of the military defeat (ibid.: 136).

Despite its split-screen identity, filmed under Nasser, screened publicly under Sadat (and only achieving wide-spread recognition as a televised film under Mubarak), *The Mummy* remains primarily an artifact of Nasser-era imaginings of tradition, modernity, and national identity. As such, it fits the ever ambivalent nature of the progressive nationalist discourse. The tribespeople are, overall, ignorant, stubborn, and corrupt. They are also, in a wider socio-political economy linked to Cairo and abroad, corrupted by a larger, overarching authority. Whether they can be brought into the modern world, or simply must observe bitterly as "their" treasure is appropriated remains unanswered.

HAREMS

The same ambivalence pervades Salah Abu Sayf's late 1960s venture into the countryside, a first for the esteemed director (not counting the 1954 *The Monster,* which is primarily a crime story). *The Second Wife* (*al-Zawga al-thaniya* 1967) remained one of Abu Sayf's favorite films (Abu Sayf, December 19, 1995). The director prided himself on the ethnographic details with which he represented village life, and the way in which his players studied and enacted rural habits and mores (al-Nahhas 1996: 159–60). Critics agreed with the former, had mixed takes on the acting, but in general found the story that Abu Sayf brought to the screen to be simplistic and melodramatic, a far cry from the social realism for which the director was known (Yusuf 1992: 331–42).[17] The critics may have been right in claiming that Abu Sayf gutted writer Rushdi Salih's complex rendering of rural tradition and pre-revolutionary social structure, in particular his re-scripted happy ending. The vision that Abu Sayf brought to the screen, however, speaks louder to a shifting emphasis at the time—however social-realist contrived—toward a more self-empowered peasantry.

Salih's story concerns Utman (Salah Mansur), an unlikeable *umda* (village chief) whose power-base is undercut by his childless status. He and his wife Ruqiya (Sanaa Gamil) not only face the jibes of public gossip—he behind his back, she to her face—they also stand to lose her 300 feddan inheritance.[18] Together, they agree that Utman will take a second wife, the beautiful young Fatima (Suad Husni), but that her child will be registered as Ruqiya's and she will thereafter be divorced. To complicate matters—and deny any residual sympathy to the troubled couple—Fatima is already married to a poor peasant, Abu al-Ila (Shukri Sirhan), with whom she has children. Abu al-Ila is coerced into divorcing Fatima, a scene powerfully captured on film. In Salih's original story Fatima bears Utman a child (the umda sleeps with her, but only in darkness). Subsequently Abu al-Ila goes mad and wanders the village in a demented state.

Abu Sayf and his collaborators reworked the story to create an entirely different tone.[19] They did not lessen the complexity of the predicament in which Utman and his wife find themselves. Rather, they turned Salih's story into a morality tale in which a crafty fallaha outwits her new husband, and in which he, not the oppressed peasant, suffers madness—and worse. In a series of encounters that border on the comical—and in which Ruqiya, against her best long-term interests, becomes an unspoken co-conspirator—Fatima manages to avoid sexual contact with her new husband. Instead, she becomes pregnant by Abu al-Ila, to whom she remains loyal, after he sneaks into her chamber on her wedding night. When her pregnancy is announced, Utman is struck mute with paralysis and confined to his bed; she bears a son, whereupon Utman drops dead amidst a fanfare of ululation. In this revolutionary tale, peasant wile, personified by the fallaha, ultimately defeats the corrupt cultural and repressive social order of the village chief and his allies, including the local clergy, who conspired with him to break up a happy modest household on behalf of a corrupt elite.

Riding on its major stars, especially Suad Husni, and the reputation of its director, the film garnered mild success (Mustafa Darwish, April 28, 1996). Yet, as noted above, reviewers attacked on a variety of fronts, and their responses reveal much about Egyptian film criticism in the late 1960s. "The film's characters are a blend of formalism and melodrama"; all save one are unrealistic representations of pure good or evil, and all are poorly acted, despite the fine cast (Samir Farid in Yusuf 1992: 331–33). Fatima is too shrewd for a "simple, ignorant, sweet peasant," while Utman is reduced to "a man entering his second adolescence" (Adli Fahim in ibid.: 336). Abu Sayf has recorded the village "through the eyes of a city boy," producing a "common tale" rather than confronting the real challenge raised by the story, "that Abu al-Ila has only two options after his wife has been taken: to rebel against the umda, in effect against an entire society based on exploitation, an impossible option; or, as his sole remaining, inevitable option . . . to live in a different world" of the mind (Faruq Abu Zayd in ibid.: 339–42). It is the oppressed, broken-down peasant whose wife has been taken from him who should stand stage center:

> Abu al-Ila is the "missing" peasant who has had his wife hatefully taken from him. He is a peerless symbol of the peasant who is ground up socially, and should have been the true hero of the film. Had that happened we would have seen a marvelous cinematic work. Instead

> Salah Abu Sayf leaned toward the screen adolescent, young Suad Husni, and the screaming sexual desires of Salah Mansur, and wasted three-quarters of the film (ibid.: 342)!

City critics challenging the city boy's cinematic vision obviously foster their own problematics, for by denying Fatima's intuition as well as Abu al-Ila's ability to actively resist, they ultimately deny the peasants any real agency in coping with an oppressive social structure that seeks to manipulate tradition to its own better end.

Shukri Sirhan would get his due in *The Rains Dried Up* (the film that opened this chapter), a little-known movie that meshed socialist realist propaganda with the avant garde and concluded with a melodramatic flourish.[20] Sirhan has played peasants before, but this is the new post-feudal peasant:

> . . . there is a peasant who comes after the revolution, the new peasant. Not the weak, broken down peasant, submitting to his fate, to his master. Rather, the peasant who builds his future and his way by his desire . . . who does not know the impossible, who doesn't surrender to it, but rather he who believes only in work, in desire, and in his ability to change his life.[21]

The "new" peasant in the new society faces familiar dilemmas in the film co-authored by director Sayyid Isa and future director Raafat al-Mihi.

State interest requires the appropriation of village land for construction of a new university. Willing villagers will be resettled in a reclamation province. "Your interest is the nation's interest," a government official announces. Village children look on with bemusement—it is they, the film implies, who will ultimately benefit—and catch the eye of the ranking officer in charge. The men try to charge the field and are held back. Later they debate their plight in the mosque, expressing a variety of heartfelt opinions. The most suspicious of the project is Shaykh Ali (Abd al-Ghani Qamr), the blind cleric, who speaks forthrightly against accommodation, with little regard for his flock. The shaykh's home, where he eats furiously (and sloppily), hectored by his evil-eyed wife (Naima Wasfi), is contrasted to that of Husayn (Shukri Sirhan), their son-in-law, and his wife Amina (Samiha Ayyub), where quiet peace prevails as the couple discuss their options. In other households villagers sort through heirlooms or sit pondering their fate. The following day, his wife coerced by her parents into staying put, Husayn leaves alone. As departing trucks pass the village cemetery an old man (Shafiq Nur al-Din) jumps down to scoop up some earth. At night the travelers are terrified by horrific images of denuded trees. The camera cuts quickly between branches, wide eyes, and clasped hands, suddenly reversing the image to the negative. The following morning they are calmed by placid images of palms, but upon arrival at their new lands discover that their lodgings are not yet ready for occupation. That night they again sit pensively as a song of sad alienation wafts through the air. In the morning many choose to return home, and are welcomed warmly by their less courageous neighbors.

Positive images of the proud pioneers follow, as Husayn and the stalwart till the soil and erect mud walls for housing. A sand storm undoes much work and a tragic fire claims several lives (including the old man). Government officials assure the community that their losses will be covered and the venture re-started, but another group abandons the site. "They're crawling back like dogs," snarls Shaykh Ali's wife. Longing for his family, Husayn grows despondent. A romantic strain develops with Haniya (Suhayr al-Murshidi), an eligible young woman who carries a torch for Husayn. He rebuffs physical affection, but increasingly comes to tolerate her attention and desire her presence. "Shall we live like the tree that has planted its roots by a new river bank," Husayn laments. "Tomorrow the tree will grow and spread its branches, and sink its roots in its [new] land," responds Haniya. Still despairing, Husayn plans to return home, until his son, having escaped the prison of his grandparents' home, arrives. Next, Amina rebels, first leaving her parents' home, then setting out with her remaining children to join Husayn. In the final scene, she meets him on the road. They all hitch a jeep ride back to the reclaimed land, the road now a comforting path to a new life.

Perseverence having paid off, with the help of government subsidy, a new land will be cultivated far from the evils of old-fashioned patriarchy (and matriarchy) cloaked in religious garb. Whatever the realities of life for landed and migratory peasants, villagers and tribesfolk, the new society onscreen bespeaks a better future. Yet Sayyid Isa's film, like Khalil Shawqi's more ambivalent *The Mountain,* has made far less impression than the highly popular and oft-broadcast films such as *Struggle in the Valley, Blood on the Nile, Call of the Curlew, The Sin,* or *The Second Wife.* To that extent the image of the new peasant, the presumed fruition of all the earlier works—and the reformist texts on which they were based—never really supplanted that of the oppressed, beaten-down, and stubbornly ignorant rural dweller.

Men of Faith

If peasants, villagers, and tribespeople garnered the ambivalence of reform-minded artists and intellectuals during the Nasser era, what of the imaging of religion? Nasserist Egypt was a secular state, and cinematic reflections of this are mirrored in popular print media, murals, and other fine arts. Many Egyptians remained personally devout, but with the Muslim Brotherhood politically outlawed, its leading members in prison or exile, Islamism played no role in the official state rhetoric that championed secular ideals, arts, and symbology. In the early years following the July coup, propagandists denounced the Brothers as "merchants of religion"; thereafter, the state, with the assistance of like-minded clerics, set out to secularize al-Azhar University, the thousand-year-old bastion of orthodox learning. Contemporary photographs of bare-headed coeds lined up in front of cloaked and turbaned admissions officers might well surprise those for whom the norm on all Egyptian campuses has been the post-"Zouzou" era. If zealous modernizers imagined a "passing of traditional society," others more attuned to the power of deep-rooted symbols, beliefs, and practices sought some degree of political-social-cultural accommodation. The cinema at once reflected the ideological power of the new and the persistence of traditional religious patterns. For some, the struggle to mediate between the two continued.

A contemporary critic viewing Salah Abu Sayf's *The Second Wife* took the director to task for perpetuating misguided characterizations of religious authorities:

> In his depiction of the character Shaykh Mabruk (Hasan al-Barudi), Salah Abu Sayf has fallen into the same dangerous trap as have so many of our major writers and intellectuals: portraying Egyptian men of religion as allied to the exploitative feudalist and capitalist classes. This is an historical error that contradicts what has really happened. Throughout its modern history, from the Mamluk state up until the July revolution, men of religion were in the forefront of the powers crying out against exploitation, and based this revolutionary position on religious law (Faruq Abu Zayd in Yusuf 1992: 341).

The critic did not aim wide in his reading of Abu Sayf's text, for Mabruk embodies the corrupt, and deplorably antiquated religious official.[22] Hovering at the edge of the morality play, the shaykh is part "witch doctor," prescribing a variety of folk-remedy potency enhancers to the distressed umda, and part evil counsel, participating in the coercion of the hapless Abu al-Ila, who yields to the pressure and renounces his wife.

The latter scene is shot as if a police interrogation. The claustrophobic room is darkened, a spotlight shining on the participants' faces. Helpless and bewildered, his eyes tear-filled, the peasant pleads with his betters, "Oh, men of religion!" Shaykh and umda stare back with cruel eyes, their visages betraying a growing aggravation. Only the muezzin, also pressed into service as a witness, divulges any sense of shame. As Abu al-Ila stands after his thumb print is put to paper, Shaykh Mabruk callously offers a cigarette; the umda hastily presses a wad of bills into his hands. Bowed but retaining a degree of dignity, the peasant waves off both, leaving them to their crime.

If the director's aim is clear, there are in his film countervailing forces at work. In its depiction of popular religious practice, especially female fertility rituals, the film adopts an ethnographic eye that is generally dispassionate.[23] And in a pivotal scene, Fatima, the second wife, visits a shrine in a nearby town to seek solace from the entombed saint. Sitting by the catafalque, she is approached by the mosque's imam, who, sensing her distress, questions her. When she outlines her predicament, he assures her that God would never sanction the umda's actions. This steels her resolve to resist the fait accompli of local coercion by whatever guile she can muster. The conjunction between *sunna* and saint, orthodox institutional and heterodox popular religious practice, expressed by the kindly, more urban imam leaves the door open for a degree of accommodation between tradition and modernity within a religious context.

That accommodation, albeit with a more cynical twist, is expressed more forthrightly in the film adaptation of Yahya Haqqi's popular novella, *The Lamp of Umm Hashim* (*[Qandil Umm Hashim],* Kamal Atiya 1968). The film's opening scene captures the uneasy coexistence of orthodoxy and heterodoxy, albeit with a bemused gaze. The first image is of towering Mamluk-era minarets, the distinctive architecture of Cairo's medieval splendor. The credits then roll over a still image of a glass lamp, the receptacle for the blessed oil of Umm Hashim, patron saint of the blind. The director's name overlays the array of minarets that grace Cairo's medieval skyscape. Next a cleric walks past a mosque; outside the doors blessing-seekers are engaged in various degrees of frenetic prostration. "Blasphemy," he mutters, and walks on. The scene cuts inside, where a portly, wide-eyed mosque attendant (Salah Mansur) silences a bedraggled, ranting dervish with a tap on the head. An old man reading the Quran looks on, as does Ismail (Shukri Sirhan), the story's hero. Dressed in a striped gallabiya, he too sits reading in a corner, but he studies medical texts. Bemused by the familiar antics around him, he rises, walks over to contemplate the hanging lamp, and greets the attendant warmly. Turning towards the saint's tomb, he notices a young woman clinging silently to the lattice gate surrounding the catafalque, then exits into the clamorous streets. The opening is exaggerated and at times comical, designed to impart cynicism and, ultimately, scorn.

If Ismail is ambivalent at the outset, he returns from his study mission in Germany—where he has had the requisite romance with a European woman—a changed man.[24] The skewed camera angle of his carriage and the commotion in the streets evoke his new-found alienation. When he discovers that Fatima (Samira Ahmad), the young woman who has been living with his family, is losing her sight, Ismail takes her to the hospital for evaluation, then himself performs—without success—a delicate, experimental operation. When he subsequently finds his mother (Amina Rizq) treating Fatima's eyes with oil from the saint's lamp, he flies into a frenzy. Now wearing a European-style suit, he marches into the mosque, disregarding the congregants, and smashes the holy lamp. The shocked assembly turns on him, beating him senseless. Regaining consciousness to find himself the object of an exorcism, Ismail again explodes. Cursing the "ignorance" that rules family and neighborhood, he flees for the modern city. There he advances in his profession, but remains troubled by his inability to cure Fatima.

Finally a rapprochement is reached. A senior associate determines that Fatima suffers from "hysteria"; the earlier operation failed because of her psychological dependence on the saint's oil. Begrudgingly, Ismail now accepts a compromise. He returns to neighborhood, family, and mosque. A visit to the saint's shrine prompts trepidation for the congregants, but his request for a vial of oil is applauded. Ismail now suggests a combined treatment of modern and folk cures, substitutes a placebo for the oil, performs a second operation—and Fatima is cured.

In order for Fatima to again see—and with greater clarity—two accommodations must be made. Ismail must allow the "superstitious" to believe in Umm Hashim's grace. Concurrently, Fatima insists, against the panicked protests of Ismail's mother, that the operation proceed. Her faith in modern science, despite its prior shortcomings, is as important as his willingness to accede to the spiritual power of belief in the healing process. As the film ends, Ismail again looks up at the towering minarets. Their majesty, reaching skyward, reaffirms a power that is not necessarily backward or dangerous, so long as it can coexist with modernity.

Religion and religious figures are multi-faced and multi-voiced in other Nasser-era films. The comical, befuddled shaykh, a common figure in romantic screwball comedies since the early days of cinema, remained a standby, even in those films that invoke social relations once considered inappropriate for the screen. At the finale of *Nights of Love,* the early Abd al-Halim Hafiz comedy in which the lowly employee romances the boss's daughter, two shaykhs appear to oversee Amal Farid's marriage to her rich Alexandrian cousin. The first, real shaykh is greeted by a similarly cloaked, turbaned, and bearded Abd al-Halim, who warns him that the fiancé is loopy and potentially violent. When the agitated cousin, confounded by a web of mistaken identities, accosts the shaykh, calling him a charlatan and tugging at his "false" beard, the panicked cleric runs off to fetch an ambulance from the sanitarium. But not too far that he cannot be recalled to perform the marriage of the proper couple once matters have fallen in place.

Overzealous protestations of piety—Zaki Rustam's demonstrative *"Allahu Akbar"* when confronted while at prayer by Farid Shawqi in *Platform Number 5*—have often been a marker of villainy. Obsessive concerns with purity and pollution—the ever-at-prayer Abd al-Qawi in *My Wife is General Director*—have been another comic trope. Clerics can also, as in the transitional scene in *The Second Wife,* lend spiritual comfort. At the same time, their attempts can be portrayed as ultimately futile.

Naguib Mahfouz has always had a soft spot for holy figures, who recur with some regularity throughout his literary corpus in important supporting roles. With a mystical bent, often speaking in veiled language, they embody a social and spiritual rootedness, a truth that is beyond the ken of the hyper-secular world (el-Enany 1993: 102–3). His most enigmatic mystic is found in the 1961 novel *The Thief and the Dogs (al-Liss wa al-kilab),* brought to the screen by Kamal al-Shaykh in 1962. The central figure, Said Mahran (Shukri Sirhan), is an urban Robin Hood ground down by a world, both criminal and supposedly respectable, that has lost its social compasses. The story is a parable of politics and power, and a revolution that has become dominated by opportunists and jaded ideologues who have surrendered the last vestiges of social responsibility. When Said is released from prison, where he landed after being betrayed by his closest friend, he finds his family in the enemy camp. He takes refuge with the neighborhood Sufi shaykh, formerly his father's spiritual guide. In both novel and film the shaykh, delivering parables, speaks to a world in which ultimate knowledge produces ignorance and in which the prison of the mind extends beyond social bounds. In the novel, Shaykh Ali lends a degree of spiritual comfort to the tortured Said, and near the story's climax provides physical asylum from a tightening police dragnet. In the film the holy man is less ambiguous and more antiquarian. In two early encounters he provides brief respite for the tortured hero, but at the climax, when Said escapes to his lodge, the fugitive is overcome by the dissonance between the fervently praying dervishes and the harsh realities outside. Rather than accept lodging, gaining a last sleep, as he does in the original text, the movie Said flees immediately to meet his death.

If the confluence of religion and politics remained fraught with danger throughout the Nasser era, several films did highlight the role of a patriotic clergy in the pre-revolutionary nationalist struggle. The most dramatic rendition of opposition to British rule appears in Hasan al-Imam's *Palace Walk.* In a stirring ten-minute montage of the 1919 popular uprising, Imam depicted the entirety of Egyptian urban society on the march, including theology students and clerics. Coptic and Muslim religious dignitaries speak from each others' respective pulpits about the unity of crescent and cross, the symbol of the national movement. Church bells peal, the *idhan* (call to prayer) sounds from minarets, priest and imam grasp hands before being hoisted on ecumenical shoulders and paraded through the streets. *Sayyid Darwish,* a classic formula biopic of Egypt's famed composer who began his career as a religious student, also depicts young clerics engaged in anti-British demonstrations. In an early scene, Sayyid's close friend and fellow theology student falls victim to an imperialist bullet while both crouch behind a barricade. Darwish's career, of course, takes him far from his clerical roots, and his artistic rebellion against the rigid strictures of his training are celebrated. Still a youth, he pawns his father's watch in order to be able to enroll in an Italian music academy, starts to perform with a back-up band, abandons his robes, and carries on with a dancer.

In the aftermath of the June 1967 defeat Egyptian cinema took a dramatic turn, the "setback" ushering in a period in which a wall of taboos toppled. An important group of films, some scripted but not approved prior to the June war, now saw the light of day. These films (they will be treated in more detail in the following chapter) expressed a growing cynicism toward revolutionary projects and many, unlike similar pre-June efforts, no longer couched social and political ills in the requisite historical garb. Amongst a powerful corpus of films, one in particular addressed questions of authoritarianism and its limits in ways that, in retrospect, seem to presage a shift from secular to religious evocation of opposition.

A Bit of Fear (*[Shay' min al-khawf],* Husayn Kamal 1969), a parable of power narrated as a timeless folktale, is set in a fictitious village in an indeterminable time marked only as pre-revolutionary by the old crescent flag fluttering in the village square. The story, punctuated by a recurrent ballad sung by a chorus,[25] traces the career of Atriss (Mahmud Mursi), the sensitive grandson and namesake of the local warlord (also played by Mursi), a violent tyrant who rules his fiefdom, Dahashna, by terror. Grandfather Atriss, fearing his heir will be devoured without toughening, forces grandson Atriss to engage in violent acts—killing a pet dove, torching peasant fields, stampeding through town—as part of his education. As he matures, the younger Atriss pledges to Fuada (Shadia), his childhood sweetheart, that he will remain gentle. But when his grandfather is gunned down by a recalcitrant victim, the grandson assures him that he will not die unavenged.

In mythic fashion Atriss assumes his grandfather's identity, following his destined—and now avowed—path. He ravages Dahashna, raising taxes, ransoming children, ordering irrigation sluices shut. Fuada ultimately confronts his brutality with her own elemental moral power by opening the sluice, then staring down the marauders, daring Atriss to shoot her. It is a powerful scene, in which the proud fellaha, clad in black and with head covered but staring outward—"Egypt Awakening"—fearful but with strength of purpose, takes actions that no man is willing to initiate.

Torn between love and power, Atriss resolves to wed Fuada and presents her parents (Muhammad Tawfiq and Amal Zayid) with a fait accompli. Fearful of retribution, her father and his summoned witnesses swear falsely that Fuada has consented. When word spreads through Dahashna that she had indeed refused, and is thus illegally held, a long-complacent population begins to mobilize. Atriss has now crossed an impassable moral boundary, the violation of religious law. Young men, shamed that it has taken a woman to activate resistance, meet in the mosque and swear to protect Fuada's virtue. Shaykh Ibrahim (Yahya Shahin), a landowner in clerical robes who had long bemoaned Dahashna's inaction but remained passive, now proclaims the marriage invalid. When his fields are destroyed by Atriss's guards, he rises in the mosque at Friday communal prayer to rally the congregation. Queried about his prior passivity, and warned about the consequences of further dissent (this by one of the warlord's henchmen), Ibrahim asserts:

> The coward as good as joins their gang because he encourages them in their excesses. Those who remain silent allow them to raise their voices. Why do we pray [together] on Fridays? To study the problems of fellow Muslims. What happens to one concerns us all, and that is God's business. People, the marriage is invalid! Do they think that by burning my fields the marriage will somehow become valid? The marriage is invalid and will always be invalid!

When his son is murdered on his wedding day, Ibrahim, bearing the corpse, leads the village in an attack on Atriss's villa. Abandoned by his guard, then locked alone in his upstairs bedroom—Fuada has escaped to join the mob—the tyrant perishes in a blaze of justice.

Based on a short story by the conservative writer Tharwat Abaza, *A Bit of Fear* is implicitly critical of the Nasserist state, and was understood to be so at the time. Within the context of a village fable, the utilization of religious strictures concerning marriage (with all the related issues of chastity and honor/shame) as the rubicon of allowable exploitation and terror, like the utilization of mosque and preacher as site and instigator of resistance, make literary and cultural sense. Nonetheless, the film takes a major step forward in expiating the "sins" of traditionalists—peasants, tribespeople, and preachers—that is so characteristic of modernist and then Nasser-era print and film literature. And without perhaps consciously intending to do so, *A Bit of Fear* presages the role of mosque and preacher in the upsurge of political turmoil that would mark successive decades, well into the present—and ultimately lead to the increased marginalization of religion from big and little screens, except in carefully packaged formats (Abu-Lughod 1993: 498–99).

The Peasant and the Land Revisited

One final film deserves mention, although at face value it seems to connote a step backward from either the new industrious, forward-looking peasant of *The Rains Dried Up* or the triumphant, ultimately optimistic anti-authoritarianism of *A Bit of Fear*. This is Youssef

Chahine's magisterial 1970 adaptation of Abd al-Rahman al-Sharqawi's 1954 novel *The Land* (*al-Ard;* translated as *Egyptian Earth* 1990). Eight years in the making (Armes 1987: 248), Chahine's film is a major re-write of the story that heightens dramatic tension by limiting the story to a smaller set of characters and by intensifying the sense of an ever-oppressed peasantry.[26] Chahine's script takes point of view away from the twelve year-old boy returning from school in the city and narrates the story instead through an impersonal camera eye. The action opens with a close up of a peasant's hands tenderly cradling a small cotton plant. This is Abu Suwaylim, the conscience of the village and the living site of memory of better bygone days. According to scenarist Hasan Fuad, Abu Suwaylim symbolizes "all peasants past and present . . . their inherited, immutable character traits and their unified behavior in the face of events" (al-Salamuni 2001: 84). The second primary character in the film, the younger, virile Abu Hadi, reflects, according to author al-Sharqawi, "the rebellious nature of the Egyptian peasant, who deeply loves the land, and who from this love finds value [in life]" (ibid.: 82). Amidst a village of richly drawn characters, these two, the elder, reflective Abu Suwaylim and the headstrong young Abu Hadi stand out in the film as the anchors of rural society and identity.

Rather than building a new society, as in *The Rains Dried Up,* the peasants in this story desperately cling to their turf as their fields are literally snatched from their grasp. Not to make way for schools and other socialist projects—the painful but necessary trade-off from the Sayyid Isa film—but rather so that the rapacious bey (here a combination of several aristocrats in the novel) can build a more direct roadway to his estate without compensation to those whose earth is trampled and with appropriate reward for those who collaborate in the scheme.

Based on a text published in the early, heady days of land reform, Chahine's film seems in some respects a throwback to the film production of the fifties, including his own *Struggle in the Valley.* He demonstrates a continued love of the land and fascination with the potential dignity of rural life, a continuous struggle to capture the contradictions between "the natural beauty" of the countryside and the "misery of the fallahin" (ibid.: 84). Yet here the focus has shifted. The evil aristocrats are kept in the background. They are heartless, enjoying the rural quietude without a concern for the crops or lives of their subjects who face increasingly steep cutbacks in water rations. Yet they are depicted as far more banal than the characters portrayed by Zaki Rustam and Farid Shawqi in the 1954 film, who seem almost caricatures in comparison. Likewise, the peasants, although still manipulated with a degree of ease by those with more education and social status, are not presented as superstitious or bound by rigid cultural mores—there is no vendetta theme in *The Land* (either novel or film). In an oft-cited scene, adapted from separate instances in the novel, two peasants who have come to blows spontaneously join forces to pull Abu Suwaylim's cow from a well, then collapse, exhausted, in each other's arms.

Sharqawi's peasants are less the victims of ignorance and out-moded traditions than of brutal force martialed by their masters to quash their defiant spirit. Helpless to defend their land, and exhausting quasi-legal options—they petition the government, but only after the bey has re-written their text to suit his purposes—the peasants rebel. Beaten in the fields and tortured in prison, the leading males retain their resolve. In a penultimate scene, one that recalls the efforts to save the cow, the villagers combine forces to help Abu Suwaylim harvest his crop before his fields are trampled by road workers, some of the latter unemployed itinerant laborers with little option but to collaborate in the demise of the landed peasantry (a cruel twist on Yusuf Idris's *The Sin*). The upbeat mood, almost, perhaps deliberately reminiscent of scenes of happy peasants from pre-revolutionary films, changes abruptly with the arrival of the military. Abu Suwaylim, left alone to face the commanding officer, is slapped, lassoed, and dragged to his death by horse as he clings to the earth—his earth—the cotton crop slipping through his bloodied fingers, a reverse imaging of the film's tender opening.

There is in the contradictions to which the director has pointed—"natural beauty" and "misery"—an ambivalence that has rendered his work hard to classify. The film has been duly honored: in 1984 leading critics rated it the best Egyptian film ever made.[27] Critics and film historians have nevertheless been unsure how to categorize it, even within Chahine's own corpus. Raymond Baker (1974: 412–13), analyzing "political film" in the early 1970s, described *The Land* as "a moving condemnation of rural feudalism—by no means a dead issue in Egypt today" in a body of work that he characterized as "depressingly uneven." Roy Armes (1987: 248), whose cultural focus is broader, called it a "masterly rural epic" and credited Chahine with a "more assured technique" and "stronger" political view, compared specifically to his earlier urban masterpiece, *Cairo Station.* That political view, rooted in Nasserist socialist reforms, is a call to further the revolution by extending nationalization; as such *The Land* stands apart from Chahine's later, more critical takes on Nasserism.[28] Others, like Duriya Sharaf al-Din (1992: 100), categorize it simultaneously as a socialist film celebrating the nobility of labor and a post-1967 work in which historical oppression becomes a mirror for the present. Chahine addressed the issue indirectly in an interview with film critic Sami al-Salamuni shortly after the film's release (2001: 88):

> I was a spontaneous socialist, a young man who returned from abroad [in the early 1950s] full of zeal and a desire to change everything. Then, through working in the cinema, I began to develop a scientific understanding of the world via work itself and by searching for answers to the questions how and why. In my films, from *Papa Amin* [*Baba Amin* 1950] to *The Land,* there is one clear strand: what happens to the honorable individual under certain conditions without losing his honor or surrendering?

Already in 1970, if Chahine does not couch his socialist leanings in the past tense, he clearly indicates that *The Land* cannot be subsumed easily with other, earlier works—his or others'—that celebrated socialist virtues in the heyday of Arab socialism.

His film is a masterpiece on many levels. Many, like Armes, have noted his surer use of the camera, color, and script (al-Salamuni 1984: 28–33). His casting is also a key element. To play Abu Suwaylim and head a roster of supporting or new players, Chahine turned to Mahmud al-Maligi. The aging actor, who had played more parts than anyone before or after in the history of Egyptian cinema, so many of them villainous pashas or rural and urban mob bosses, now dramatically shifted character, hiding his thin, sneering lips beneath an enormous

Manhood embodied: Mahmud al-Maligi as Abu Suwaylim in *The Land.* Courtesy of Arab Film Distribution.

bushy mustache, and transforming his familiar caustic glare into a defiant but weary gaze. When Abu Suwaylim returns from prison, having been arrested along with other troublemakers for sabotaging the bey's road works—not out of peasant obscurantism, but self-preservation of economic livelihood—his shame is exemplified by his effort to veil himself with his scarf from fellow townsfolk so they cannot see that his face has been shaven in prison. Yahya Shahin, the powerful Shaykh Ibrahim, who is roused from slumber to lead the rebellion in the recently released *A Bit of Fear,* here plays the turncoat Shaykh Hassuna, who is recalled from Cairo to support the peasants, but sells them out for assurances from the bey that his land will remain untouched. Abd al-Warith Asr, usually sympathetic, here acts the corrupt umda. Many other players in the ensemble cast—Izzat al-Ilayli as Abd al-Hadi, Salah al-Saadani, Nagwa Ibrahim—were newer faces, indications of another generational shift in the industry.

That shift took place at a time of dramatic transformation in Egypt: the defeat of June 1967, the death of Nasser in 1970, and the sudden demise of black-and-white movies. If *The Land,* with its depressing finale, seems out of place with many of the films noted above, its power may well rest in its reflection of an uneasy gaze both backward and forward. Some solace may be found in Abu Suwaylim's monologue, coming at a pivotal moment in the film, after his humiliation in prison. Now, pondering their options, Abu Suwaylim reminds his neighbors how in prouder days they all fought the British on behalf of the nation:

> We must rouse ourselves anew. But how? Where? Those were the days, long ago, days which have not been re-awakened. We had manly strength and spirit then—we were Men! The pride of the village, [protector of] its honor and chastity. Now we stand and talk, complain and paint our faces like idle women who say "tomorrow" and "patience is good"; who say anything, who don't know how to say anything! We sleep with words, wake up with words, live with words. Our life has become nothing but talk. . . .

Despite Abu Suwaylim's chastisement, despite his own ultimate humiliation, the peasants—men and women—do retain their dignity, and thus do represent, in a manner, the new fallah and fallaha. In the end nothing is gained and everything lost, but *The Land* remains a call to action, inspiring not only in its ability to arouse anger at unfeeling social and political elites, but also to awaken a sense of communal responsibility to "balad"—village or, in its variant meaning, country. In the aftermath of the disaster that was June 1967, the peasant remained beaten, but unbowed, the spirit of the nation.

NOTES

1. *Al-Musawwar,* September 10, 1965, p. 47.

2. *Al-Musawwar,* June 4, 1965, back cover.

3. The statue was replaced by a colossus of Ramsis and moved to the promenade outside Cairo University in 1955.

4. The gallabiya has often been a target of social reformers who perceived it as old fashioned. According to a 1954 government report, "Six million males in Egypt wear galabias. This dress is not practical as it handicaps certain kinds of industrial work and may cause accidents" (*Egyptian Gazette,* December 21, 1954).

5. And continues to pose a similar problem in contemporary drama, especially in television serials. Abu-Lughod (1998) views one, aptly titled *Dream of the Southerner,* in which many of the images cited below—selfish disregard for historical relics and the blood feud—persist as markers of positive urban and negative rural national characteristics.

6. Although an early role for Sirhan in what would be a long career encompassing some 150 films between 1949 and 1988, this is the character highlighted in the title of a recent volume written by the actor's son (Sirhan 1999).

7. The National Union (1956–1961) was the second single party administration founded by the Nasser regime, superseding the Liberation Rally (1953–56) and predating the Arab Socialist Union (1962–1978).

8. For the difficulties of rendering the work into another language see the introduction by A. B. as-Safi to his English translation (1997).

9. Baracat's film won state prizes in 1960 for best director, producer, male and female leads, female supporting actress (Zahra al-Ila), and scenario.

10. In his study of rural laborers, Jim Toth (1999: 237) questions the prevalence of female migrant workers as depicted in the film. However, he misplaces the action, putting it in Upper Egypt when in fact the migrants hail from Gharbiya Province in the Delta, thus the appellation, *Gharabwa,* given them by the villagers (Ishaq in Idris 1984: viii).

11. To induce a miscarriage she tries jumping and falling on her stomach and pressing a stone milling wheel onto her belly.

12. *The Sin* won state prizes for best director and film score for the 1964–65 season. In 1984, the panel of critics sponsored by the magazine *al-Funun* judged it the fourth best film in Egyptian cinema history.

13. Fathy (1973: 173–74) notes that his project captured the attention of the king in 1947, but mentions nothing of any royal visits. The depiction of the princess and her retinue seems more in keeping with post-1952 literary and film convention than with historical grounding.

14. Salah Qabil and Samira Ahmad, while neither were blockbuster marquee stars, both had their share of leads in the 1960s. Their roles here, especially Ahmad's, were decidedly secondary.

15. For a thorough study of Shadi's career, including the scenario for this film, see the special triple issue of *al-Qahira,* February 1996. For an English translation

of the scenario and a collection of excerpts from interviews with Shadi, see *Discourse 21* (1) 1999, pp. 89–139. My translations are from the Arabic screenplay.

16. See, among others, Abd al-Rahman (1996). Shadi had worked under Rossellini's direction during filming of the Egyptian episode of *Man's Struggle for Survival* (1970).

17. Amongst the selected essays in Yusuf there is one dissenting opinion (343–44), ironically penned later, after a television broadcast in memory of the actor Salah Mansur (d. 1989).

18. By the time of the film's release, of course, that inheritance was 250 feddans over limits imposed by a series of land reform decrees.

19. His original collaborator was Saad al-Din Wahba, but he completed the script with Mustafa Sami.

20. The director, Isa, had studied film in the Soviet Union and directed two prior films. He made a final film in 1983.

21. *Akhir saa,* August 23, 1967, p. 33.

22. Barudi also played the wily estate clerk, Masiha Effendi, in Baracat's *The Sin,* a character only slightly more likeable, thanks to his sympathetic turn near the story's end.

23. Abu Sayf has noted how when villagers (the film was shot in a village in Qalyuba province) turned out en masse, even giving kids a school holiday, many were incorporated into the film performing "real" dances and fertility rituals (al-Nahhas 1996: 160).

24. One critic complained, among other things, that the European interlude took up far too much of the film; see *al-Musawwar,* November 15, 1968, p. 41.

25. The powerful ballad, which is sung throughout the early portions of the film, was written by the poet Abd al-Rahman al-Abnudi, with music by composing giant Baligh Hamdi.

26. See the comments by scenarist Hasan Fuad in a 1970 interview with critic Sami al-Salamuni (reprinted in 2001: 84–85). Also Fawwal (2001: 72–80).

27. The poll results appeared in a special edition of *al-Funun,* May–June 1984, which has been cited extensively throughout this work. The top 10 films, in order, were: *The Land, The Beginning and the End, The Mummy, The Sin, The Thug, Call of the Curlew, Cairo Station, The Postman, The Bus Driver,* and *Heroes' Struggle.* Most noteworthy, all of these works, with one exception, Atif al-Tayyib's *The Bus Driver* (1983), are from the period under study in this book. To my knowledge, no similar survey has been undertaken since. Duly skeptical of the value of such endeavors, I would nonetheless expect that even after another two decades of filmmaking, a majority of "top" films would still be rooted in the Nasser era.

28. In view of this implicit critique of Nasser's failure to extend his reforms to the nationalization of land, it is not surprising that the novel's setting of 1933 has been retained; nevertheless, the film emerges as of far more than merely historical interest.

SIX

Unhappy Endings
The Rise and Fall of Nasserist Cinema

We all love the revolution, don't we? . . .

Miramar, 1968

The dear government is busy boosting the economy and building a socialist society. It's not free to trouble us here.

Chatter on the Nile, 1971

Socialist Endings

Any film that serves a political, humanistic, national or social cause serves our new society, and is by intent a socialist film. However, one must place this aim within the framework of a good, stimulating cinematic story. Because if the public is to like the film it must be able to both absorb the content and be entertained. There are people who believe that a socialist film should be nothing but speeches and preaching, but in my opinion such films serve no socialist cause. Socialism is not torment—it aims to raise up the people. Therefore, it is necessary that when we see such a film we walk away happy, so that we may accept our lives with enthusiasm and joy.[1]

Gamal al-Laythi spoke from a position of growing importance in the film industry. A former Free Officer, he had left the army for film production, then entered the public sector. In two years he had produced nineteen films, making his mark and setting the stage for a near monopoly of Egyptian film holdings from the black-and-white era and early 1970s. While Gamal controlled production strings, his younger brother Mamduh would soon emerge as a major script-writer, responsible for adapting for the screen several of the most popular and controversial literary works of the late Nasserist era. Mamduh followed well his brother's version of a socialist credo, working an uplifting finale into the bleakest of stories and scoring an enviable string of hits.

How happy the ending? In Hollywood on the Nile, happy endings represented a nearly inviolable convention. Several of Naguib Mahfouz's early tragic novels demanded fidelity. Nafisa (Sanaa Gamil), then her brother Hasanayn (Omar Sharif) jump to their deaths in *The Beginning and the End;* Said Mahran (Shukri Sirhan), the bandit hero of *The Thief and the Dogs,* is eventually snared by a police dragnet and gunned down;[2] the headstrong but beloved Rushdi (Hasan Yusuf) succumbs to tuberculosis in *Khan al-Khalili* (Atif Salim 1966); and Fahmi (Salah Qabil), the eldest son of al-Sayyid Ahmad Abd al-Gawwad in *Palace Walk,* is killed by British fire during a demonstration. Heroic martyrdom figured in a popular post-Suez war film, *Giants of the Sea,* when an entire squad of patrol boats is wiped out after sinking an enemy warship. In a particularly unsettling sixties ending, Fatin Hamama falls half-consciously to her death from a Ferris wheel when she learns the dirty truth of her mother's disappearance years earlier. *The Confession* then ends with a final shot of her mother (Madiha Yusri), a prostitute, walking the dark streets. These endings remain striking rarities in a corpus almost schematically dominated by comfortable, uplifting resolutions designed to send the audience home reassured and satisfied.

By raising the issue of socialist endings, Gamal al-Laythi confronted directly a much broader debate about the proper role of the state in guiding, administering and, ultimately, dictating the course of film production. After a decade-long discourse about the artistic consequences of a privately financed "entertainment" industry, the state finally stepped in to promote a more artistically creative, politically progressive cinema by nationalizing the industry in 1962. That intrusion into an industry that was paramount in the Arab world, however "low-quality" the product, remains a highly volatile subject. Nationalization, argue some, chased away stars and directors, and brought those who stayed under a reign of fear, thwarting the creative energies that had taken the Egyptian cinema in bold new directions by the late 1950s. Others, recognizing the system's faults, reply that the public sector produced some of the finest films ever screened—some hits, some not—and helped nurture a new generation of talented filmmakers. The public sector also produced a series of films that became vehicles for an emergent political and social criticism of Nasserism that characterized the latter years of Nasser's life, particularly following the 1967 war. In such films, always minority offerings amidst a plethora of "entertainments," filmmakers still battled with censorial whims and audience expectations. Working between these twin constraints, many found an allowance to push prior taboos and, perhaps more gratifying, an audience willing to break out of traditional viewing patterns.

NATIONALIZATION

"The period of the public sector of the 1960s is considered the beginning of the 'setback' of the Egyptian cinema" (Fayid 1999: 47). This author's blanket statement, in a recent book published for popular consumption by the Egyptian General Book Organization, is punctuated by the potent utilization of "setback"/*naksa,* the term used since the late sixties to signify the Arab defeat in 1967. Nationalization of the film industry came in conjunction with the broader agenda proclaimed in the 1962 Socialist Charter (Abdel-Malek 1968: 320–50).[3] As in other commercial and industrial realms, public and private sectors coexisted side by side. Decree 48 of 1963 established the General Egyptian Organization for Cinema, composed of four societies: Cinematographic Production (primarily documentary filmmaking), International Production, Studios and Property, and Distribution and Projection. A year later two new societies were added: Independent Distribution and Cairo Production, the latter headed by Gamal al-Laythi.

From the outset those responsible for guiding the public sector found themselves caught between two competing and seemingly mutually exclusive goals, those of enhancing the artistic and literary quality of individual productions, with the adjunct goal of scoring higher in international competitions and gaining larger foreign (non-Arab) audiences, or, conversely, of directing energies toward producing a greater quantity of films, with an eye toward maximizing profits. Under the directives of the culture ministry, led from 1962 to 1966 by Abd al-Qadir Hatim, quantity took early precedence over quality. Hatim, who oversaw the expropriation of studio facilities by the state, purchased from private owners at artificially deflated prices, charged the public sector to produce the largest number of films possible.[4] His successor, Tharwat Ukasha (who had served previously as minister of culture from 1958 to 1962), adopted the counter policy, focusing on quality and reducing the number of bureaucratic functionaries. Among Ukasha's most important directives was the call to bring to the screen adaptions of the best Egyptian literary works. Even the harshest critics of the public sector champion Ukasha's watch over that of his predecessor.

In retrospect, the public sector is viewed by many—even the harsh critics—as having made a positive contribution to the Egyptian cinema, irrespective of the upheaval, the unfairness with which some were treated, and the conflicts that followed greater state intrusion into decision making at a variety of levels (Abou Chadi 1995: 121). Directors working for the public sector produced a string of films that are among the best ever produced in Egypt. Of the films already noted in prior chapters, these include: *Cairo 1930, The Sin, The Second Wife, My Wife is General Director, The Mummy, The Impossible,* and *A Bit of Fear.* Between 1962 and 1972 the private sector produced 289 films to the public sector's 141.[5] Yet the private sector produced far fewer films of critical note. Of the eighty-one directors working during the public sector decade, twenty-one never worked for the public sector, while twenty-six worked solely under public auspices. Among the twenty-six directors who graduated from the public sector Cinema Institute (compared to only seventeen who debuted in the private sphere) were Husayn Kamal, Khalil Shawqi, Galal al-Sharqawi, Said Marzuq, and Ali Abd al-Khaliq (Abou Shadi 1995: 121; 1998: 51–52).

Several leading personalities, Fatin Hamama and the director Baracat most notably, left Egypt voluntarily, to pursue projects in Lebanon.[6] None made any films of note, certainly not from an artistic perspective. Many retain quarrelsome grudges against leading public sector personalities, if not the venture itself. Here the most famous discord is that between the director Tawfiq Salih and production sector head Salah Abu Sayf. Stripped of his assignment to direct *Palace Walk,* and refusing to go quietly, Salih found it difficult to secure another directorial or script-writing assignment for three years. Salih insists that he was blacklisted (January 7, 2000), if only informally, a charge that runs counter to a widely held credo that no one was ever formally banned from working, forcibly retired, or otherwise ousted from the industry (Abou Chadi 1995: 121). Among Egypt's film stars, the most prominent critic of the public sector remains Fatin Hamama. She returned to Egypt after 1967, and her career flourished as she embarked upon a series of more mature roles.[7] Unlike other actors—Tahiya Carioca, Nadia Lutfi, Nur al-Sharif, Amina Rizq—she has never been politically active or outspoken. Nevertheless, she quarreled with director Khayri Bishara during filming of his 1988 *Bitter Day, Sweet Day (Yawm murr, yawm hilw)* because the scenery called for a background portrait of Nasser, cast in sympathetic light (Khayri Bishara, January 2, 2000).

If the quality of films produced under Ukasha's ministry far outweighed that of Hatim's, many would agree that the real maturation followed upon the heels of June 1967. This includes the harshest recent critic, Duriya Sharaf al-Din, who has cast the 1960s as a "cinema of fear" (1992: 35). Pointing specifically to the role of novelist Naguib Mahfouz, who took over as chair of the Higher Cinema Institute in 1966, she notes an improvement in the intellectual caliber of films (ibid.: 72). However skeptical she may be about regime motives—she is not the first to sense a tactic to "defuse the latent anger" of a politically oppressed population—she nonetheless admits that the "green light" to treat issues of political oppression after 1967 did produce an "intellectual agenda" that set its gaze toward the future (ibid.: 96).[8] Rescripted attitudes must always be taken into account, as must the opportunity for freer expressions of doubt or dissent. Called before Sadat's inquiry commission, Naguib Mahfouz expressed hostility to the concept of nationalization (Abou Chadi

1995: 119). In the 1960s, however, he spoke out forcefully on behalf of public sector ambitions and achievements. The public sector, he argued in late 1967, aimed to produce better films than a profit-driven private sector. And, ever-conscious of charges that the talent pool remained limited, he noted successful efforts to bring new faces to the screen.[9]

A year earlier, film critic Mustafa Darwish had proclaimed the "return of the spirit" to Egyptian film.[10] The context was a review of the public sector comedy, *My Wife is General Director.* Fatin Abd al-Wahhab is, Darwish wrote, one of the few directors who can make people laugh "without resorting to vulgarity." Praising both script and comic ensemble acting, he singled out a character player whom he had noticed for the first time. Adil Imam, king of comedy since the 1970s, earned an early rave review: "His very presence in any scene, even momentarily, reduces the audience to uproarious laughter and uncommon entertainment."[11]

"Tear it down; We'll Build it Anew"

The "green light" refers to a small but influential group of films produced in the wake of the 1967 disaster that mark "the beginning of the desire of the 'system' to loosen the 'iron grip' relating to the freedom of expression in film" (Sharaf al-Din 1992: 126). Scripted by influential social and literary critics, in most cases prior to 1967, these texts were then brought to the screen by some of Egypt's most established or emerging directors and featured many of Egypt's biggest and budding stars. Several of the films, remaining faithful to their literary sources, depicted an Egypt from the era prior to the Nasser revolution. Now, however, they clearly spoke to the present state of affairs. More arresting to viewers were those films set in the immediate present, replete with the symbology and iconography of Nasserist Egypt. Self-criticism had not been a prominent feature of the Nasserist state, certainly not in the realm of cinema, and did not come easy, however logical the transformation appears in hindsight. When critics and historians speak of a "green light" we must recall the painstaking process by which filmmakers and government censors reached accommodation in order to even begin production, as well as the often cavalier decisions that allowed for or blocked final screening.

The thaw, in retrospect, sometimes appears to be more the sum of a few, politically charged parts, than a recognized or recognizable policy in the minds of those who ruled.

As Duriya Sharaf al-Din is quick to note, the great majority of films screened after the 1967 war continued to treat common themes, perhaps with greater urgency. None of the films screened in 1967 (and here we must note that many were pre-war projects) treated what she calls "the most important events" of the era (1992: 128). Of the thirty-three films released that year she counts the following categories: adolescent dramas (8), love stories (8), love stories about artists (6), and police/crime dramas (4). She does recognize that young, politically conscious filmmakers and critics chafed at the bit (ibid.: 120). One of them, Madkur Thabit, a graduate of the Cinema Institute, recalls the debut of himself and several colleagues in May 1968, before a seminar chaired by Samir Farid, most vocal of the new guard critics (Thabit 1984: 93–99). Three directors premiered the first works, all shorts, fully produced by Institute graduates, in what he has likened to a final exam. Nearly a full year after the defeat, the event remains ingrained in the memories of those who would comprise a new generation of cineastes. Yet for the time being artistic power, whether state or private-backed, remained in the hands of the establishment. And it was key figures from within that establishment who would turn the moment to artistic advantage.

I focus here on seven films made by five directors: Galal al-Sharqawi, Kamal al-Shaykh, Salah Abu Sayf, Tawfiq Salih, and Husayn Kamal. Each film, however different from the others, spoke directly to issues of corruption, authoritarian rule, opportunism, and social decay—a revolution betrayed by its servants, if not its leaders, and now openly chided by outspoken characters who represent broader trends of discontent. The political backdrop is the fall-out of the June war: a wave of recriminations, show trials, student upheaval, and youth rebellion.[12] If such films defused rather than spawned social discontent, this is not simply the result of state hegemony or a "lack of confidence" by filmmakers rooted in the "legacy of prohibition" (Sharaf al-Din 1992: 121). Rather, it is because in the search for a new, forward-looking civic focus, many of Egypt's most creative—and popular—film artists sought to right rather than to topple the Nasserist agenda. However cynical the vision, most of these films reflect a plea for a fresh start down similar, but better-tended roads. In some cases the clearest proof of this is an uplifting "socialist" ending, or at least one that allowed for a degree of optimism, if only to clear censorial hurdles. Few could, at the time, really envision any alternatives.

"OF COURSE, WE'RE ALL CORRUPT"

When Mahgub Abd al-Daim, the social-climbing anti-hero of Salah Abu Sayf's *Cairo 1930,* denounces the pervasiveness of social corruption, he wears an old regime costume and finds himself brought low by the sexual peccadillos of a lustful aristocrat. In Galal al-Sharqawi's rendition of Yusif Idris's *The Shame* (*al-'Ayb* 1967)—a transitional film, produced and released prior to the June War—the time-frame is the Nasserist present and the corruption even seedier. Nasser's portrait, not Farouk's, hangs in the government office where a group of opportunistic bureaucrats sell government permits for LE 75, then attend liquor-splashed parties hosted by the bribe-profferers. When challenged by the idealistic Sanaa (Lubna Abd al-Aziz), a young university graduate appointed to their office, they respond with varying degrees of self-righteousness and jaded paternalism that they have families to support, medical bills to pay, kids to put through school, none of which is possible on their meager government salaries. They are not by nature bad men. Muhammad al-Gindi (Rushdi Abaza) is seen visiting a bed-ridden mother in the hospital. The chief clerk (Shafiq Nur al-Din) plants loving kisses on a brood of grandchildren. Why should Sanaa, who has to support her mother and pre-teen brother, a young boy who dreams of a brand-new school uniform, be any different?

Al-Sharqawi's film is at once a dramatic break from the heavily historicized depictions of official corruption and a natural extension of social films that treat the entry of the "new" woman into the male work space. The casting underscores and lends dramatic power to the latter aspect. Lubna Abd al-Aziz, in what would be her final film role, still radiantly convincing as a recent graduate, reminds viewers of her early, defining role in *I'm Free.* In the pre-credit opening, she and two female colleagues also on their first working assignment withstand the prurient attentions of an entire bureau. In an early scene she is gently barred from entering the office by the orderly, who informs her that a "men's committee" is in session. When she is finally brought into the web of deceit it is by callous design—she will sign the record books, thereby becoming not only an accomplice but legally culpable for every permit "sold." In order to secure her consent, the men agree that one of them—they naturally select the dashing Muhammad—must successfully woo her. Why else, he argues, do young women go to work? Only too late, after their engagement, does she recognize how the office really operates. Shafiq Nur al-Din, her prayer bead-clutching supervisor, reprises his comical role in *My Wife is General Director,* only here the humor is absent and there will be no personal redemption. When Sanaa confronts the fatherly chief clerk over his culpability he lays out his own financial constraints—"I'm overburdened, Sanaa, my daughter." When she presses him, he turns increasingly authoritarian—"We know everything about you—the rent is late, so are the accounts with the grocer, for bread. . . ." As his persuasive powers fail and his tone becomes more derisive, Sanaa's face is framed for several seconds by his prayer beads, a common explication of pseudo-religious hypocrisy.

Pressed by personal circumstances and the persistence of her corrupt colleagues, Sanaa ultimately accepts a bribe (albeit at a reduced rate of LE 50 per permit). She is set up, left alone in the office with Ibada Bey (Salah Mansur), a regular Thursday visitor. When she protests that she has no proper forms, the orderly appears with fresh copies; when, in a panic, she spills ink on the documents, more are procured. The same scene in the book, which Roger Allen (1987: 154) has described as "comical," is played on screen for dramatic tension. Sanaa signs in the presence of the orderly, who stands over her desk, an imposing witness, and after Ibada has slipped an envelope into her white purse. Left alone, staring at her handbag, unable to touch it, she is startled by the shrill ring of the office phone, which sends her running out of the building, breathless. By now, however, she is not the only tortured soul. Muhammad, the engagement off, has pangs of guilt. Wildly drunk after a party at Ibada Bey's, he is refused entry to the hospital to visit his mother for lack of proper papers. Instantly, he recognizes the terrible irony:

> To be born you need a license! To die you need a license! To work, to marry, to divorce! Everything requires a license!

When he returns the next morning, he finds his mother's hospital bed empty. Now, while Sanaa ponders her situation, he more soberly reassesses his life. "Of course, we're all corrupt," he reasons. "We try to cleanse ourselves by praying afterwards. We can't do anything but corrupt others, as we've been corrupted—we're garbage, garbage."

Idris's ending is bleak, but Hollywood on the Nile salvages the scenario. In the climactic scene, Sanaa hands the bribe back to Ibada Bey, then refutes his pronouncement that she will better understand reality when she is "grown up":

> No, Ibada Bey. I know myself well. It's true, I'm not as strong as I imagined. But I'm not as weak as you all thought either. Your money is like a disease that makes me realize the value of my health. It's like a prison that makes me value my freedom. My integrity is my property; I'm not humiliated by anyone! So, what do I care for you or your money, Ibada Bey? I can't stand its smell. Frankly, I can't stand your smell. . . .

Muhammad now breaks rank and follows her out. Apologizing for his earlier actions, he informs her that he has resolved to turn himself in to the authorities. In the final shots he marches up the steps of the High Court while Sanaa looks on through the iron fencing, already viewing her lover through prison bars, but recognizing that both have managed to find redemption.

"LONG LIVE THE VIRTUOUS CITIZEN"

Fathi Ghannam's *The Man Who Lost His Shadow (al-Ragul alladhi faqad zilu),* published in 1962, is the cynical story of a liberal era social climber whose road to ruin is predicated on class animosity and romantic disappointment. Kamal al-Shaykh's 1968 adaptation took the novel's Rashomon structure and turned it into a linear tale with perspective shifting between the amoral Yusuf (Kamal al-Shinawi) and the victimized peasant woman, Mabruka (Magda), who becomes his father's wife, then mother to his half-brother.

Yusuf is not a totally despicable character. As the fourth voice in the novel, his narrative fills in a number of important gaps and rounds out the reader's understanding. Because the film foregrounds him, formative experiences such as his unrequited love for the daughter of his rich uncle lend heightened sympathy. Other early scenes underscore the disparities between Yusuf, who lives with his father (Imad Hamdi) in a modest flat, and his far richer cousins, whom his father tutors and whom Yusuf often visits. When Mabruka, whose earlier tribulations are not revealed in the film, comes to live as a servant to Yusuf and his father, his world is further upturned. When she becomes his father's mistress, then wife, he moves out. Shortly thereafter he gains employment at a leading newspaper, where he becomes understudy and eventually replaces the powerful editor-in-chief, Muhammad Nagi. Throughout, Yusuf seems more the prisoner of his fate than the ruthless social climber presented in the novel. When he loses his fiancée to his former boss, he is again crushed, and clearly recognizes the price he has paid in order to achieve financial wealth and professional recognition.

His climb has also been on the backs of those for whom he truly once cared: Mabruka, his father, their young son, and a group of college chums who have become revolutionary activists. Yet here, too, the film veers from Ghannam's cynicism to promote a more uplifting vision. In the novel, Yusuf turns his back on Mabruka and his half-brother. When she is then taken in by Shawqi, a former comrade who now works as an illustrator for the same paper, she is able to make ends meet. Yet, soon after, Yusuf informs on his friends—not eagerly but ultimately willingly—and Shawqi is arrested. Mabruka, who admits her love for Shawqi has withered, turns to prostitution. Halfway through the novel's chronology she vanishes from the story. In the movie, Mabruka becomes an accomplice in anti-regime activity, helping Shawqi (Salah Zulficar) print leaflets after his comrades have been arrested. The shame of her degradation as a prostitute is traded for a scene in which she is tortured at police headquarters, her head forced repeatedly into a bucket of water—all this before she understands Shawqi's political inclinations. When he is eventually nabbed (not by Yusuf's accusation, but after a long period of surveillance), Mabruka is again left alone. But now a committed revolutionist, her future seems less precarious.

As in the novel, Yusuf gets the last word. However, two important emendations have been made. Whereas Ghannam's text carries over into the revolutionary era, with Suez as backdrop to the final action, Shaykh's film ends during the repressive last years of the old regime. However poignant the story, it therefore remains couched in historical garb. The scene in which Mabruka is brutalized recalls images from Youssef Chahine's 1958 *Jamila*—with Magda again the victim—but here the villains are not colonial authorities—and not yet Nasser's torturers—but Farouk's political police. When Shawqi is finally arrested he leaves with chin up, a final gesture of defiance that may be read as presaging the July coup. Finally, although Yusuf is given the last tortured words, they are not his cynical proclamation: "I can do what I want. I am very powerful," followed by a despairing cry for the "hidden," "mischievous" inner child (Ghanem 1966: 352). Rather, Yusuf presages, perhaps, a transformation:

> They got married to avenge me. Success is easy; the difficult thing is to love. I have become a servant to the rich and influential. If the day comes when the people are victorious, I'll attack imperialism, the rich and the influential. I'll prove to the people that I'm honorable, and have worked hard to leave poverty behind. I'll be honored to claim Mabruka as my father's wife and Ibrahim as my full brother. I'm a son of the people who have suffered and been subdued, and I've endured humiliation. The good, kind-hearted people will raise me up on their shoulders and shout fervently: "Long live the virtuous citizen! Long live the hero!"

Rescripted for the film, Yusuf's last thoughts remain ambivalent, perhaps delusional, but, as in *The Shame,* they do leave room for redemption.

"I'M SICK, JUST LIKE YOU!"

Tawfiq Salih retains a special place in Egyptian cinema history, the "director of prizes" who refused steadfastly to bow to popular demand, a cineaste who alienated major stars, preferring to work with secondary players, and who demanded fuller artistic control than most producers—or state officials—were willing to allow. His production output speaks to an uncomfortable relationship with the film industry, something to which the director freely admits. After two critical successes seven years apart (*Alley of Fools,* 1955 and *Heroes' Struggle,* 1961), Salih won a plum assignment. Salah Abu Sayf, busy with administrative duties, handed him the finished scenario for Naguib Mahfouz's *Palace Walk.* Salih, however, did not like the script (written by scenarist Yusif Gawhar), and a struggle for creative authority ensued that led Abu Sayf to turn the directing assignment over to veteran melodramatist Hasan al-Imam. Salih subsequently found himself in the doghouse for three years, until a new public sector administration gave him permission to film *The Rebels,* an adaptation of a story by journalist Salah Hafiz. The director wrote his own screenplay, with dialogue assistance from the story's author.

An allegory of revolutionary travail and, ultimately, failure, *The Rebels* depicts an uprising within a tuberculosis sanitarium, a desert outpost that is ruled as a penal colony by an odious director and apathetic staff. At the film's outset the inmates are slowly dying of thirst due to the withholding of water rations. The local director blames the government, but agrees to bring in water when confronted by the vocal opposition of Doctor Aziz (Shukri Sirhan), a recent arrival, who is both a member of the medical staff and a patient. When a young boy is struck and killed by the water truck, tempers boil. Doctor Aziz spontaneously becomes the spokesman for the inmates. "Listen to me—I'm Aziz—I'm sick, just like you!" he shouts, calming the crowd and freeing the innocent driver. When the director tries to cover up the boy's death, the inmates stage a hunger strike. When he threatens them, Aziz rises to shout him down:

> Listen, men. . . . It's finished—we won't ask anything from anyone! We won't petition the director or the minister. We'll do it ourselves, protect ourselves. . . . We'll create a system that we like!

When a patient asks about the administration, Aziz proclaims: "There's no administration—it's finished, we're the administration!" Led by the doctor and several other charismatic, educated patients, the oppressed seize the facility, oust the director and erect barricades.

Shortly thereafter, however, the rebellion stalls for lack of direction and from a breakdown in revolutionary discipline. The doctor's insistence on maintaining a hunger strike begins to alienate his followers, and his own unwillingness to impose martial order, while demonstrating his compassion, ultimately weakens his authority. Unity is briefly restored by the arrival of a detachment of troops; utilizing slingshots and rudimentary catapults, the inmates score an initial victory, chasing off the soldiers and suffering the martyrdom of one leader. Nonetheless, Aziz's self-centered preoccupation with his personal life—his fiancée on the outside refuses to answer his letters—exacerbates discord and ultimately leads to the restoration of the old order. When the director returns, backed by greater military force, Aziz looks on helplessly as he resumes command and secures the rebel's transfer.

Set in an undefined pre-revolutionary time and place—police officials still wear the fez—Salih's film resonated with contemporary allusions, proving both prescient and problematic. The desert setting for the sanitarium, the hard labor in which the patients engage, and the barbed wire that encloses their barracks, purposefully resemble the desert camps that the Nasser regime inherited and maintained as political prisons. A scene in which Doctor Aziz and his ruling council—steadfast but bewildered, and unsure of their next step—sit around the director's table immediately after seizing power recalls familiar images of the Free Officers in the early morning hours of July 23. When his comrades look to him for direction, Doctor Aziz shrugs his shoulders, underscoring a lack of ideological orientation that will prove disastrous.

Many have suggested (e.g., Darwish 1995: 96; Baker 1974: 415), and Tawfiq Salih has admitted, that the doctor, a heroic, yet ultimately stymied rebel, was written to represent Nasser. Aziz's public statements—"I'm just like you" and others—recall well-known speeches. His sense of resignation in defeat, others argue, presaged Nasser's own public offer to step down in the wake of the June 1967 disaster (Abu Shadi 1999: 13). Conceived before the war, the script was approved by the chief censor without emendation (Mustafa Darwish, 17 April 1996), a remarkable exercise of political integrity and administrative savvy. Despite Tawfiq Salih's animus towards directing stars, the casting of Shukri Sirhan, the leading male player of the decade (certainly after Omar Sharif's departure for Hollywood), as the doctor underscored the character's heroic sincerity. Sirhan had, since the early 1950s, played a succession of serious roles, many of which have been noted in these pages, in which he represented the common man, often desperately poor but sometimes upwardly mobile or middle class, caught in the vortex of social change or oppressed by outmoded social and cultural mores.

Filming was completed in 1966, but the film only saw the briefest light of day in 1968, after the 1967 defeat and following a protracted struggle with a less responsive censor board (Mustafa Darwish, who had approved the film, was no longer chief censor). The dispute reached the office of Culture Minister Tharwat Ukasha, who demanded the removal of twenty-five minutes and a more optimistic finale. A bleak ending is suddenly salvaged—from a censorial, if not artistic or political standpoint—by an almost dream-like post-script in which the doctor, suddenly working in a real hospital, talks of continuing the struggle and learning the lessons of the past. The film failed commercially and has never been broadcast on television. Perhaps because of this, Salih's star remains unique in the pantheon of fellow directors:

> Working on the margins of the film industry there have always been a number of innovative directors trying to truthfully and objectively express Egyptian reality, to participate in the construction of a national cinema, to convey political, social, and economic transformations, the fundamental developments in the building of Egyptian society. Some of them believed in the revolution, then broke away to support successive trends, or presented careful analyses of affairs in Egypt prior to the revolution to which July 23 was the natural result, and to the struggle of other nationalist forces. One of them had the courage which many others lacked, and set out to discuss the very experiment for the first time prior to the events of June 1967. True, he was forced by the constraints of censorship to package it as a symbolic work. True, they managed to block the film, *The Rebels,* to confiscate it and demand of the

> director, Tawfiq Salih, that he submit to the excision of several scenes and to modify or abridge several others. In addition, they demanded a new ending (Abu Shadi 1999: 12).

Having been shut out of the industry for so long, Salih, as he later recalled, "was forced to accede" to the demands of higher authorities. "The film lost much of its impact, but I recognized that despite the alterations *The Rebels* retained a fundamental value with regard to the Third World as a whole" (ibid.: 13).

"TEAR IT DOWN, UNCLE MUNAGID"

Case 68 (Salah Abu Sayf 1968), a critical failure and box office bomb, warrants retrospective attention as an attempt to allegorize the failures of the socialist experiment, not least because it was directed by the chief of the public production sector. Salah Abu Sayf, the master "realist," adapted an absurdist drama by the influential leftist writer Lutfi al-Khuli before the June war, but the film did not open until the following year. When it did, critics and government officials hooted—at a rowdy premiere, a disruption that Abu Sayf believed was orchestrated by party officials and the police—the public showed disinterest, and the film closed within a week (al-Nahhas 1996: 125).

Abu Sayf and his collaborators, including the original author, had attempted to broaden the dramatic scope from an indictment of the persistent stranglehold of outmoded regulations to a full-scale assault on political opportunism and influence-peddling within the current ruling structure. The drama, revolving around a local political committee's debate over whether to renovate or raze and rebuild an apartment building that does not meet code, serves as symbolic representation of the larger order. Caught between two factions, the greedy, establishment-oriented renovators and the younger, idealistic levelers, is Munagid, committee head and building owner. Salah Mansur, who often played shady secondary characters (he had recently been Ibada Bey in *The Shame* and the umda in *The Second Wife*), here is the well meaning, but flustered Munagid, who watches helplessly as, first, his committee disintegrates, then his building literally comes apart at the seams. The idealists are played by Hasan Yusuf and two new faces, future stars, Mahmud Yasin and Mervat Amin. In the last scene, having suffered a breakdown, a discomfiting image of leadership at any level of government, the building owner is led away as the neighborhood denizens, trying to console him, shout in unison: "Tear it down, Uncle Munagid! We'll build it anew!"

"WE ALL LOVE THE REVOLUTION"

With *Miramar* (1969), Kamal al-Shaykh went even further than in *The Man Who Lost His Shadow* in exploring social and political ills. Naguib Mahfouz's 1967 novel, like Fathi Ghannam's, is a Rashomon story told from four different perspectives. But unlike Ghannam, Mahfouz set his story in the Nasserist present. With characters who represent both pre-revolutionary and revolutionary regimes all given voice, the lively debates that ensue resound far louder than in other works. *Miramar* stands out as the first film to attack the Nasserist order, not merely for corruption, as did *The Shame,* but for spawning a culture of opportunism, while making direct political reference to the present.

Named for the Alexandria pension at which all the primary characters reside, *Miramar* is ostensibly the story of Zahra (Shadia), a beautiful village girl fleeing an arranged marriage, who takes refuge in the big city. Serving as a maid, she is wooed, pinched, and in some cases sexually assaulted by three of the five male boarders. The two elders, Tulba Bey Marzuq (Yusuf Wahbi) and Amr Wagdi (Imad Hamdi), represent the pre-revolutionary generation. Both eased aside by the new, they do not, however, revere the same old regime legacy. The blustery Tulba, a former under-secretary of state, is a royalist who has had his property expropriated. Amr had been an influential journalist affiliated with the majority nationalist party, the Wafd. Now he observes the world around him silently, taking solace for his age and the times by reading the Quran. In a scene taken from the book, but rewritten to add timely political punch, the two men sit in a sea-side café. The dominant statue of Saad Zaghlul, nationalist hero and Wafd founder, prompts a not-unfriendly debate:

> *Tulba:* Do you know who is the cause of the misfortunes we face today?
>
> *Amr:* Which misfortunes?

Tulba: Cut the nonsense! The misfortunes in our country.
Amr: Who?
Tulba: Saad Pasha. He kept heaping attack on the king and cursing the English; all the talk of revolution and democracy, just so the people would applaud him. The people are still clapping—they will applaud almost anything.
Amr: God rest his soul. He was a patriot and a revolutionary—and he was trustworthy.

Into their midst suddenly appear three younger men, each representing a different aspect of present-day Nasserist society and politics. Sirhan al-Buhayri (Yusuf Shaaban), deputy head accountant at the nationalized Alexandria textile mills and a member of the Arab Socialist Union political committee—something he continually trumpets—is the Nasser-era opportunist. Aware of his good looks, he woos Zahra, then, breaking her heart, becomes engaged to the language teacher who comes to the pension to give her private lessons. He also plots with an associate to embezzle goods from the factory, but the scheme fails. Husni Allam (Abu Bakr Izzat), scion of Tanta gentry who still holds 100 feddans, left his family after land reform. He is a hip swinger, his characterization punctuated by the phrase "ferekiko" (cool, dig it) and a thumb-snapping swagger. Allam makes an unsuccessful pass at the maid and shortly after beds Sirhan's recently thrown-over girl, when she appears at the Miramar to make a scene. Finally there is Mansur Bahi (Abd al-Rahman Ali), the brooding young leftist who has been sent away from Cairo by his family (and arrives accompanied by his police officer brother), yet who continues to rendezvous with a jailed comrade's wife.

Young men and elders circle each other, suspicious of political leanings as well as sexual-romantic inclinations. Eventually blows are exchanged, for which poor, virtuous, but foolhardy Zahra ultimately reaps the blame. Sirhan's death, for which Mansur claims responsibility, but which turns out to be a case of suicide, provides the dramatic climax. Before that the film revels in a new-found openness to address politics with fewer holds barred. A Thursday evening Umm Kulthum concert provides the occasion for a communal gathering around the radio.[13] Husni Allam provides the spirits, and as drinks are consumed the talk becomes freer:

Sirhan: Umm Kulthum never sang like she sings for the revolution. Her feelings for the revolution. . . .

Tulba (exasperated): So everything with you comes down to the revolution?!! That no doubt comes from your engagement in politics. . . .

Sirhan (not rising to the bait): You're right. From the Liberation Rally to the National Union to the Socialist Union. . . .

Mansur: So you weren't involved in politics before the revolution?

Sirhan: When I was in college I was a member of the Saadist student committee. After I graduated I joined the Wafd. With the revolution I joined the Liberation Rally.

Mansur (curious, but with a cynical edge): Sirhan, did you believe in socialism before the revolution, or only after it?

Sirhan: To be honest, I came to believe in socialism with the revolution.

Tulba: Wonderful, wonderful, my brother! In any case, all of us here believe in the revolution. Even Zahra. Right, Zahra? Don't you also love the revolution?

Zahra (nodding innocently): Yes. . . .

Tulba: See! Its true that they forced me into early retirement, and stripped my rank as bey. Its also true that they sequestered me [my property]. But all that was for whom? For the people! So [*with sarcastic emphasis*] all of us love the revolution. . . .

Yusuf Wahbi, aged relic of a bygone theatrical and cinematic era, plays the role of Tulba with relish, giving the former government under-secretary a loveable, if inscrutable persona, and voicing sentiments heretofore unheard on the silver screen. Imad Hamdi, by now a paternal figure, rarely anything but good-hearted, lends gravitas to Amr Wagdi, particularly in the scenes where he sits contemplatively reading holy text.

This conversation and many others in the film are far more open and hostile to the Nasserist present than those in the written text from which they are adapted. The above encounter, which is narrated with slight variation by different characters, is in the novel far less focused on the young Sirhan. The real focus in Mahfouz's original text is Amr Wagdi, who speaks at length—or so he and Husni Allam relate in their separate narrations—about the Wafd party and its failings. Tulba's intrusions are more circumspect. He confides later to Amr that he fears one of the young men may be connected to the secret police, and even considers moving to new lodgings (Mahfouz 1978: 24).

Sirhan al-Buhayri is also less circumspect in his self-pronouncements. In the novel he is certainly full of himself (Husni Allam, no gem either, refers to Sirhan as "dreamboat" and the others are no less skeptical of his motives.) In the film, however, he constantly reminds his fellow lodgers that he serves on the Arab Socialist Union political committee, something to which he only alludes in print. This, too, is a tactic employed by scenarist Mamduh al-Laythi, younger brother of Cairo production chief Gamal, to turn the full focus of the story onto Buhayri, who is given little opportunity here to stake out a complex personality.

Zahra, the personification of the nation, is abused at every turn. In the end, however, she triumphs, helped by a happy ending that goes far beyond the novelist's original intent. Leaving the pension, by order of the proprietress—the woman suffering for the inappropriate behavior of men—she is comforted one final time by Amr Wagdi, the only lodger who never looked at her with lustful intent. Imad Hamdi speaks lines right out of the novel: "Remember that you haven't wasted your time here. If you've come to know what is not good for you, you may also think of it all as having been a sort of magical way of finding out what is truly good for you" (Mahfouz 1978: 130). Scenarist al-Laythi then adds a positive twist in the character of Mahmud Abu al-Abbas, the newspaper vendor played by the comic Abd al-Munim Ibrahim. In the novel, Mahmud expresses romantic interest in Zahra, is rejected, and subsequently disappears from the story. At the film's finale he encounters Zahra as she leaves the pension and helps her carry her bag. He has traded his gallabiya in for modern clothing and embarked upon a new path:

> Yesterday I went to night school. I got this notebook and paid the 125 piaster tuition. We'll start studying together, struggling together—and growing together.

As they walk off together, Zahra again lifts her head up, lending a very different air to Amr Wagdi's final musings on fate and history.[14]

Miramar owed its approval to the personal intervention of Anwar Sadat, at the time vice president. Sadat reportedly saw the film in a private screening and liked it, then solicited Nasser's approval. This is noteworthy because the film retains the distinction of being the first to openly criticize the system "without resort to symbolism or allusion," becoming, in effect, the first step in the "cinema of apostasy" that would emerge in the aftermath of Nasser's death and Sadat's ascension to power (Abu Shadi 1999: 18).

"A BIT OF FEAR DOES NO HARM"

Fresh from the critically lamented but publicly adored *Father's Up a Tree,* Husayn Kamal brought to the screen a troubling parable of power and its abuse in *A Bit of Fear* (1969; a film already discussed in Chapter 5). Presented as a timeless folk legend with the powerful refrains of an epic song punctuating the action, Kamal's film suggests, unlike Tawfiq Salih's *The Rebels,* that a people long bent under oppressive rule will eventually rise up to oust their masters. Kamal's vantage point is decidedly not to restore or rebuild the existing order, but rather to cry out against tyranny and warn Egypt's rulers of the seeds their oppression has sown. If the ending of *A Bit of Fear* is to be considered happy, the triumph is tempered by harsh recognition of the price that has been paid by those who have submitted, through force or conniving, to an order that rules by terror.

Two strong personalities dominate the film. Mahmud Mursi, not yet a major star, but with several important roles behind him (especially Isa al-Dabbagh in *Autumn Quail*), plays the dual Atriss roles, the ruthless chieftain of Dahashna, and his gentle grandson who is groomed against his will to rule the roost. With blackened teeth, a weathered face, and a cruel, hoarse laugh, Mursi's elder Atriss is a vicious tyrant. "A bit of fear does no harm," he reminds his men as they set off for the funeral of a man they have just murdered. His outrage at the gentility of his heir is founded on both sadism and pragmatism. "If you're not tough they'll swallow you—they'll surround you like wolves," he lectures the boy. When the elder Atriss is finally gunned down by a desperate subject, he compels his grandson to vow revenge. As the young Atriss lets loose his guard on the village to exact collective punishment, remorse gradually gives way to habit. The cycle of terror, never having been broken, proceeds apace. The second personality is Fuada, childhood playmate, later sweetheart of the grandson. Portrayed by Shadia, as in *Miramar* a fallaha, but here far less the victim, she exudes fortitude and courage, the very traits needed to bring down the oppressor.

The pinnacle scene occurs halfway through the film. Atriss has ordered the irrigation sluices shut. As the crops dry out, peasant men and women sit helplessly. Suddenly Fuada climbs atop the gate and opens the wheel. As the water flows the people come to life, but the camera returns to Fuada, proud and steely-eyed, even as Atriss and his men ride up, and the chieftain levels his rifle at her breast. Fuada's "manly" courage leads Atriss to attempt to dominate her via marriage; the violation of her "womanly" honor leads villagers to finally rise up and topple the tyrant. Led by Shaykh Ibrahim (Yahya Shahin), a man with enormous moral power, heightened by the loss of his son, Atriss's latest victim, the mob sets fire to the ruler's stronghold. Locked in his tower by his own men before they beat a hasty retreat, Atriss is enveloped by flames. The final scene recalls the classic *Frankenstein* (at least as James Whale meant his movie to end, without the lighthearted postscript and with no hint of a sequel; Schatz 1989: 94–95), with the monster eliminated and order restored.

"BLOOD IS CHEAPER THAN INK"

Tawfiq Salih's *Diary of a Country Prosecutor* (*Yawmiyat na'ib fi al-aryaf* 1969) is often overlooked in works treating the period. This is due in part to the attention that has been focused on the director's prior, more obviously political *The Rebels.* Yet the latter film garnered more critical success and is in many ways the most accessible of the five films the director made in Egypt between 1955 and 1969. With *Diary of a Country Prosecutor* Salih moved onto surer, less politically explosive ground, to produce a venerated literary text while adding a distinctly contemporary note. Tawfiq al-Hakim's scathing 1937 satire of judicial practices in the pre-revolutionary countryside provided the director, who co-wrote the script with novelist Alfred Farag, a natural vehicle through which to examine the abuse of power by public officials for whom jurisprudence is at best an inconvenience.

Hakim's diary is written by a jaded prosecutor assigned to a motley rural posting. The action commences with an attack upon a villager, who dies without naming his assailant. Prosecutor and local officials realize that the case will likely remain unsolved. From a dramatic standpoint the case serves merely as window to a broader legal system in which judges rule without hearing testimony, one eye on the clock, so that courtroom proceedings end in time to catch the train back to the city. In one of many trial scenes, adapted faithfully from the original text, the prosecutor and his younger assistant look on as the judge deals peremptorily with an accused peasant. Their whispered conversation is interspersed amongst shots of judge and defendant:

> *Assistant:* The man has a right to defend himself!
> *Prosecutor:* That's none of your business. Your business is to bring the indictment, lay out the charges, and nothing else.
> *Assistant:* And what about justice?
> *Prosecutor:* All right, all right, we'll talk about justice later. Pay attention now to what's going on in this session.

As in Hakim's novel, such interchanges, punctuated by the blustery protests of rural plaintiffs and defendants, prompt simultaneous laughter and outrage.

If Hakim's prosecutor is inured to the system, Salih's retains the potential for outrage. This is partly because near the end of the film director and scenarist take the story beyond Hakim's boundaries. The camera films innocent peasants being arrested and herded into prison. The sullen prosecutor is led to proclaim "There's no difference between the criminals' weapons and the weapons of the police." In one scene he stands in a window overlooking the prison yard. Somber music underscores his still potent sense of frustration. As he turns away he is lectured by a local official:

Official: Times are bad and politics is strangling the country. There's no need for. . .
Prosecutor: You mean leave the people to arrest without their being charged with a crime?
Official: Your Excellency, as you well know, the commissioner serves the interior minister, who also happens to be the prime minister. Our boss is the minister of justice, plain and simple. In situations like this the government has transferred justices to Upper Egypt. . .
Prosecutor: So we should just enter our reports and keep quiet?
Official: Your Excellency, we're no better than those who have preceded us. They were no smarter than us. . . .

In the film's final scene the prosecutor enters his inconclusive report on the murdered peasant with what Hakim (1989: 135) described as "a tone of bitter mockery." His filmed voice-over is adapted and slightly reordered from a longer written soliloquy:

> Blood has been spilled . . . Blood [that] is cheaper than the ink with which this case has been recorded. We don't take people's lives seriously. We spend money with abundance on frivolous matters, but if the money is required to uphold justice or improve the people's lot, it suddenly becomes dear. That's because "justice" and "the people" are words whose meaning remains incomprehensible to us in this country.

He notes the date, October 1935, yet in so caustic a tone that the ruse of post-dating the events is obvious. Salih's film, a deft mixture of dark humor and bleak sobriety, with an ensemble cast featuring (finally, he might say) no major stars, opened only after a successful pilot projection to over 100 members of the Arab Socialist Union.[15] Salih recalls a boisterous positive response (January 7, 2000). Afterwards Nasser arranged a private screening, whereupon he personally approved the release (Abdennour 1993).

If Salih seemed poised to finally attain success, the moment proved short-lived. His next project *Sayyid Balti* (*al-Sayyid al-Balti* 1969), the story of the exploitation of a fishing community, garnered a new set of problems. Salih hesitated to film what he has termed an "old script sitting in a drawer," then tried to rewrite as he shot. Working within a fixed schedule and an approved schema of scenes and shots, he found himself limited to rewriting dialogue. Constrained in his ability to depict social problems he resorted to discussion. As a result, the finished product is "too talkative." Censors later insisted he delete a scene that depicted women applying a honey depilatory to their legs, an ethnographic touch deemed overly provocative. When several copies of the film screened prior to the censor's cuts having been removed, the film was pulled, after only a few days in the theaters (January 7, 2000). Shortly thereafter, Salih left Egypt for Syria (where he made his next film, the acclaimed *The Duped* [*(al-Makhdu'un)* 1973]), far less an opponent of the regime than a victim of personal and bureaucratic animosities.

"THE CONSCIENCE OF THE NATION"

The last significant film from the period following the 1967 defeat and through the death of Nasser, Kamal al-Shaykh's *Sunset, Sunrise* (*Ghurub wa shuruq* 1970) is an historical drama with very little political commentary on the present order. Yet, as a retelling of the revolutionary myth, replete with dissident, conspiratorial junior officers, the film casts a disturbing shadow on the last year of Nasser's rule. It makes a particularly interesting counterpoint to the quasi-official film *With God on Our Side* produced in the immediate wake of the Free Officers uprising. Similar plot conventions and the re-casting of Mahmud al-Maligi as the villainous pasha-father turn the film into an obverse mirror of the original. An ambivalent ending, politically upbeat but romantically sour, also marks the film as a decidedly counter-revolutionary melodrama.

The young officer-heroes of this film are not schooled in revolution in either the barracks or on the Palestinian front. They are two dashing commercial pilots, Amin (Salah Zulficar) and Samir (Ibrahim Khan), and a crack mechanic Issam (Rushdi Abaza), apolitical playboys who share a bachelor flat in an upscale neighborhood. The film opens to scenes of Cairo burning on Black Saturday, but the heroes' selfish disinterest in the national question is underscored by their garrulous response to political leaflets signed "The Conscience of the Nation" that are left on their car. Leaving the flat with their current girlfriends they carelessly toss the papers to the wind as they drive off.

Trouble starts when Samir falls for Madiha (Suad Husni). Unbeknownst to him, or to his flatmates, she is the daughter of the chief of secret police, Azmi Pasha (al-Maligi). Quickly engaged and married, they find themselves under virtual house arrest in the pasha's villa. When Samir leaves on assignment, his restive bride seeks entertainment by flirting with Issam, who has no idea she is his best friend's wife. When Samir discovers his wife alone and in a nightgown in his old bachelor flat, he drags her home and renounces her in front of her father. Before the friends are ever able to set the record straight, the pasha orders Samir's murder. When his two friends visit the widow to pay respects, her cover is blown. Azmi Pasha now forces Issam to marry her. The seeds of political discontent are thus sown within the context of an unseemly romantic triangle and the abuse of official power by a father who fears scandal. Issam and Madiha eventually come to feel true affection for each other. But by this point nationalist politics have interceded.

When dissident officers, one of them the pasha's chief bodyguard, convince Amin and Issam that Samir's death was no accident the two friends join a secret political cell. To discredit his father-in-law, Issam breaks into his home safe—a reversal of *With God on Our Side,* in which the daughter robbed her father's safe—and photographs incriminating documents which he then hands over to the movement. Brought down by the scandal, the pasha is arrested before he can harm his antagonist. There is no shoot out at the end of *Sunset, Sunrise.* Nor has the revolution occurred. Most important, Madiha and Issam, having been thrown together by coercion but now in love, do not walk away together. With a decidedly unromantic twist, Madiha remains loyal to her father. The goodbye is sad but not prolonged. Madiha looks on from an upstairs window as Issam and Amin, comrades and brothers first and foremost, leave the house together. As the police van pulls away the pasha's bodyguard nonchalantly tosses a matchbook at their feet. Amin picks it up and the two committed revolutionists take note of their latest instructions.

With a string of literary adaptations after 1967, Kamal al-Shaykh established himself at the forefront of a political movement in the arts that would soon turn against the Nasserist regime. Prior to the late 1960s he had rarely concerned himself on celluloid with social or political issues. His films are marked by suspense and mystery, whether noir or gothic, a fascination that he traces to Fritz Lang's *The Woman in the Window* (January 23, 1996). His 1962 adaptation of Mahfouz's *The Thief and the Dogs* is, in retrospect, remarkable for its early condemnation of revolutionary era opportunism. Yet in other respects the story of a sympathetic criminal on the run, primarily in the nighttime hours, proved a natural vehicle. Shaykh himself has always denied being a political director, asserting simply that those films of his that have been labeled political films have, more properly, treated social issues. If he has begged the issue of what constitutes political cinema, he nonetheless has earned the reputation as a man of the "right," compared to "leftist" directors such as Tawfiq Salih and Salah Abu Sayf.[16]

Of his three prominent post-defeat films, *Miramar*, with its direct exposition of contemporary political malaise, is most significant. In many respects, however, *Sunset, Sunrise* lends more poignant closure to the Nasser years. The film has been viewed as a morality tale of political corruption and the abuse of martial authority, veiled behind old regime symbology. In a recent retrospective of Shaykh's work published by the Cairo International Film Festival the film was described as such:

> The film stays clear of direct politics. Within the framework of a good, suspenseful drama, it suggests the corrupting tendencies of power and the abuse of power that destroys those closest to the chief of the political police—his daughter Madiha, who desires nothing but freedom from his oppressive authority and pays the price for this—and also the three friends. They are transformed from normal people working in the shadow of the existing order into true enemies of the regime. Not only that, they share in demolishing this regime. In addition, the events of the film occur before the revolution. Yet, despite this, they point to

> issues of power and corruption in organs similar to those [depicted] that arose after the revolution (Adli 1995: 67–68).

Set in the old regime's dying days, the film is a revolutionary anti-history. Unlike the romantic melodramas of the early revolution where hero and heroine defy social conventions—and occasionally the political police—to walk off into a new dawn, here the romance has turned sour. The revolution will take place, but love does not triumph. It is in some respects Kamal al-Shaykh's grimmest finale. And a prelude to the onslaught that would follow the sudden death of Gamal Abdel Nasser (six months after the film's release), the demise of the public sector, and the onset of a new, less certain era.

Karnak: The Opening Salvo of Apostasy

Nasser's death, on September 18, 1970, threw Egypt into a state of shock. Few Egyptians had realized the extent of their leader's illness. Cairenes stayed in the street for several days, until they had accompanied the leader to his tomb. In the back rooms, Nasser's associates selected Vice-President Anwar al-Sadat, the man seen as least likely to upset the fragile balance of power, as successor. Sadat, who had reportedly collapsed upon learning of Nasser's death, set about assuring the nation that it remained in steady hands. Few at the time expected him to last in power, and fewer might guess the extent and speed with which he would set out to transform the face of the Nasserist state.

Within a year of assuming the presidency Sadat moved against the "centers of power," leading figures in the security apparatus and secret vanguard organization of the Arab Socialist Union. His "corrective revolution" of May 15 effectively eliminated the very figures who felt they could manipulate him, and won him tremendous accolades both amongst the intelligentsia and population at large. The new president followed through by lifting press censorship, opening political prisons, and, in a dramatic gesture, overseeing personally the destruction of illegal wiretap and coerced confessional recordings and transcripts held in the interior ministry. In the most famous essay of the period, the venerable writer Tawfiq al-Hakim heralded a "return of consciousness" from a dreamy state of intoxication (al-Hakim 1985). Sadat's ascendancy was not without its skids, the worst his unfulfilled promise to resume the "battle" against Israel. Nevertheless, with his expulsion of Soviet advisors in July 1972, then his triumphant leadership of the "crossing" in October 1973, the new president succeeded in capturing public enthusiasm. With the October Paper of 1974, the "hero of the crossing" carried his political capital over into the domestic sphere, setting in motion the *infitah,* the "opening" of Egypt to foreign investment, the realignment with the capitalist West, and ultimately the dismantling of much of the Nasserist public sector.

Even before this, in 1972, Sadat had abolished the public film sector. Works in progress saw themselves through to completion. Final recapitalization would await a series of government inquiries to determine compensation for sequestered studios and equipment. Yet, for all intents and purposes 1972 marks the end of the ever-controversial public film project. In assessing and reassessing that project, none can fail to note the role that the cinema played in paving the way toward the "de-Nasserization" that ensued.[17] The "green light" films had all in one way or another examined aspects of popular discontent. If many did so in order to put the revolution back on track, if they were utilized by the state to defuse public antipathy—and the lack of success here may be gauged by, for example, the extent of student protests on campus in the year following the June 1967 war—others were more correctly read by their audiences as stern critiques of a system that needed dramatic overhauling, and expositions of a society that had lost its moral bearing.

Here again Naguib Mahfouz provided the most potent vehicles for expression. Husayn Kamal's adaptation of Mahfouz's 1966 *Chatter on the Nile* (*Tharthara fawq al-Nil* 1971),[18] marks the onset of the transformations that would occur under Sadat. Mahfouz's tale of a lost generation of young Egyptians, intellectuals, artists, and professionals who spend their nights cavorting on a houseboat, speaks to a pervasive nihilism quenched only by an excess of drugs, alcohol, and casual sex. At the novel's climax, the party spills out of the houseboat, where most action occurs, and into an automobile in which the main characters race, terrified but exhilarated, down country roads. Gatsby-like, the car strikes an innocent bystander, a peasant, whom the perpetrators leave for dead by the roadside. Pangs of guilt intrude, more for some than others, but are eventually dismissed as the author seeks no redemptive path for any of his characters.

Kamal's film, scripted by Mamduh al-Laythi, has been criticized for an exploitative focus on debauchery at the expense of message. Director and scenarist might be excused if we recall the time frame in which their film emerged. Kamal had filmed alcohol-splashed parties in his debut film, *The Impossible,* and gone further in the sexually explosive *Father's Up a Tree.* In *Chatter on the Nile* the political stakes are higher and the story line far less compelling than the imagery. An ensemble cast, composed of elder stars and character actors joined by relative newcomers, parties incessantly and with reckless abandon, even more caustically after the accident, which takes place earlier in the film, and in which a young woman rather than an older man is killed. There is a moment of stunned silence after they return to the houseboat, as Ragib al-Qadi (Ahmad Ramzi), the playboy actor who was behind the wheel, looks forlornly at his front bumper. Yet, as the water pipe is passed spirits rise. When one of the passengers suggests the authorities might uncover their crime, the hasty reply is politically charged: "The dear government is busy boosting the economy and building a socialist society. It's not free to trouble us here."

If al-Laythi and Kamal took pains to mock the socialist project, they nonetheless provided the redemptive finale that Mahfouz originally avoided. Redemption comes through the characters of Anis Zaki (Imad Hamdi), the elder government functionary who serves as Greek chorus and master of ceremonies, and Samara Ragab (Magda al-Khatib), the righteous journalist who has been introduced to the houseboat and who falls for the charms of Ragib al-Qadi, but keeps a notebook in which she sketches critical social profiles of the party-goers.[19] Near the film's end, she takes Anis along on a bus tour to visit a residential area in the Suez Canal zone destroyed by enemy bombs during the 1968–69 War of Attrition. On the return trip he confesses his part in the peasant girl's death and resolves to go to the authorities, then disrupts the cavorting on the houseboat by insisting the perpetrators own up to their crime. A short brawl ensues, after which the stoned assembly takes up Anis's heartfelt insistence—"The fallaha has died and we must turn ourselves in"—as a mocking bacchanalian chant. As Anis and Samara depart, the boab lets loose the mooring; the houseboat drifts downstream, its occupants unaware. Anis wanders the city streets confessing their crime and exhorting the pubic at large to sober up and regain consciousness.

Written before the June disaster (as is the case with *Miramar*), Mahfouz's novel took on greater meaning when produced in its aftermath. If an abundance of sex and dissolute cavorting provided the greatest attraction, this succeeded in filling theaters—and furthering Kamal's new-found career as a successful commercial filmmaker. If many of his colleagues continued to produce a preponderance of profit-driven entertainments in the late sixties (Sharaf al-Din 1992: 114), others did strive to produce something new. And if none touched directly upon the June war in its immediate aftermath, films like *Miramar* and *Chatter on the Nile* clearly reflected a changed Egyptian ethos. Kamal also struggled with the censors, who demanded the excision of two scenes that he has considered among his most inspired (Farid 1993: 114). Even so, his film remained a powerful, if somewhat exploitative statement on the state of the nation.

The real transformation in political attitudes and filmmaking came with the sensational adaptation of Mahfouz's 1974 novel *Karnak* (*[al-Karnak],* Ali Badrakhan 1976), the third project scripted, and now produced, by Mamduh al-Laythi.[20] A sparse, subtle novel set primarily in a Cairo coffee house where the patrons, particularly a group of students, gather to discuss politics, the story—which remained unpublished for three years (LeGassick 1977: 205)[21]—now exploded onto the big screen, stripped of innuendo and blessed by a government that sought to distance itself from the worst excesses of its parent regime. If Mahfouz wrote his story to exorcize the demons of an order that had turned increasingly repressive as its dreams and programs came crashing down, the filmmakers exercised new found freedoms to depict graphically the crimes committed by those affiliated with the "centers of power." In the hands of al-Laythi and Badrakhan, Mahfouz's "intimate portrait of what it meant to live in Cairo in the middle and late 1960s" and "scathing critique of the repression of Nasir's police state" (ibid.: 206) became an outline, from which their own creative imaginations set to work to flesh out a story of punishment without crime and, ultimately, salvation through corrective revolution and war.

Scenes that correspond to the original text follow with a great degree of fidelity. The lead students, Ibrahim (Nur al-Sharif), Hilmi

(Muhammad Subhi), and Zaynab (Suad Husni), leave campus to join a larger multi-generational gathering at the café, presided over by the well-known writer Taha Gharib (Imad Hamdi, again the sagacious witness). Lulled by a sense of false security, the accompaniment of popular political anthems, and display of propaganda posters, they debate the successes and failures of the revolution with little regard for who may be listening. The students' naivete is underscored by an uneasy encounter with the university rector. When the devoutly loyal students suggest that the cloth they are using for political banners be utilized instead for clothing and bandages in depressed rural areas, the rector tells them to mind their own business. Still imbued with a naive enthusiasm for the revolution, wearing their Nasserist youth league ribbons, Ibrahim and Zaynab are taken aback.

Not so Hilmi, their fiery comrade who has already lost his faith. Later, at a study session in the flat he shares with his father, Hilmi reproaches Zaynab for asserting that the July revolution exceeds others in progressiveness:

> *Hilmi:* What!! You still believe that? It started out progressive, my dear. But those who direct it are hardly progressive.
>
> *Ibrahim:* You mean they're all reactionaries?
>
> *Hilmi:* I didn't say all of them, and I didn't say reactionary. Most of them, as individuals, are not really counter-revolutionary. . . .

Hilmi's arguments fall on doubting ears, until the trio is later arrested on successive occasions, physically abused, and forced to either confess or condemn their friends as enemies of the state. The fluctuating charges, first affiliation with the Muslim Brotherhood, then with communist organizations, are not merely groundless; they appear to be purely manipulative tactics designed to destroy any sense of independent thinking and produce docile subjects who will later be coerced into serving as campus informants.

Sitting atop the terror structure is Khalid Safwan (Kamal al-Shinawi), son of a palace official, now the man most responsible for rooting out—or, in Orwellian fashion, manufacturing, then eliminating—enemies of the state. The encounters between Safwan and his "guests" turn increasingly violent. What Mahfouz leaves to his readers' imaginings is played out graphically on screen, as the action moves from verbal interrogation to savage beatings to electrode torture and, finally, in the case of Zaynab, rape.

The film's casting provided a clever mixing of old and new cinema. Suad Husni, whose repertoire had included a variety of sullied characters—Ihsan in *Cairo 1930* and, more recently, Madiha in *Sunset, Sunrise*—could still act the innocent school girl. She had recently played the popular co-ed with a sordid background in *Watch Out for Zouzou.* There—also a Zaynab—she had triumphed over class prejudice and religious rigidity to lead the positive party to victory. Here she is debased, forced to rat on her friends, and driven to engage in backseat sex with a sleazy patron of the Karnak café (in the novel she does worse, becoming a paid mistress for two men). As Khalid Safwan, Kamal al-Shinawi, once a light romantic lead (as in *The Good Earth*), now followed the logic of his later casting by Kamal al-Shaykh—the hypocritical, opportunistic Rauf Ilwan in *The Thief and the Dogs,* and the self-centered Yusuf in *The Man Who Lost His Shadow*—as the amoral product of the revolution. Ever handsome, but no longer as youthful, al-Shinawi had mastered a cold, manipulative look. The other students are played by relative newcomers: Nur al-Sharif, Muhammad Subhi, Yunis Shalabi, and Wahid Sayf. Zaynab's emotionally distraught parents are played by Farid Shawqi and Tahiya Carioca. Shawqi, the heroic "beast of the screen," gets his licks in against a corrupt local market boss who wants to marry Zaynab—a classic film trope hearkening back to *Determination*—but is reduced to pained impotence before the organs of state repression. No less empathetic is the performance by Carioca, the great belly dancer now cast in maternal roles—she had also played Suad Husni's mother in *Zouzou.* Hilmi's father, who loses his teaching position due to his son's presumed political activities, is played by Muhammad Tawfiq, a veteran character actor who had once specialized as the loveable sidekick (in, for example, *The Noble Thief*), but who had also played Fuada's/Shadia's oppressed father in *A Bit of Fear.*

Free to attack the "centers of power," *Karnak* pulls no punches. The students are released on successive occasions with mock apologies for their detention—"Congratulations, we've found you innocent"—and apologias for their treatment—"We appear to have beaten a number of people without cause, but the majority have benefitted. . . ." An elected official (Salah Zulficar) to whom Ibrahim and Zaynab turn for help in securing Hilmi's release is dismissed derisively by Khalid Safwan; as the legislator exits, a hooded prisoner is brought in for interrogation. In a powerful politically charged scene, Hilmi is beaten to death by concentration camp guards as the June War erupts. Having heard rumors of war and ashamed that they are unable to defend the nation, the prisoners demand, even plead, for information. Struck repeatedly by wooden clubs, Hilmi looks across the yard toward Ibrahim, who lies half conscious, unable to help his friend. Images of their bloody faces and the beating administered by Egyptian guards are juxtaposed with footage of Israeli planes bombing Egyptian soil. In contrast, the most poignant scene in the novel—the chance encounter at the Karnak between Khalid Safwan, purged after the "corrective revolution," and his victims—is here dramatically altered. In Mahfouz's text, Safwan winds up joining the Karnak circle, where he offers excuses for his misdeeds and, remarkably, is allowed a degree of atonement by his listeners (if not by the amazed narrator; ibid.: 211). In the film Safwan is confronted not at the café, but in prison by fellow prisoners, who treat him derisively and even strike him physically before the announcement of their imminent release (but not his) halts the attack.[22]

Although *Karnak* was not the first film to indict the Nasserist police, it became the defining moment of cinematic exposition, and as such marks the real end of the era of Nasserist cinema. The film, writes Ali Abu Shadi (1998: 21), represents the "first salvo" in a "savage attack on the July revolution." Traditional cinematic villains—corrupt and brutal officials—overnight became Nasserists or servants of the Nasserist state who are routinely seen torturing victims by various means. The apex in *Karnak* is the "immoderately long" scene (ibid.: 22) in which a police thug assaults and rapes Zaynab while Khalid Safwan sits calmly behind his office desk.[23] The film garnered great commercial success; as a result it spawned an entire genre of "Karnak" films *(al-Karnaka)*. The recipe for success, notes Abu Shadi wryly, was simple: "add a bit of torture and a bit of the 'centers of power' to an old script" (ibid.). A headline grabbing lawsuit also helped, brought by Salah Nasr, the chief of Nasser's secret police, who charged, not without good reason, that Khalid

Safwan was meant to be him. Sadat's court dismissed the case after a great deal of publicity, all of which generated ticket sales.

To underscore their political convictions, while at the same time providing the still normative happy ending, Badrakhan and al-Laythi bracketed their film with imagery of the October 1973 war. The film opens with a disheveled Ibrahim sitting alone in the Karnak, staring dreamily into space. Suddenly, as the radio announces the outbreak of war, his eyes come to life. He rushes to a military hospital, but is refused entry, despite his medical credentials. Spying Zaynab inside hospital grounds, he calls to her. In order to secure permission for him to enter she relates their story to the head physician, setting in motion the flashback that constitutes the entire film. That story ends with Ibrahim, suffering from survivor guilt and the deep-seated fear that he would, if coerced, have denounced Hilmi, now breaking his engagement to Zaynab. As the film cuts back to the present, she runs to the hospital gate to hand Ibrahim his orders, and together they rush to lend medical assistance to the wounded. In a final flourish the film cuts to Egyptian troops storming the Bar Lev line, erasing the shameful defeat that is now squarely laid at the feet of the Nasserist order.

Portraits of Power Revisited

Having embarked upon his presidency in the shadow of Nasser, Sadat increasingly began to distance himself and allow for the indirect denigration of his predecessor. As his own image began to proliferate throughout the country, the Nasserist icons came down. As noted earlier in this text, where they could not be totally erased, such as the monument to Soviet-Egyptian friendship at the Aswan High Dam, the successor was superimposed over the likeness of his predecessor. Nasser's passing prompted an incredible outpouring of emotion. In the aftermath of his death, however, he found no major monument dedicated to his memory.

Nasser's picture had begun to crop up in several instances in films produced in the late sixties. In *The Shame* he looks on—in this case a familiar dignified profile—while bribes are passed and corruption is defended by petty bureaucrats as a reasonable solution to economic inequity. Yet he also looks over Rushdi Abaza's shoulder, no doubt with approval, as the repentant official resolves to turn himself in and blow the whistle on his associates. In *Karnak,* Nasser appears in an early scene alongside posters of Soviet flags and leaders. With the primary events portrayed predating the June War, as well as Sadat's July 1972 expulsion of Soviet advisors and his reorientation toward the West, the image is designed to remind viewers of the folly that produced the defeat. All this before that folly is graphically depicted as torturous oppression.

The most poignant scene in the film adaptation of *Karnak* occurs near the end, a quiet moment in a movie that has suddenly turned gruesome. Zaynab and Ibrahim have returned home late at night. They had gone to Hilmi's apartment for a study session, but found a political meeting in progress. Both privately fearful of hearing and seeing too much, they excuse themselves to go study at another friend's unoccupied flat. Alone, they begin to make love, but memories of prison beatings invade Ibrahim's consciousness. The friends walk home in silence, then separate without comment, enter their respective flats (each still lives with parents) and retreat to their bedrooms. Ibrahim paces and smokes. Zaynab sits at her desk in front of a notepad, starts to write her report for Khalid Safwan, then looks up at the official portrait of Nasser that hangs over her desk. In this portrait, a common icon, his features touched up by an artist's pen to make him look a bit younger, Nasser smiles. Zaynab's eyes reflect a combination of lingering adoration, disbelief at the ruler's potential complicity, and the intense pain of betrayal. It is a brief exchange, all of a few seconds, and ends inconclusively. Zaynab crumples the paper and puts her head on her arms. Is her act one of complicity with, or resistance to the icon? Little matter, for the following day when she submits her report—in which she has tried to exonerate Hilmi—to Khalid Safwan, she learns that both Hilmi and Ibrahim have again been arrested. At worst the Leader is an active participant in the debasement of Egypt's children, loyal children of the revolution; at best he is impotent, detached, unaware. Either way he is clearly culpable.

Sadat's moment in the sun would not last long; by January 1977 the "hero of the crossing" would be chastised by bread rioters, the opening scene in his own sudden skid toward popular execration. The following decade would be marked by the "infitah films," cynical expositions of the failed dreams of de-Nasserization and nihilstic remakes of the most popular films of Egypt's modernist liberal past (Malkmus 1988; Armbrust 1996). Throughout it all, Nasser's banishment from the big screen persisted. Until finally, a national malaise began to recall the fallen leader through very different lenses.

NOTES

1. *Akhir saa,* August 31, 1966: 38.

2. One change, however, is significant. The good-hearted prostitute, Nur (Shadia), who provides a hideaway and comfort to Said, vanishes mysteriously in the novel, lending her relationship with Said a discomfiting ambivalence. In the film she is there at the end, first calling on the thief to surrender, then a grieving "widow" after his death.

3. Abdel-Malek, however, has nothing to say about the film industry.

4. A commission of inquiry concluded in 1981 that the studios were worth ten times their acquisition price (Abou Chadi 1995: 118).

5. Six public sector films were in fact co-produced by public and private sectors.

6. Omar Sharif did not leave, but rather stayed away, as noted in footnote 15 of Chapter 1, because he felt that if he returned he might find himself cut off from his blossoming Hollywood career.

7. Among the most famous are Husayn Kamal's *Empire of M's* and Said Marzuq's *I Want a Solution* (1975).

8. Abu Shadi ([Abou Chadi] 1995: 120–21), one of the public sector's staunchest champions, also notes this about Sharaf al-Din, whom he succeeded as chief censor in 1996.

9. *Akhir saa,* December 27, 1967: 35.

10. Here he is echoing the title of Tawfiq al-Hakim's classic and highly influential 1932 nationalist novel.

11. *Akhir saa,* February 16, 1966: 45.

12. For student activism in particular, see Abdalla (1985).

13. Umm Kulthum's live Thursday night radio concerts had been a regular feature of Egyptian life for people of all classes from the late 1930s onward (Danielson 1997: 86–87).

14. See the comments on the particular verses he cites by translator Fatma Moussa-Mahmoud (Mahfouz 1978: 138, 141).

15. The lead in this film, if there is one, the character of the local inspector, is played by veteran character actor Tawfiq al-Daqn, one of Tawfiq Salih's favorites.

16. Abu Sayf used the term "rightist" to refer to his colleague—without rancor I should note—in a conversation with me (December 19, 1995), shortly before his death.

17. For "de-Nasserization" in general, see Waterbury (1978: 235–56).

18. The novel has been translated into English as *Adrift on the Nile* (Mahfouz 1993).

19. Her name has been altered for the film from Samara al-Bahgat.

20. Ali Badrakhan, the son of famed director Ahmad Badrakhan, made his first film in 1973. *Karnak* was his second feature.

21. According to LeGassick, an "unusual notation on the [novel's] final page" informs the reader of the delay in publication.

22. In reality, Salah Nasr, on whom Khalid Safwan is based, was released shortly thereafter; thus allowing the Safwan character to freely visit the cafe.

23. For a clip, see the CD-ROM "Cinderella al-shasha al-Arabiya."

SEVEN

Nostalgia in Black and White
Nasser's Streets and Public Memory

We serve the Republic around the clock!

Life or Death, 1954

All my life I have obeyed the government. The present one, the one before it, and I'll serve the coming one. Suppose I didn't obey, what would happen?

Terrorism and Shish Kabob, 1992

"A Beautiful Dream"

In the climactic scene of the satirical fantasy *Land of Hypocrisy* (*[Ard al-nifaq],* Fatin Abd al-Wahhab 1968), Masud, a beleaguered civil servant, dumps a bag full of "morality powder" into the Nile. Within moments the essence has permeated Cairo's drinking water; one gulp and a sneeze later, people suddenly speak and act without inhibition. Masud and the mysterious purveyor of potions, a wizardly chemist with a pharmacy that sits on the desert's edge, tour the city to see the potion's effect. At the funeral of Masud's boss, the grieving widow, having sipped from a cup, suddenly erupts in curses to the dead, while the undertaker protests loudly that he cannot provide a proper funeral for the paltry sum provided. Elsewhere in the city morality breeds a different result. The curious wanderers come upon a sparkling block of public housing with "vacancy" signs. How can so many flats be available at once, they wonder. "These were all flats of ill repute," the boab intones. "When the people became moral, they left the flats—and the [housing] crisis lifted.[1] That's the story."

All too soon, however, the potion has dissipated. Newspaper hawkers run by shouting that normalcy has returned. "What a shame. It was a beautiful dream; I wish it had lasted," notes the wizard, who departs to "look for new work." Masud, who had initially pilfered several vials of "hypocrisy" potion and climbed the social ladder of success, then carelessly imbibed a vial of "morality," finds himself back where he started: a target for pitched garbage in a raucous back alley, an oppressed clerk at work, and a badgered husband at home. Desperate, he returns to the wizard's oasis only to find the laboratory boarded up, closed due to "lack of public morals."

A comedy vehicle written for Fuad al-Muhandis, Egypt's king of comedy in the sixties, successor to Ismail Yasin, *Land of Hypocrisy* speaks at once to timeless universal truths and specific Egyptian realities. Masud might fit into Gogol's Russia or Sembene's Senegal. Compared to a film like *Case 68,* which was adapted for the screen to pillory stasis within the ruling party, the Muhandis vehicle could easily be set in the pre-socialist 1950s, even the pre-Nasser era. The film's social commentary is tame, hardly representative of other socially relevant films produced after June 1967. Nonetheless, the imagery, from the animated credits to the fashions sported by socialist-era nouveau riches, elicits clear recognition of time and place. The social commentary implicit in uproarious satire and sardonic ending is tame compared to other socially relevant films produced after June 1967. Still, there are clear traces of the malaise pervasive in Egypt during Nasser's last years

Today, for many, that malaise, viewed in hindsight on television or home video, seems enviable. *Land of Hypocrisy* remains one of a score of "classic" films from Egypt's golden era of cinema. Something starring Fuad al-Muhandis, whether a film or tape of one of his many famous stage plays, is screened virtually daily on one TV channel. Virtually all of those classic roles, many opposite the brassy, domineering Shweikar, his wife for many years, originated in the black-and-white cinema or television of the 1960s. From 1962, the date of their first film collaboration, they worked together regularly, producing a film annually through the early seventies.[2] By that time a majority of Egyptian movies were produced in color. With that change-over Egyptians have long considered the golden era of cinema to have come to a close.

Egyptians certainly did not reject color. The two biggest hits between 1969 and 1973, *Father's Up a Tree* and *Watch Out for Zouzou,* were both color films. The seventies spawned a new generation of stars—Nur al-Sharif, Husayn Fahmi, Mahmud Yasin, Mervat Amin, Nagla Fathi, Boussy—and directors. Still, something had died, if not in the film industry then in the country at large. It is significant that the artistic transformation corresponded to political changes in the air: the ascension of Sadat, de-Nasserization, the brief fluorescence of political confessionals that spawned the "Karnak" films, and the infitah, the economic open door that would ultimately generate a far more lingering malaise, and with it, a new genre of socially critical filmmaking. Because these attitudes, this Egypt, was filmed in color, the break with the past was only accentuated. Black and white films, for all that was good and bad about them, were buried with Nasser and the revolutionary experiment. If what followed was more sober than even the post-1967 "green light" films, the harsh tones of "living color" would forever mark the transition.

During the first two decades of color production, a younger generation of Egyptian directors, many the products of Nasser's state-owned film sector, moved with increasing frequency out of the studio and into the streets. They captured on film a "new reality" (Gaffney 1987: 69–73), a far more "real" society than that portrayed in earlier eras, producing powerful "new" films in which "yesterday's filmic conventions are no longer valid" (Malkmus 1988: 31). As one consequence, sound quality depreciates considerably. Cairo has always been a noisy city, but the shift produced a literal cacophony. The streets of the city, still the setting for most films, increasingly became places of moral discord and physical danger. While their deliberate neo-realist bent has always been in some respects a response to, if not outright criticism of, the studio system, many leading filmmakers have also evoked a growing degree of nostalgia for the Egypt that "was." A counter-balance to the "Karnak" phase of social-political filmmaking, their work is born out of the disappointments and social dislocations of Sadat's liberalization.

A seminal work here is Atif al-Tayyib's *The Bus Driver* (*[Sawwaq al-autobis]* 1983), a powerful family drama set against the backdrop of increasingly crowded and unruly streets, jam-packed public transportation, and the beginning of a proliferation of consumer goods, many ill-gotten. Hasan (Nur al-Sharif), a 1973 war veteran, drives a city bus and moonlights as a taxi driver. In the opening scene, as credits unfold, he guides his bus through early morning traffic, already crowded, as his *kumsari* (ticket collector) weaves through the throng of passengers to collect fares.[3] When a woman cries out that her purse has been snatched, the driver pulls over and locks the exit doors, but the thief, having worked his way to an open window, jumps through and vanishes into the crowd of pedestrians.

Overcrowded buses, often with a requisite pickpocket, had long been dramatic, often comic, sites for filmic interludes. In *Uncle Abduh's Ghost,* heroes and heroine meet when the young woman accuses them of having snatched money from her purse on the bus. In *My Wife is General Director,* the hapless husband, the family jalopy having broken down, looks on from the landing of a packed bus as his wife speeds past in her chauffeur-driven limousine. A more demonic, claustrophobic depiction occurs near the climax of *The Shame.* After reluctantly accepting a bribe from Ibadi Bey, Sanaa runs from the building, hurtles across a busy street and catches a bus. Hoping to catch her breath, she suddenly looks around, and imagines that her co-riders, particularly a group of burly, menacing peasants, filmed at upward angle to accentuate her sudden claustrophobia (she has ridden the bus without care or incident in prior scenes) have designs on her purse. In Tayyib's film, the bus plays a far more central role. If it does not symbolize the nation, it certainly situates the citizen clambering to make his or her way through the crowded, ever more corrupt streets of that nation.

The driver's personal struggle is played out on two levels. The first is his own struggle to get by, one that necessitates working two jobs, both of which—a clever turn by scriptwriter Muhammad Khan—have him combating traffic in the streets in order to get others where they are going. The second concerns his efforts to prevent greedy family members from selling off his father's wood shop—on which the family learns it owes unpaid back taxes—to speculators. With his family rent apart by avarice, the driver turns to army buddies for assistance. The trope of October War veterans encountering social defeatism at home remains key to many such "infitah films," the poignancy of the domestic predicament underscored by scenes in which the demobilized soldiers recall their—the nation's—triumphant moment, when they scaled and planted the Egyptian flag atop the Israeli Bar-Lev fortifications on the eastern bank of the Suez Canal. The wealth of consumer goods stashed in his sister and brother-in-law's Port Said flat does not simply point to a society that has quickly lost its moral compass. While Port Said, the gateway to the Canal, and a duty-free city with Sadat's reforms, has long been associated with a certain "free market" spirit, critics—and many Egyptians, no doubt—noted a clever, troubling juxtaposition between the corruption spawned by the "open door" and the heroic resistance the city mounted in 1956, captured in films like *Port Said* and even *The Prisoner of Abu Zaabal* (Ramzi 1984a: 65–66).

The ending to *The Bus Driver* is ambivalent. The hero manages to raise enough captial to prevent the sale of the family workshop, but not before his father, played with quiet pathos by the great Imad Hamdi, dies. The final scene then reprises the opening, only now Ahmad is able to collar the thief who has been preying on his line. He chases the man down the street, grabs him, and administers a beating. Some critics saw this as the ultimate triumph of the virtuous citizen (ibid.: 67), a post-socialist happy ending? It might easily be read more negatively: "the driver vents his anger by savagely beating a pickpocket" (Gaffney 1986: 72), or even as a meaningless scuffle in the face of the rampant corruption that has already impacted society.

City Streets

The urban focus is not exclusive, yet in the "infitah films" the city re-emerges as the symbolic center of Egypt. The shift from countryside to urban metropolis is telling. In a broader context, Janet Abu-Lughod, writing at the end of the Nasser era, spoke to the revolution's symbolic ties to "the land" and uneasy relationship to the city (1971: 221):

> Perhaps in reaction against the previous exploitative role of the capital as the center of alien dominance, there has been a certain reluctance—which now seems to be passing—to give the city her due. For too long the countryside represented the Egypt of the Egyptians, whereas Cairo symbolized a parasitic growth whose conspicuous consumption was achieved through conscienceless mulcting of the fallahin. There existed an ambivalence—a pride in the greatness of Cairo but also a rejection of her symbolic association with "the government." Even after the revolutionary regime succeeded in making that government indigenous, some residual ambivalence remained. . . . This early ideology has apparently now given way to a more balanced view.

The cruel irony is that the city, always the setting for a majority of films, re-emerges in a far more harsh light, the conspicuous consumption not that of the old elite, but the commoner aspiring to join the swelling ranks of the nouveau riche, or "war profiteers" *(ghani harb)* in colloquial Arabic. That consumption is reflected in starkly negative depictions of the "social homogenization" Abu-Lughod had described (ibid.: 238–39) in more sympathetic terms.

Those who might imagine that the "street theater" (Waterbury 1978: 171) of Cairo—the pulsating crowds, the seeming disregard for order of pedestrians and drivers of motorized and animal-drawn vehicles alike—emerged only in the Sadat era when the number of private vehicles spiralled, should look back to frequent pleas for "discipline" in the popular print media of the Nasser era. In January 1956 *Akhir saa* complained that "Chaos Sticks its Tongue Out at the New Traffic Law."[4] In the same journal, over a year later, Salah Muntasir, now a veteran journalist, asked "Why Do People Run in the Streets of Cairo?"[5] Admitting that he, too, had become swept up in the sprint of daily life, the foot race to catch public transport, the author pointed to both a marked increase in traffic and a chronic lack of faith in the traffic cop, and predicted only worse for the future:

> Day after day, the speed of everything will increase. And all the people will run in the streets, ever faster than the day before—or the hour before. Soon we won't even be able to focus on the steps people take while they run!

History bore out Muntasir's premonition. At frequent interludes throughout the sixties, photojournalists attempted to capture the "unbelievable" scenes of urban street life,[6] and frequent government calls for "self-discipline," whether directed at drivers, pedestrians, or both, have proven fruitless.

Nonetheless, depictions of traffic-choked, crime-ridden streets in films produced since the early eighties differ markedly from images of the street in the old films, particularly from the fifties and sixties, when filmmakers began to include city vistas, and a greater number of individual scenes were filmed on location. These latter images—however crafted or edited—are striking to anyone who has lived in contemporary, post-Nasserist Cairo, whether one remembers the past or accesses it only through visual media. Statistics tell one side of the tale, a city that had grown from 3.3 million people in 1960 to over six million by 1972, and in which the growth in the number of private vehicles could by the late seventies already be characterized as an "explosion" (ibid.: 126).[7] A city in which public services are strained to the limit, in which crimes against strangers have risen precipitately, and in which citizens have in recent years for the first time turned away rather than confront displays of public violence.[8] To all these citizens, the stresses of contemporary life—particularly in the big cities and especially in Cairo—is mirrored daily by an antithetical set of images, none more powerful than the orderly flow of traffic in a spotless, unpolluted city where justice ultimately prevails before the curtain falls or the final credits roll.

In Salah Abu Sayf's *A Woman's Youth,* Shukri Sirhan arrives from the village to pursue university studies. The film opens in the countryside, where a cow is sold to pay his expenses. Upon his arrival in Cairo at the central rail station, the camera follows the journey by horse-drawn carriage to his lodgings in a quarter of the medieval city. Overhead shots capture the wide, uncrowded boulevards; street-level shots the ornate turn-of-the century and sparkling post-war era high-rises of the Western city, then the procession down Muhammad Ali street towards the Citadel. In more conventional melodramas the uncrowded streets serve as private promenades for young lovers. In *The Empty Pillow,* Abd al-Halim Hafiz slowly extends a hand to Lubna Abd al-Aziz, who slips beside him on their secret rendezvous. When Abd al-Halim pedals Shadia on his bicycle in *The People's Idol,* moving footage of a car-free, Nile-side boulevard runs behind a fixed-bike in the studio; similar footage backs Anwar Wagdi and Layla Murad in *Daughter of Nobility,* although here the couple rides a motor scooter. Earlier in the latter film, however, Wagdi and Ismail Yasin pedal side-by-side through real streets, at times extending arms to touch shoulders, while Murad sings in the background. Likewise, Abd al-Halim sings a solo number in *The People's Idol* while riding carefree through downtown Cairo and then down a flower-lined lane. The working class neighborhood to which he returns is a studio set, but the street footage—even if orchestrated by a degree of directorial control—is real. Melding with the characters—and tunes—of the great crooners, romancers, comics, and toughs, such scenes create an imagery of intense power which translates into an equally powerful nostalgia.

SITES AND SOUVENIRS OF MEMORY

In defining "sites of memory" *(lieux de memorie),* Pierre Nora notes the problematic of "the embodiment of memory in certain sites where a sense of historical continuity persists" (1989: 7). Cairo—its streets, squares, buildings, monuments, gardens—may not represent such a site (or melange of sites) in the strict sense he denotes. Nora looks more specifically at those sites designated by political or academic officialdom, to be repositories of "history," "the reconstruction, always problematic and incomplete, of what is no longer" (ibid.: 8). Sites of events, "remains [of] the ultimate embodiments of a memorial consciousness," become sites of memory when memory appears to dissipate; in response, the purveyors of public history act "deliberately" (ibid.: 12) to "stop time, to block the work of forgetting, to establish a state of things, to immortalize death, to materialize the immaterial" (ibid.: 19).

Nasser's Cairo certainly has its sites of commemoration. In the first year after seizing power the military officers initiated a major overhaul of geographic nomenclature. Streets were stripped of royal allusion and renamed for the military (Farouk Street became Army Street), the new non-monarchical state (the intersection of King Fuad I and Ibrahim Pasha became 26 July and Republic), revolutionary achievements (the new Evacuation Street), or paeans to revolutionary friends (Garden Street renamed for Iraqi leader Abd al-Salam Arif). The monuments planned for the newly renamed Liberation (*Tahrir,* previously Ismailia) Square never got past the design stage, but that square, along with the plaza in front of Abdin (now Republican) Palace and the vast area by the central train depot all carry great commemorative power, at least for those who recall the throngs who greeted Nasser and his fellow officers at the rail station, or who attended or watched newsreels of political rallies marking Revolution Day or other holidays at Liberation or Republic Square.

Such memories are infused with the optimism of the period, however jaded in retrospect. The re-countings of such memories are often cathartic, even for someone like Safinaz Qasim, the literary critic who later embraced the Islamist movement:

> This was Farouk Square, renamed Army Square after 1952. It's one of the loveliest places of my childhood. All that remains from that time are these two fine buildings. There were so many beautiful buildings. They were part of what made us proud and happy, to walk through this neighborhood. Every morning I crossed this square. In the center there was a clock and we'd hear this song. . . . The parade of Free Officers passed by here in July 1952. The officers of the revolution—Nasser and Neguib were there. In July 1952 we were 12 or 13. We were very happy. My mother and big brothers were very excited. We jumped and waved so Neguib would notice us. Nasser saw us. He saluted us. We went, "Not you, him!" He laughed, that made us like him, and he pointed us out to Neguib (Rached 1997).

For all Egyptians, whether or not they lived the Nasser era, the contemporary reality of such sites—congested, litter-strewn, vehicle-smogged—contrasts with both recalled and filmic identity: "There were *so many* beautiful buildings."

For Egyptian cinema no place perhaps holds as much emotive power as the central train station. For his 1958 classic, *Cairo Station,* a sordid tale of sexual deviance set against a backdrop of labor unrest, Youssef Chahine utilized the station's old name: Bab al-Hadid. Four years earlier, however, the revolutionary regime had replaced the classic Mukhtar sculpture, "Egypt Awakening," with a colossus of Ramsis II, and renamed both station and square for the pharaoh. Today the statue of Ramsis is dwarfed by a web of overpasses designed to bypass a nearly impassable series of intersections below. Before that it was encircled by a hideous blue iron pedestrian bridge. The fountain, with its gushing jets of water projected outward from the statue's base, which, according to young wits—turning an artist's dream into a vernacular nightmare—made the glorious pharaoh appear to be urinating, has long been shut down.[9] On black-and-white film, however, Ramsis retains his royal demeanor. He gazes outward with solemnity as poor, demented Qinawi (played by Youssef Chahine) flirts with the voluptuous soda girl (Hind Rustam) in *Cairo Station.* And in purer romantic guise, Ramsis, lit splendidly with fountains gushing, serves as backdrop as a disconsolate Salah (Abd al-Halim Hafiz) roams the quiet square after putting Nadia (Zubayda Tharwat), his new-found love, on a train in *A Day in My Life.* The same holds for run-down Nile-side casinos, the Cairo Zoo, the Zamalek grottos, the Japanese gardens at Helwan, and countless other sites where lovers courted, flirted, and reconciled.[10]

If some sites have fallen into decay, testing the imaginative powers that might invest them with a "symbolic aura" (Nora 1989: 19), others have vanished entirely. One such site is the iron-sided Abu al-Ila Bridge, a magnificent structure associated, at least in popular imagination, with Eiffel, that spanned the Nile from Bulaq to Zamalek. Topped by a modern flyover that then continued across Gezira Island to the river's west bank, the iron and wood bridge had been restricted to sure-footed pedestrians in its final years. When it finally came down in 1997 some decried the loss of yet another modern-era architectural wonder. I found no direct appeals to its cinematic iconography as the structure traversed by Farid Shawqi to strains of "The Man I Love" during his upwardly mobile journey as *Boss Hasan.* Yet somewhere that, too, is a part of the collective memory of a population that has been, and is still, bred on the oldies.

Those oldies that are set in the city, by far the great majority, are marked by a plethora of settings, general and specific, that have become infused with "the necessarily insatiable demands of nostalgia" (Stewart 1984: 135), and are, as such, vernacular "sites of memory." They might also be considered social "souvenirs" brought to life on the little screen. As Susan Stewart delineates, the souvenir "will not"—perhaps cannot—"function without the supplementary narrative discourse that both attaches it to its origins and creates a myth with regard to those origins." That narrative, so clearly encapsulated in memories of a beautiful, now dysfunctional city, "displaces the point of authenticity as it itself becomes the point of origin for the narrative" (ibid.: 136).

> The double function of the souvenir is to authenticate a past or otherwise remote experience and, at the same time, to discredit the present. The present is either too impersonal, too looming, too alienating compared to the intimate and direct experience of contact which the souvenir has as its referent. This referent is authenticity (ibid.: 139).

Again, the tales of Nasser and his era, narratives that are so intimate in comparison to what has followed. This one, narrated by Shahinda Maklad, widow of an agricultural labor activist murdered by landowners in 1966, during the latter days of land reform, here with a rural setting, but also rooted in site:

> In 1965 President Nasser was supposed to pass by here on his re-election campaign. We decided to prepare a welcome to pledge our support. There were peasants lined up on all four corners. The motorcade wasn't supposed to stop in Kamshish, but we'd decided

> otherwise. Nasser was traveling with his friend Che Guevera. I slipped through the crowd and stepped right in front of their car. The body guards were taken by surprise. One officer tried to pull me away. Nasser told him, "Leave her." We began to sing hymns and songs. We burst into song. He listened to us and then drove on (Rached 1997).

Yet, while the countryside was always replete with tensions between progress and tradition, steadfast labor and stubborn superstition, the city—Cairo especially—with few exceptions became a setting in which the individual and, by implication, Egyptian society might charge forward. Desmond Stewart (1957: 26), an old Cairo hand and later the city's biographer, sensed this in the late fifties: "Now the city seems to belong to the people: there are differences between the rich and the poor: there are slums: but the spirit is new, and the spirit is powerful. This is the new Cairo of the twentieth century: a Cairo in which the Cairenes themselves are owners, and therefore hosts."

Life or Death in the City

If the city remains a vast site of memory, that site is inextricably linked to its people. As recalled in the cinema, these people, despite the requisite (and dramatically obligatory) villains, and despite the late sixties cynicism, reflected a positive, optimistic sense of civic duty—responsibility toward fellow citizens and a sense of community. No film expressed this civic sense better—and none is cited more often in this respect, especially by Egyptians who lived the Nasser era—than Kamal al-Shaykh's early masterpiece *Life or Death* (*Haya aw mawt* 1954).[11] Based on a true story, the film evokes much of the director's early penchant for suspense; at the same time it reveals, however crafted, a fine eye for the type of social realism that is more often associated with Salah Abu Sayf or Tawfiq Salih. When all is said and done, the film is about the city and its denizens. Together they represent the nation.

The simple story concerns a young girl's errand to purchase medicine for her gravely ill father and a conscientious pharmacist's desperate effort to trace a prescription that he realizes soon afterward has been incorrectly filled and will certainly prove fatal. The film starts with the image of a ticking clock. Opening shots then provide a panoramic vista of common people in a vast metropolis. The camera hovers over the Qasr al-Nil bridge, then the primary link to Giza, taking in the traffic, then zooms in on busy downtown streets. The narration speaks of the faceless crowd:

> In a crowded city like this, Cairo, inhabited by two and a half million souls, from all walks of life, yet intertwined, the struggle between life and humanity is ever intense. This overwhelming life, just like this immortal river, and the people who cross the bridge between it and the unknown—the procession of life in widespread Cairo is ceaseless. Within it struggle the souls of millions of people, each proceeding toward an unknown fate.

As the narrative hones in on its subject, a distraught father who cannot afford to buy his daughter a holiday gift, the camera finds Ahmad Ibrahim (Imad Hamdi) starring wistfully into a downtown department store window, eyeing a girl's party dress. As the narration ends, he walks away dejectedly, then enters the office of the firm from which he has been dismissed. A former colleague greets him warmly, offers a cigarette and, referring obliquely to an operation, asks about his health. Preoccupied and not a little embarrassed, Ahmad informs him the operation was unnecessary, a fact that will soon be brought into serious doubt. When the boss is finally able to see him, Ahmad learns that company rules will not permit him to collect his severance pay until after the holiday. Despondent, but too proud to take a token handout, offered clumsily after a tip to the porter, Ahmad pawns his watch in order to purchase the dress, and returns home with only a few coins in his pocket. His daughter Samira is pleased with her gift, but asks innocently about the matching shoes and bag. Unable to hide his shame, Ahmad retires to his room. His wife (Madiha Yusri) tries to comfort him, but the two quarrel, whereupon she leaves for her parents. As father and daughter fantasize over a future of wealth—he will own a dairy from which none will be fired—he is suddenly gripped by chest pains. Reaching into his pocket, he gives Samira some change and instructs her to fill his prescription at the local pharmacy. When she arrives she finds it closed and is directed to the other side of Cairo. Thus begins a suspense-filled journey into the heart—and soul—of the city.

In some of the earliest and most extensive on-site shooting to date, Kamal al-Shaykh's camera films the young girl in a variety of locations as she navigates the streets, helped by a series of well-meaning strangers—in one case given a lift on a man's bicycle—then travels across modern Cairo by tram. The pharmacist (Husayn Riyad) allows her to underpay with a promise to return the following day. Only after she has exited and vanished into the crowd does he realize that in preparing the prescription he has dropped a decimal and mistakenly added a toxic dose to the medication. Failing to contact the prescribing physician, the pharmacist sets out by car with his assistant to somehow find the patient before his daughter delivers the poison. The camera now cuts back and forth between street scenes and a series of encounters by both girl and pharmacist, some comical, some serious, with a variety of average citizens. When Samira, who has no change left for a return tram ride, accidentally walks into a man on the sidewalk, he first scolds her for her inattention, then helps direct her homeward. Later, after her medicine bottle cracks, another bystander takes her into a liquor store where the syrup is poured into an empty spirits bottle. Spotting a young girl carrying (presumably) alcohol, a wino swipes the bottle; he, however, is unwittingly saved by two good Samaritans who chase him down and return the bottle to its rightful owner. Meanwhile, the pharmacist, trying to trace the patient by his all-too-common name, encounters a series of unhelpful boabs—a comic trope in film and real-life—who barely deign to get off their benches, let alone reveal the identity of their buildings' inhabitants, and an overworked police sergeant who is busy questioning common thieves. In desperation, the pharmacist enters municipal police headquarters, where he finds the highest police officials in the city engaged in the pursuit of an escaped convict. Presuming that he has approached them with a clue, they agree to see the man.

Dumbfounded to learn his real purpose but moved by the pharmacist's predicament, the police chief (Yusuf Wahbi) commits significant manpower to finding a young girl with a medicine bottle (which, of course, she no longer has) and contacting her father about the danger of her delivery. Humor and good civics again intersect as police officials endeavor to visit every Ahmad Ibrahim in the metropolis. In one instance law enforcement officers break in upon an adulterous couple, only to leave them to the wronged husband, a wrong Ahmad Ibrahim. Fortunately, they also inadvertently come upon the escaped convict, who is apprehended after a shoot out. The civic camaraderie of the streets almost proves their undoing. Passersby notice with surprise a series of young girls holding bottles being escorted into police vehicles; one witness, a young boy, helps Samira avoid interception, guiding her through back alleys and pointing her on her way home. Desperate, the police decide to broadcast a public announcement over the radio, warning a certain Ahmad Ibrahim not to take his medicine. Ahmad's wife, who in a prior scene had turned off the radio at her parent's, now turns it back on and hears the announcement. In the climactic scene, she runs home. Finding the door locked, she breaks through the glass with her bare hand, then rushes in and, to the shock of husband and daughter, slaps the proffered glass out of Samira's hand. Before she can explain, the police chief arrives, along with the pharmacist, who carries the proper prescription. With a characteristic Yusuf Wahbi swagger, the chief, saying nothing, turns on the radio so all present may hear the announcement. Husband and wife embrace warmly. Addressing the chief as "Sergeant" *(ya Shawish),* Samira thanks him. When mother echoes daughter, the police chief responds simply: "It's our duty, ma'am. We serve the Republic around the clock," then salutes and exits.

With all the common touches, Kamal al-Shaykh succeeded in mastering the suspense genre by highlighting the human face. "Provocative . . . Tough . . . Real!" heralded a promotional blurb:

> This is the movie that all have been awaiting. The movie in which the camera plays the lead role, taking its story from the street and its hero from the people you see and encounter every day. It is the story of the struggle—in which, without even realizing it, you might well be one of the heroes.[12]

The film garnered great success both at home and at international festivals, and established the director's credentials. Most of his later films would be played out on a much smaller canvas. Yet, in *Life or Death* Kamal al-Shaykh captured the civic sensibilities of a generation that saw the nation moving forward. There is nothing particularly "revolutionary" about the story, except that the police are here not engaged in political activity in the least, nor in crimes that, however universal, needed to be more comfortably set in a royalist, pre-revolutionary past. It is not inconsequential in this respect that the police chief speaks to serving not the Nation, but the Republic. Most striking in retrospect is the positive depiction of officialdom. There is the comical, maddening desk sergeant, too preoccupied to hear the panicked pharmacist. Yet, compared to the filmic depictions of police functionaries at all levels since the late sixties, and especially after *Karnak,* Shaykh's *Life or Death* is positively wistful.

FAST-FORWARD: NASSER AND THE NIGHTINGALE[13]

For all that was new about the "new" cinema of the late seventies and early eighties, much remained the same. The star system remained in place and the state retained a degree of control over production from which few—Youssef Chahine is the primary exception—could break free. Many films did feel different; at the same time younger directors clearly continued to work within, or around, long-established paradigms, genres, and cinematic clichés. Cinematic referencing of the classics remains an important vehicle for self-expression. Hollywood has always been a major source for adaptations, but Egyptians have also tapped their own vaults for inspiration. Walter Armbrust (1996), who has traced the ways in which popular pre-Nasserist films were rescripted in the wake of the infitah to reflect the disillusion with economic liberalism and persistent authoritarian politics, explicates how the modernist dream, expressed first in fashion and print media, then adopted by early filmmakers, had incontrovertibly soured. By the late eighties and early nineties a different mode of referencing began to emerge in the work of socially conscious filmmakers for whom the Nasser era, with all its aspirations of social justice, progress, and national purpose, rather than the Sadat era, became the focal point.

The films I highlight below are full of cinematic references to past masters and masterpieces. The unifying feature is the utilization of the iconic figure of Abd al-Halim Hafiz as the key symbol of the Nasser era. As noted earlier in this work (Chapter 3), Hafiz embodied—and continues to embody—the aspirations of lower-middle- and middle-class youth during the period. As a vocalist, a singer of love songs and nationalist anthems, he remained unsurpassed throughout the better part of three decades. Unlike Umm Kulthum and Farid al-Atrash, his greatest contemporary rivals, but both well-established before his emergence as an artist, Hafiz became a star with the advent of the revolution. All three died within years of each other in the early to mid-seventies, but Hafiz was only forty-seven, which made his passing all the more tragic.[14] His funeral marked the last time that Egyptians have publicly taken their grief into the streets—or have been allowed to (in the recent case of Suad Husni) accompany the body of a worshiped hero to the grave.

In death, Abd al-Halim has transcended superstardom to bridge a gap between artistic fame and political longings. Two decades gone, he continues to personify the archetypical, youthful Nasser-era hero that he was in life—and that he played onscreen. His ongoing stature as the dominant cultural icon of Nasserist Egypt cannot be divorced from his chronological and ideological positioning in Egyptian history. Abd al-Halim has always been more than a recorded voice. It was on the silver screen that he sang his most popular love songs and where he fashioned a persona that, combined with the beauty and pathos of voice and face, touched the heart of the nation. Successive generations have encountered him first on television, both from frequent broadcasts of films and recorded concert footage, and more recently via home video screenings and satellite dishes. It is also on screen—in movies that then work their way to television and video—that a younger generation of filmmakers have utilized the Nightingale as a symbol of long-lost Nasser-era (if not Nasserist) aspirations. He remains an unassailable icon—in ways that Nasser is not—by which to decry the predicaments of post-Nasserist Egypt.

Abd al-Halim's films are replete with images that are ingrained in the minds of successive generations, no less than his lyrics and tunes. As such he remains a "site" of collective memory, a "souvenir," an interface with the nation's collective present. His films, like others in the classic black-and-white corpus—perhaps even more than others—remind viewers of a far more liveable social environment, a nation of manners, cities of wide, uncrowded streets where one might navigate a bicycle while singing one's heart out. Not surprisingly, in some of the most powerful cinematic works of recent decades Abd al-Halim Hafiz has become the personification of lost innocence, crashed dreams, and a particular era that, whatever its warts, was far better than the present. Such films speak in varying degrees to matters of past and present, positing a dreary today in relationship to a romantic—and romanticized—yesterday. Each references Abd al-Halim through music, film clips, concert footage, and several through textual allusion are more direct homages to the man and his genre of cinema. All ultimately rely on the high degree of pop-cultural literacy that Egyptians of all social classes and ages seem to command.

Wife of an Important Person
(*[Zawgat ragul muhim],* Muhammad Khan 1987)

Muhammad Khan's troubling story of a young woman who leaves university studies to marry a rising star within the national security police places Abd al-Halim at the forefront of dramatic action and character development. The film opens with a nostalgic cinema flashback: in 1962 two young school girls run to catch an afternoon matinee. They arrive a reel late, but slide into empty seats and immediately become engrossed in the feature. The film is *Today's Girls,* the scene a pivotal one in which Abd al-Halim discovers the good sister's poetry, sits at the piano and on-the-spot composes and sings what became one of his signature tunes, "I Love You" ([Ahwak]; lyrics by Husayn al-Sayyid, music by Muhammad Abd al-Wahhab). As Magda swoons on the theater screen, one of the school girls, framed in close-up, sits transfixed. Nodding ever so slightly, betraying the trace of a smile, she hints that she knows the film; but tears still fill her eyes. Suddenly, as Khan's credits end, time spins forward fifteen years and a young adult Mona (Mervat Amin) watches an older, disease-ravaged Nightingale sing the same song in a televised concert clip.

Abd al-Halim will become the film's coda, the mirror to the downward spiral of Mona's life and marriage, her husband's increasing brutality at home and on the job, and the parallel crisis of Egyptian society. Mona first encounters Hisham (Ahmad Zaki) in a neighborhood shop, when she runs out, mid-radio concert, to buy a blank cassette. Hisham pursues her—he is attracted but there is a clear evocation of stalking in his manner—then proposes to her parents, who bless what appears to be an excellent social match. The marriage initially appears to be a good one. When Hisham discovers his new bride's obsession with the Nightingale he chides her, an omen of not-kindred spirits, but also plays a tape to gently wake her up in the morning. However, as their marriage decays, Mona takes increasing refuge in her tape player, further arousing Hisham's scorn.

As the film progresses, Mona's marriage—and, one might say, her not-secret love affair with the singer—comes to embody the detachment of Egypt's nouveau-elite from the aspirations of common citizens. At a contentious 1977 New Year's gathering of high police officials, Mona defends the Aswan Dam, another key Nasserist site and the subject of a popular Abd al-Halim nationalist anthem. Within the month, the country erupts in violence—the January 1977 bread riots. Hisham, having risen in the ranks, disappears for days at a time. Watching the angry crowds riot below her balcony, Mona quietly invokes a famous Nasser Suez War speech, urging the masses to "fight on." Her ideological leanings, like her adolescent infatuation with the Nightingale, are accentuated by the casting of Mervat Amin in the role. Amin, as all Egypt recalls, had played Amal, Abd al-Halim's girlfriend, in his last film, the sexually explosive *Father's Up a Tree.* This intersection of "star-as-self/star-as-role" (Custen 1992: 47) that links Amal-Mona-Mervat Amin and all of them to Abd al-Halim makes Mona's descent into depression and her undying fantasy-love for the singer all the more poignant.

That fantasy ends with the singer's death in March 1977, two months after the riots. Mona learns of his passing after casually observing a young school girl (dressed in a uniform reminiscent of her own in the film's opening) running hysterically through the street tearing at her hair. Snippets of the funeral follow: throngs of Egyptians accompanying the coffin, then a quick cut to a young woman leaping from the balcony, all to the tune of another early love song. Hisham, who is fired for his handling of the January disturbances, remains dismissive of his wife's—and, by extension, Egypt's—grief. His world crashing down around him, in one scene he ejects an Abd al-Halim cassette from the player and yanks the magnetic tape out of its case. When, in the climactic scene, he shoots Mona's father, then turns his gun on himself, her silent screams are covered by strains of "I Love You," the song that opened the film in flashback.

Ice Cream in Glym
(*[Ice cream fi Glym]*, Khayri Bishara 1992)

Khayri Bishara's hip revival of the musical, out of fashion for nearly two decades, is in many respects an Abd al-Halim film updated for the MTV generation. Not a remake of any particular movie, it is a general homage to singer, star, and genre that recalls the classic Abd al-Halim screen scenario. Sayf, played by pop star Amr Diab, lives alone in a converted Maadi garage, delivers videos for an unscrupulous music producer, and dreams of true love and stardom. He exercises with an old spring chest extender, bathes in a bathtub rigged with a bucket shower, and boils water for tea with an electric coil. His entire persona, from his black leather jacket to his wall posters of 1950s Hollywood icons (Marilyn Monroe, Paul Newman, James Dean, Elvis Presley), to the Elvis tunes he plays on his Walkman while riding his motorcycle, initially invoke an imported nostalgia, one that speaks particularly to Bishara's generation. Yet the film speaks concurrently to a more indigenous set of memories. Sayf is, as the first Elvis tune asserts, just "a poor boy." His beat-up Jawa is an updated bicycle, the normal Abd al-Halim mode of transport; the rich kids who harass him for attracting the girls drive around in an open Jeep 4x4, a trendy update of the open convertible that Samiha drives off in when she breaks Salah's heart in *The Empty Pillow*.

As in many Abd al-Halim musicals, the mood remains light, optimistic, although tinged with sadness, and ends with a note of romantic and artistic triumph. A recent migrant from a Delta village (the Glym of the title), Sayf has been smitten (in flashback) by a chance encounter on the Alexandria corniche with a chicly-dressed beauty who he sees fleetingly at an ice cream bar. She remains his creative muse as he struggles to get by, to keep his upwardly mobile girlfriend (played by the singer Simone), who eventually rides off in a sports car with a rich older man (Izzat Abu Ouf), to express himself musically, and maintain a positive love for homeland amidst the grumblings of his outwardly mobile band buddies. Abd al-Halim allusions are ever-present, from plot convention to mood, to his prominent photos in the video shops where Sayf makes his drops. Although he cruises to Elvis, his friend Nur (Ashraf Abd al-Baqi), a leftist poet with a *kufiya* draped over his shoulders, rides behind him listening to Abd al-Halim's political anthems on the Walkman.

Although Sayf rejects ideology, opting to follow an apolitical path, Khayri Bishara does not intend his audience to reject the political poet's politics, and certainly not the Nasser-era anthems. The one collaborative composition that Sayf and Nur produce, "Platform Number 5," despite its comical performance—Sayf acts a cripple while his bandmembers feign blindness—is a serious number, reminiscent of the collaborations between poet Ahmad Fuad Nagm and musician Shaykh Imam. The song's title also recalls a popular Farid Shawqi film from the mid-fifties in which the hero, a disgraced coast guard non-com, topples his nemesis (the ever villainous Zaki Rustam) and restores his honor.

Ultimately, however, the film keeps to its melodramatic course. The two friends quarrel over romantic jealousies and part ways. Yet Nur always comes back, and Sayf sticks up for him against the band's nefarious manager (Husayn al-Imam). And Nur is there on the sidelines cheering when Sayf wins true love and finally scores commercial success. That success is sited on the same Alexandria beach where Sayf first found artistic inspiration (although a second encounter with his muse—he takes an ice cream cone in the face—shatters his illusion). More important, it is also the site in which Abd al-Halim found his voice—and where his screen persona repeatedly suffered romantic anguish and won true love.

Violets are Blue
(*[Lay ya banafsig]*, Radwan al-Kashif 1993)

If Khayri Bishara paid doting homage to the Abd al-Halim film as genre, Radwan al-Kashif's directorial debut took a more hard-boiled approach, cynically re-working one of the Nightingale's debut films,

Our Sweet Days (Ayyamna al-hilwa), to underscore differences between a sweet past and sour present.[15] In the 1955 film, Abd al-Halim, Omar Sharif, and Ahmad Ramzi play struggling students who share a flat—and romantic interest—in Huda (Fatin Hamama), their downstairs neighbor. The competition, initially good natured, soon turns serious. Huda's engagement to Sharif's character precipitates the breaking of the friendship, until her life-threatening illness draws the comrades back together in a desperate effort to raise money for an operation (Ramzi takes a beating in the boxing ring, while Abd al-Halim returns to his village to wed a girl he does not love in order to secure his inheritance). The operation is a success, but Huda, despairing of her projected future life as an invalid, disobeys doctor's orders to remain in bed. As the three reunited friends, unaware of her true condition, walk off arm in arm, she watches from the hospital window, then falls dead.

Kashif's version turns the story on its head. His trio lives not in a respectable student flat that they rent from a cheeky but maternal landlady (Zaynat Sidqi), but here in a one-room hovel in an unpaved back alley on the edge of Cairo. To get by the friends share the meager profits of a *kushari* (a dish of rice-macaroni-lentils) cart, a double bed, and the good will of a close-knit community. Unfortunately, they also share affections for the beautiful, but materialistic Nadia (Lucy). Rather than fall for Ahmad (Faruq al-Fishawi), who most approximates Omar Sharif in the original, she weds Abbas (Nagah al-Mugi), a crass reworking of the muscle-bound Ramzi character, who commandeers the flat and, at Nadia's prodding, siphons off the business and attempts to monopolize the food wagon. The strained friendship is not helped by Nadia's sexual overtures to Ahmad, unthinkable in the earlier version. Outraged by the couple's behavior, Abbas's former roommates finally expel them from the flat.

Allusions to *Our Sweet Days* are explicit. On the two occasions when Ahmad visits a friend in the projection room of a local theater an Abd al-Halim film is being screened. The second time the film is *Our Sweet Days* (a brief snippet in which the jealous rivals reconcile and embrace).[16] Said (played by the diminutive Ashraf Abd al-Baqi, Nur in *Ice Cream in Glym*) incorporates the Abd al-Halim persona. He suffers most from unrequited love and the loss of brotherly camaraderie. In one scene he roams the Nile corniche as an Abd al-Halim tune plays in the background. In the film's most moving scene, he and Eid (Hasan Husni), the elderly blind conscience of the neighborhood, visit the Nightingale's grave, lean a picture of the departed saint against the tombstone and seat themselves before it. The elder man beseeches God to "open the gates of opportunity, as you did for Abd al-Halim Hafiz." The atmosphere in the tomb, he asserts, is blessed: "The beautiful sounds of his songs swirl around us . . . magical, like something sweet." In the background a young man sits reverentially, clutching a tape player to his chest. Two young women stand off to the other side, swaying in silent grief.

As in *Our Sweet Days,* death serves to reunite the friends. But it is not the tragic mortality of the beloved, rather the intrusion of ultimate social corruption. Said finds a disconsolate Abbas mopping floors at the neighborhood café—Nadia has dumped him—and brings him home. Ahmad, who had left for the city after torching the kushari cart, returns carrying his dying brother, a neighborhood denizen who had been lured into the underworld and has now been fatally wounded in a gang-related shoot-out. After an emotional reunion, bonded by blood, the three friends suddenly appear, surreally, in the desert, where they play the pipes and drums of a traditional wedding band.

Violets are Blue is a difficult film to categorize, for it is at once reverential and blasphemous. In his deconstruction of the mid-fifties melodrama and, by implication, an entire genre, Kashif reflects the cynicism so prevalent in an entire corpus of remakes produced since the seventies that speak to the shattered dreams of a cosmopolitan modernist ethos rooted in the early decades of this century (Armbrust 1996). That lost world was first personified by Muhammad Abd al-Wahhab, Abd al-Halim's musical patron, but has become more resolutely exemplified by the Nightingale, the former's cosmopolitan modernism giving way to the latter's social revolutionary aspirations. As the earlier screen personification of the middle class son, Abd al-Wahhab aspired for more, and when he attained higher social status he wore it well. In his wide-lapel suits and tilted tarbush, he was as dapper as Fred Astaire. Abd al-Halim's characters also attained success, but when he makes it, as in *The People's Idol,* trading his threadbare suit for silks and his modest repast for an elegant buffet, he still prefers to hang out with old chums and eat from the common bean pot. In this respect, the Nightingale's persona corresponds to ever-present populist images of Gamal Abdel Nasser. The positioning of Hafiz/Nasser in the films described above is clearly marked by textual and visual juxtapositions: the anthems, references to Nasser-era projects and, in *Violets are Blue,* pictures of the two side-by-side in the three friends' one-room hovel.

Terrorism and Shish Kabob
(*[al-Irhab wa al-kabab],* Sharif Arafa 1992)

To the generation that both rules and struggles against the constraints of a still too-dominant state, Abd al-Halim Hafiz personifies the romantic, idealistic dreams of lost youth. No one personifies contemporary cynicism better than the comic superstar Adil Imam. Imam's career began with bit parts in the mid-1960s, then took off with the stage play *School for Troublemakers (Madrasat al-mushaghibin)* in the seventies. For the past two decades, on stage and screen, he has been the most satirically vocal and physically comical exponent of commoner outrage. No wonder he has personified the downtrodden everyman in the most successful and illuminating cynically-altered re-makes of the optimistic classics of pre-Nasserist cinema (Armbrust 1996: 165–73, 206–12, 124–27). Imam's movies, especially his recent collaborations with director Sharif Arafa (son of Nasser-era director Saad Arafa) and scenarist Wahid Hamid, speak forthrightly, if in comic mood, to the disjunctures of a society whose social revolution, for all its faults, has been systematically dismantled since the infitah. In Imam's most enduring work, *Terrorism and Shish Kabob,* he and his collaborators took on the behemoth symbol of all that has gone wrong in Egypt, the Mugamaa, the towering bureaucratic nerve center of internal affairs that sits astride Tahrir Square in what has been since the Free Officers Revolution the center of downtown Cairo.

The Mugamaa is an unadorned modernist fourteen-story superstructure in which thousands work or come daily to file for documents, apply for licenses, or petition for social services. Although many associate the structure with the Nasserist public-sector bureaucracy, the building pre-dates the Free Officer revolution. In fact, by July 1952 the Mugamaa had already gained a reputation as an unkempt, inefficient edifice, precisely the opposite of its designers' intentions. "Filth Overwhelms the Building that Cost Millions," chided one weekly. Accompanied by photos of official papers piled high in the hallways, long lines of petitioners, and filthy water closet facilities, the text noted that elevators were scarce—one for every 700 employees—and hard to find, and wastebaskets lacking. "The most beautiful building in Cairo is filled with the rubble of routine."[17]

Terrorism and Shish Kabob revolves around the struggle of an average Egyptian named Ahmad, a civil engineer for the Cairo waterworks, to secure the transfer of his children to a neighborhood school. After a week of fruitless visits to the Mugamaa, where he joins an endless parade of robot-like petitioners, and where he fails to find the elusive Mr. Midhat, receiving no assistance from either his phone-bound secretary or his eternally-at-prayer assistant, the petitioner explodes. In the ensuing melee he winds up with a security guard's Kalashnikov. The guards flee, as do many of the thousands of people in the building, and Ahmad inadvertently winds up seizing the building and holding its remaining occupants hostage.

The ensuing pathos-tinged comedy makes several cinematic references to the golden oldies. One comic subplot involves the efforts of a portly young man to commit suicide by jumping from the tower. Played by a popular character actor, Alaa Wali al-Din,[18] the young man first struggles with his suicide note, a blistering letter to his mother who has forced him to marry a cousin who is fatter than him, then fails to physically lift his leg over the ledge in order to leap. Lest any clues be missed, the suicidal character provides explicit reference to the 1958 Salah Abu Sayf movie on which his character is playfully modeled. He concludes his note by explaining that "The idea [to jump] came to me from the television, from the film *Between Heaven and Earth.*" To those who really know their film history there is even an ironic twist: recognition that this movie (*[Bayna al-sama' wa al-ard],* Salah Abu Sayf 1959), now a classic of comic ensemble acting, failed at the theaters, but later gained popularity via television broadcasts.[19]

The other primary Nasser era referent is Abd al-Halim Hafiz. With his comically expressive face, Adil Imam in no way recalls the Nightingale; rather, he is comic successor to Nagib al-Rihani, Ismail Yasin, and Fuad al-Muhandis. Nonetheless, the Nightingale lurks in the wings. He croons in the backdrop one Thursday night when our hero catches a few moments of quiet at a local sandwich shop. Returning home to a sleeping flat, his weekly Friday respite upcoming, Imam's character turns to Abd al-Halim, first singing love lyrics ("I Love You," the same song featured in *Wife of an Important Person*) while undressing—though noisily and with increasing irritation—then resorts to a tape player to set a romantic mood. Alas, he fails to rouse, let alone arouse, his sleeping wife. "What's with Abd al-Halim at this hour?" she complains, finally awakened. "Abd al-Halim is always with us in our thoughts," Imam protests. "Life's pressures make us forgetful, but we remember him as soon as things are not so bad."

Terrorism and Shish Kabob ends on a sober, but mildly triumphal note. The "terrorist" wins over his captives by demanding the government supply them with meat—shish kabob—for lunch. A frustrated interior minister, played with understated wit by Kamal al-Shinawi—the villainous Khalid Safwan in *Karnak*—tries unsuccessfully to assuage them with a counter offer of box dinners from Kentucky Fried Chicken. The state is pilloried throughout, from the inhumanity of the security officers to the ineptitude of their foot soldiers, to the suspect piety of government ministers, who use the minaret of the adjacent Umar Makram mosque as their command post. Lower-level officials veil their own incompetence behind outward demonstrations of piety or spend hours on the phone bemoaning the prices of staple goods. They, at least, come to see themselves equally as victims of a soul-less state, this through the eyes of their "captor."

In the dramatic denouement, the exhausted "terrorist" informs his hostages that he will allow them to leave. Government officials, tired of the standoff and no closer to understanding their adversary, have threatened to storm the building with no thought to innocent casualties. "You may be worthless in the eyes of the government, but you are very precious to me," the beleaguered engineer tells his assembly. No orator in prior scenes, he suddenly embarks upon an eloquent monologue, during which he roams amidst his captives, smiling and patting them on the shoulder:

> My demands? I have no demands. I came to get a certificate for my children. I want to have them moved to a school nearer home. But since matters have come to a climax, our demands too must be dramatic! All

> my life I have obeyed the government. The present one, the one before it, and I'll obey the coming one. Suppose I didn't obey, what would happen? Nothing. I'd be left to stew in my own juices. I commute to work crammed in the bus, saying "Glory to He who has subdued them unto us."[20] Prices are spiraling, what of it? I have only a couple of children—I obey the Government Planning Authority. I have only a boy and girl, thank God they're fine. The class is overcrowded, with eighty-four pupils in it. The children come home worn out, dizzy, and pale from the overcrowding and the air pollution. Still, thank God, they're all right. Nothing gives me trouble but obtaining bread. I stand in a long queue. I suffer getting it, and I suffer eating it. Like the rest of you, I'm humble and content. [Sitting down.] My only demand is for the recognition of my humanity. I don't want to be abused at home, at work, or on the street. I think for such demands I should not be penalized or reprimanded or censured. But since matters have come to a head, come on, demand what you will. I'm at your service. . . .

The dramatic power of this theatrical monologue recalls a similar episode in Youssef Chahine's *The Land*, when Abu Suwaylim, equally beleaguered, beaten down by government oppression, stands amongst his fellow peasants and recalls the days when "we were men." And, as Abu Suwaylim rallies his neighbors, now Ahmad's Mugamaa captives refuse to abandon him. Instead of remaining alone inside the structure, easy prey for police sharpshooters, the "terrorist" descends the stairway and exits the building along with the others. As he walks through the police cordon, visibly tense, but unrecognized, a journalist sticks a tape recorder in his face and asks him if he saw the "crazy terrorist." "Yes, I saw the crazy terrorist," our hero replies. "He is neither very tall nor very short; neither very bulky nor very lean; neither very dark nor very fair. He was like any of us."

Thereafter he vanishes across Tahrir Square into the bright lights of downtown Cairo. In a burst of civic enthusiasm in the 1954 classic

Life or Death, the police chief of Cairo stopped his manhunt for an escaped convict in order to save the life of a doomed pharmaceutical patient, a faceless man in the crowd. "We serve the Republic around the clock," Yusuf Wahbi proudly tells the grateful family, then exits, gallantly, back to work. Three decades later, in Atif al-Tayyib's *The Bus Driver* the faceless crowd provides haven for the anti-social predator, until the righteous individual finally acts quickly enough to out him. Ten years after that, in *Terrorism and Shish Kabob,* the crowd provides ultimate sanctuary to the faceless rebel, a man "like any of us" who has persuaded them that they are dearer to him than to the Republic. Police experts scrutinize the exiting citizenry, who pay them no heed, once oblivious, now hostile to government efforts to regulate order in an unfriendly metropolis.

Terrorism and Shish Kabob captured public attention in the way only a formula genre film can when a cast that combines star power (Adil Imam, Yusra, Kamal al-Shinawi) with polished character players (Alaa Wali al-Din, Ashraf Abd al-Baqi, Ahmad Ragab, et al.) meets a particularly clever script at a particularly potent time: in this case an upsurge of religious-based political violence and the equally violent response of state forces. The film also, perhaps inadvertently, captured official attention in unexpected ways. In the years immediately afterward, the cacophony of randomly parked cars, quick-food stands, and tripod box cameras snapping identification photos (with Rushdi Abaza's "everything needs a license" echoing) that characterized life outside the Mugamaa were replaced by a pave-stone plaza, named ironically not for Nasser, whose public sector the building is usually taken to symbolize, but for his liberalizing successor, Sadat, whose infitah opened so many perilous doors. The behemoth itself, covered with layers of Cairo dust and smog, also got a face lift, whitewashed from top to bottom. Inside, alas, little has changed.

CINDERELLA COMES HOME

In the past decade Egypt—and the Arab world, still the only audience for most Egyptian productions—has lost several more of its golden age cinema stars: the actors Farid Shawqi, Layla Murad, Ahmad Mazhar, and Tahiya Carioca;[21] and the directors Salah Abu Sayf, Henry Baracat, and Hussam al-Din Mustafa. No one doubts that their likes will not be replaced. They represent a special era to those who still revere their work. This is not a forthright statement of politics, but it is certainly imbued with a politic.

The end of the millennium afforded many opportunities for retrospective, including the motion picture arts. The popular picture magazine *al-Kawakib,* a venerable journal with a long tradition of covering the arts, published a special issue dedicated to "The greatest beauties of Egyptian cinema in the twentieth century." On the cover, in a purple, yellow, and black polka-dot sleeveless dress, her hair blown wistfully across pink lips, pale skin, and almond eyes—very sixties—was Suad Husni. Why her, amidst all the others?

> We selected numerous photos for the cover of this issue! Among the multitudes of beautiful starlets in our cinema history, which should we choose? Which photo should grace the cover of this retrospective issue? The selection was difficult. Each one of them deserved to be selected. We didn't take long; our gaze turned quickly to her. She about whom Kamal al-Shinawi once said: "When she sits before the mirror she does not make herself up the way other beauties do. Rather, she makes herself up to diminish her beauty, so the resentful won't envy her." To her, in London, where she now resides, battling the pains of love and hope, optimism and smile. To Suad Husni. We think you will agree with our choice. We think all the starlets will welcome our choice. Salutations of love and admiration and esteem to "Cinderella"—to Suad Husni, for all that she has accomplished and achieved, suffered and enjoyed.[22]

As the editors note, the competition was stiff, but few could argue with the selection.

Suad Husni, who stood in the same league with Fatin Hamama, the greatest actress of Arab film, might be considered the cinematic heroine of the generation that came to the silver screen in the 1960s (Ramzi 1997: 118,121). The big difference is that Fatin Hamama, who

Suad Husni—the fairest of them all (*al-Kawakib,* December 1999). Courtesy of *al-Kawakib.*

still acts on occasion, only when drawn to a particular role, carries with her no element of melodramatic tragedy. Having first captured Egypt's heart as a nine-year-old in 1940, she successfully made transitions to romantic lead in the fifties and sixties, then mother and grandmother, and has aged with grace. After two early marriages, to the director Mahmud Zulificar and then Omar Sharif, she settled into a long-term relationship with a man who has no professional relationship to the arts. Suad Husni, unfortunately, had a far rougher ride, even, according to those who best knew her, in her glory years.

Talent ran in her blood, but so too did emotional scars. Her father, a famous calligrapher, was a classic monstrous backstage parent. As a three-year-old, Suad sang on the radio with her siblings, including the famous Nagat al-Saghira, a half-sister. The troupe was a hit, but away from the microphone their father, hoping to keep his children petite and dependent, deprived them of food and denied them an education. Suad supposedly never learned to read or write until she was sixteen; by then she had been taken in by the renowned composer and dramatist Abd al-Rahman al-Khamisi who spotted the actress behind the voice.[23] She broke into films at eighteen—some insist she was younger—in the romantic Baracat vehicle *Hasan and Naima* (*Hasan wa Na'ima* 1959), playing a village girl who elopes with her lover (the singer Fuad Muharram) to avoid forced matrimony to her father's foreman. A year later, the photo-feature weekly *Akhir saa* listed her first among twenty "new faces" for the sixties.[24]

She went on to become the "Cinderella of the Arab screen," transformed into a princess through the magic of the movies. She could sing and dance, do comedy and romance, and evoke tremendous pathos. Ever youthful and petite, perhaps a cruel irony given her upbringing, in her early twenties she could play a frustrated actress masquerading as a young girl hoping to capture a television role in *Too Young for Love* (*[Saghira ala al-hubb]*, Niyazi Mustafa 1966), one of her most enduring parts. In dramatic roles she increasingly came to personify helpless individuals trapped by oppressive political and social power structures: the working-class courtesan in *Cairo 1930,* the peasant woman forced to divorce her loving husband in *The Second Wife,* the spoiled but suffocated pasha's daughter in *Sunset, Sunrise.* No role is recalled more fondly than Zouzou, the saucy co-ed ashamed of her dance-hall roots. And for many no role is recalled with more discomfort than the equally idealistic Zaynab—Zouzou more formally named—who is raped and tortured, then turned state's agent in the seminal de-Nasserist film, *Karnak*.[25]

Suad Husni was not easy to work with. "She was considered a difficult actress, and she was difficult," recalls Muhammad Khan, who directed her once, in the early eighties.[26] Salah Abu Sayf told me he heard the same thing from Niyazi Mustafa *(Too Young for Love* and *Crazy Kids),* but he managed to pull two powerful performances out of her *(Cairo 1930* and *The Second Wife).* Her string of hits—and important films—continued through the seventies and into the eighties, although at a slower pace. She also scored big on the little screen, in the blockbuster seventies serial *He and She (Huwwa wa hiyya)* opposite a young Ahmad Zaki, lately the portrayer of presidents.[27] She did not, however, handle aging or artistic mortality with grace. Her penultimate film, *Third Class* (*[al-Daraga al-thalitha],* Sharif Arafa 1988), closed after one week, a failure from which some suggest she never recovered emotionally.[28] In her final film, *The Shepherd and the Women* (*[al-Ra'i wa al-nisa'],* Ali Badrakhan 1991), she played a middle aged widow who competes with her daughter and sister-in-law for the love of an ex-con, a prison pal of her dead husband, who comes to visit, then stays. It is, argue many, a great mature role, one in which the haggard widow becomes increasingly radiant as she rediscovers the depth of her feelings for the new man of the house. But the once eternally youthful actress hated the way she looked on screen and abruptly announced her retirement.

She did not quite vanish like Garbo or Layla Murad; nor did she don a veil and shun public life as Shadia has done in recent years.[29] A series of ailments that resulted in substantial weight gain and partial paralysis fueled her depression. She appeared onstage at the 1996 Cairo Film Festival to receive the accolades of an adoring crowd, but shortly afterward went into seclusion, spending long periods of time abroad, particularly in London, for treatment, but also to hide away. There, friends report, her telephone answering machine greeted callers with a snippet from the title song to *Watch Out for Zouzou.* And there, "in the city of fog . . . far from her homeland," where "exile produced the bitterness of solitude that was greater than the ailment itself," she fell to her death from a sixth-story balcony in June 2001.[30]

If her decision to abandon Egypt for Europe in the early 1990s left a void—there were surely other roles to play, as there have been for Madiha Yusri, Huda Sultan, Layla Tahir, Nelly, and the incomparable Fatin—Suad Husni's death sent the nation into mourning unlike any show of grief seen since the seventies. "We killed her" ran a headline in *Akhir saa:*

> We killed her. We killed Suad Husni. In the climactic moments of her frailty, at the height of her excruciating pain, which left her paralyzed. And at the time in which she was most in need of helping hands to caress her broken back, and for warm hearts to drive away the coldness of loneliness and melancholy. . . . We killed her. We killed Suad Husni.[31]

Egyptians continued to love her, to miss her, throughout her exile. Such sentiment was explicit in her selection by *al-Kawakib* as the fairest of all. Yet the posthumous tributes smacked implicitly and explicitly of survivor guilt. Some close associates in the arts simply could not countenance her demise, particularly, as most presume, by suicide. And so, in the all-pervasive culture of conspiracy, she was murdered, most likely by the mysterious friend—mysterious because she was not a public personality—in whose flat Suad had taken refuge and from whose balcony she must have been pushed. If not an unfamiliar Egyptian expatriate, why not the Israelis, the Americans, radical Islamist terrorists? After all, many protested, Egyptians do not commit suicide (except, of course, in the movies, where they are always trying!).[32] When Cinderella's body arrived at Cairo airport, a delegation of actors commandeered the coffin. Guild officers, led by al-Sayyid Radi, promised an investigation. Her funeral, not downtown at the official Umar Makram mosque (just adjacent to the Mugamaa), but at the less stuffy Mustafa Mahmud mosque across the river in Mohandisin, was by all accounts a "popular processional" attended by thousands, celebrities and common people mingling together in an outpouring of grief.[33] If the funeral did not rival those of Umm Kulthum, Nasser, or Abd al-Halim, that is in part due to the times—this is a more jaded age—and in part due to the rapidity with which police officials spirited the actress's coffin into the hearse so it could be driven, not accompanied on foot, towards her final resting place, well outside Cairo on the road to the Fayoum.

Her double exit—first self-imposed exile, then suicide—remains emblematic of a bygone age. On television she remains and will remain an oft-viewed souvenir. The anniversary of her death may well become an annual occasion for tribute, as the month in which Abd Halim Hafiz died has been.[34] That she jumped (or fell) on his birthday, June 21, only adds to the mystique, and fuels the undying speculation about their relationship. Suad Husni's self-imposed exile from homeland, even if for personal, psychological needs, then her willful decision to leave this life, have left Egyptians with a profound sense of loss. They wanted their Cinderella—loveable, funny, sexy, tragic—to grow old with them, as Abd al-Halim—and even Nasser—could not. In this sense Egyptians demonstrate a profound ability to utilize melodrama and movie stardom—the primary characteristics of their cinema—as a focal point for nostalgia, a compass for civic identity, a black-and-white souvenir of public memory in a once optimistic, but ever after troubled post-revolutionary society. "The era of the Arab has begun, and with it their sweetest days," trumpeted *al-Musawwar* in 1958, borrowing the title of an early Abd al-Halim-Fatin-Omar hit film. Cinderella's tragic return from exile only serves to underscore that those sweet days were so very long ago.

Notes

1. For the housing crunch that existed by the mid-1960s, see Abu-Lughod 1971: 230–37.

2. Their last film together appeared in 1976. Both continued to act in films into the mid-1990s, but these tended to be smaller roles and not in tandem.

3. For the best description of the system, as well as the general predicament of riding public buses, see Waterbury (1978: 161–75).

4. *Akhir saa,* January 11, 1956, p. 30.

5. *Akhir Saa,* July 17, 1957, pp. 23–24.

6. See the *"Mish ma'ul"* series of photo-essays in *Akhir saa* in the spring of 1967.

7. For population and public and private vehicle statistics, see Waterbury 1978: 145–46, 151–53.

8. In one of the more shocking—and still uncharacteristic—scenes in recent years, in early 1992 a young woman was assaulted on a bus at the densely crowded Ataba terminus while people kept to their own business. The incident, no doubt rescripted according to the telling, was recounted frequently on the streets for months afterwards.

9. This less-than-flattering view of Ramsis was first reported to me by Ibrahim Sadek, son of one of Farouk's ministers and no Nasserist, but in this case fondly recalling classic adolescent jibes at official public culture.

10. In recent years the zoo, the first on African soil, has been revamped. And for years city and antiquities officials have discussed removing Ramsis to a more suitable, less polluted environment.

11. Mahfuz Abd al-Rahman first pointed me towards this film as a significant social text.

12. *Ruz al-Yusuf,* November 1, 1954, p. 62.

13. I would like to thank Khayri Bishara for his comments on this section.

14. Hafiz died on March 30, 1977. Al-Atrash, who died in December 1974, aged fifty-nine, was also an accomplished screen presence and master vaudevillian. He starred in thirty films, almost one yearly from 1942 through 1975, mostly light melodramatic musicals in which he played against many of Egypt's leading ladies. He was often paired, in Crosby-Hope or Martin-Lewis fashion, with Ismail Yasin. Umm Kulthum died in February 1975 at seventy. A superstar for six decades, she made only six films, all released between 1936 and 1947.

15. Kashif's dedication is to "the writers of the 60s and the joy of composition," but his plot inspiration is clearly rooted a decade earlier. The title refers to a song performed most famously by Salih Abd al-Hayy (lyrics by Bayram al-Tunsi, music by Riyad al-Sunbati).

16. The first clip is the infamous slap delivered by Imad Hamdi to Abd al-Halim in *The Sins.*

17. *Akhir saa,* March 18, 1953, pp. 14–15.

18. With the recent hit comedy *Abboud on the Borders* (1999), Wali al-Din has emerged as a comic lead.

19. The film, which revolves around a group of people trapped in an elevator, starred Hind Rustam, Mahmud al-Maligi, Abd al-Munim Ibrahim, Abd al-Salam al-Nabulsi, and Said Abu Bakr, and is based on a story by Naguib Mahfouz.

20. Earlier Imam films have featured satirical routines on crowded buses. This film contains a particularly sober scene in which a old man explodes in a tirade against the breakdown of social order and civic responsibility.

21. At her death, Tahiya Carioca received rare recognition for an Egyptian star with a major obituary in the *New York Times* (September 22, 1999). However well-deserved, this stands in stark contrast to the total lack of coverage for others of equal or greater renown.

22. *Al-Kawakib,* December 28, 1999, p. 66.

23. For al-Khamisi's recollections, see "Qissat iktishafi li-Suad Husni," *al-Arabi,* July 1, 2001, p. 15

24. The others who indeed went on to become noted stars were Zizi Badrawi (9), Shweikar (18), and Nadia Lutfi (20). None of the men listed became steady leads. *Akhir saa,* November 9, 1960.

25. In 1996, to mark the centennial of Egyptian cinema, critics counted nine of her films amongst the top 100 produced by the industry. They were: *Cairo 30; The Second Wife; Sunset, Sunrise; My Wife and the Dog* (Said Marzuq 1971); *The Choice* (Youssef Chahine 1971); *Watch out for Zouzou; Karnak; Whom Should We Shoot* (Kamal al-Shaykh 1975); and *People at the Top* (Ali Badrakhan 1981).

26. "In the present tense," *al-Ahram Weekly,* June 28–July 4, 2001, p. 12.

27. The popular musical soundtrack to this series, with lyrics by Salah Jahin—after al-Khamisi her mentor and surrogate father—has long been available on cassette. Upon her death the cassette was included along with a special commemorative issue of *Akhbar al-nugum* (June 30, 2001).

28. *Al-Sinima wa al-nass,* July 14, 2001, pp. 24–25.

29. Muhammad Khan recalls a brief period during which she adopted conservative dress. "It was the beginning of a thing, you know, with religion," he notes. "But that didn't last long" (*al-Ahram Weekly,* June 28–July 4, 2001, p. 12).

30. *Akhbar al-yawm,* June 23, 2001, p. 18.

31. *Akhir saa,* June 27, 2001, p. 6.

32. Such arguments raised seemingly inevitable links to American insistence—and official Egyptian denials—that the Egyptian pilot of Egypt Air flight 990 had deliberately crashed into the Atlantic in the Fall of 1999. For one variation on this theme, see Muhammad Wagdi Qandil, "Ishtibah fi masraʿ Suʿad," *al-Akhbar,* July 10, 2001, p. 25.

33. The night before there had been a memorial service at Umar Makram. It drew a crowd, but not nearly the numbers that were at the funeral the following day.

34. A biopic of her life, with Mona Zaki, lately the young Jihan al-Sadat, in the lead, was reportedly in the works within a month of Husni's death (*al-Sinima wa al-nass,* July 21, 2001, pp. 4–5).

REFERENCES

Sources Cited

Abd al-Al, Ahmad. 1984. "Thawrat Yulyu wa thalathun amman min al-tarikh." *Al-Funun* 5 (20), pp. 14–18.

Abd al-Rahman, Magdi. 1996. "Al-Mumiya' abr thalatha tawarikh." *Al-Qahira* 159 (February), pp. 220–30.

Abd al-Rahman, Mahfuz. 1996. *Nasir 56.* Cairo: Dar al-Mawqaf al-Arabi.

Abd al-Salam, Shadi. 1996. "Sinariyu al-Mumiya'." *Al-Qahira* 159 (February), pp. 254–304.

Abdalla, Ahmed. 1985. *The Student Movement and Nationalist Politics in Egypt, 1923–1973.* London: Al-Saqi.

Abdel-Malek, Anouar. 1968. *Egypt: Military Society.* New York: Vintage.

Abd el Qoddous, Ihsan. 1978. *I Am Free and Other Stories.* Tr. by Trevor Le Gassick. Cairo: General Egyptian Book Organization.

Abdennour, Samia. 1993. "Tawfiq Saleh: The Idealistic Realist." *Al-Ahram Weekly,* November 18–24.

Abu al-Futuh, Amira. 1982. *Ihsan Abd al-Quddus yatadhakkir.* Cairo: al-Hai'a al-Misriya al-Amma lil-Kitab.

Abu-Lughod, Janet. 1971. *Cairo: 1001 Years of the City Victorious.* Princeton: Princeton University Press.

Abu-Lughod, Lila. 1993. "Finding a Place for Islam: Egyptian Television Serials and the National Interest." *Public Culture* 5, pp. 493–513.

———. 1995. "The Objects of Soap Opera: Egyptian Television and the Cultural Politics of Modernity." In Daniel Miller, ed., *Worlds Apart: Modernity through the Prism of the Local.* London: Routledge. Pp. 190–210.

———. 1998. "Television and the Virtues of Education: Upper Egyptian Encounters with State Culture." In Nicholas S. Hopkins and Kirsten S. Westergaard, eds., *Directions of Change in Rural Egypt.* Cairo: American University in Cairo Press. Pp. 147-65.

Abou Chadi, Ali. 1995. "Le secteur public 1963–1972: esquisse d'analyse economique et artistique." In Magda Wassef, ed., *Egypte: 100 ans de cinema.* Paris: Institut du Monde Arabe. Pp. 118–23.

Abu Shadi, Ali. 1996. "Genres in Egyptian Cinema." In Alia Arasoughly, ed., *Screens of Life: Critical Film Writing from the Arab World.* Quebec: World Heritage Press. Pp. 84–129.

———. 1998. *Al-Sinima wa al-siyasa.* Cairo: Dar Shariqiyat.

Adli, Nadir. 1995. *Kamal al-Shaykh.* Cairo: Mahrajan al-Qahira al-Sinima'i al-Dawli.

Allen, Roger M.A. 1982. *The Arabic Novel: An Historical and Critical Introduction.* Syracuse: Syracuse University Press.

———, ed. 1987. *Modern Arabic Literature.* New York: Ungar.

Altman, Rick. 1987. *The American Film Musical.* Bloomington and Indianapolis: Indiana University Press.

Amin, Galal. 2001. *Whatever Happened to the Egyptians: Change in Egyptian Society from 1950 to the Present.* Cairo: American University in Cairo Press.

Amr, Munir. 1995. *Al-Nisa' fi hayat Abd al-Halim Hafiz.* Cairo: Madbuli al-Saghir.

Ang, Ien. 1985. *Watching Dallas: Soap Opera and the Melodramatic Imagination.* London: Routledge.

Armbrust, Walter. 1995. "New Cinema, Commercial Cinema, and the Modernist Tradition." *Alif: Journal of Comparative Poetics* 15, pp. 81–129.

———. 1996. *Mass Culture and Modernism in Egypt.* Cambridge: Cambridge University Press.

———. 1998. "When the Lights go Down in Cairo: Cinema as Secular Ritual," *Visual Anthropology* 10: 413–42.

———. 2000a. "The Golden Age before the Golden Age: Commercial Egyptian Cinema before the 1960s." In Walter Armbrust, ed., *Mass Mediations: New Approaches to Popular Culture in the Middle East and Beyond.* Berkeley and Los Angeles: University of California Press. Pp. 292–327.

———. 2000b. "Farid Shauqi: Tough Guy, Family Man, Cinema Star." In Mai Ghassoub and Emma Sinclair-Webb, eds., *Imagined Masculinities: Male Identity and Culture in the Modern Middle East.* London: Saqi. Pp. 199–226.

Armes, Roy. 1987. *Third World Film Making and the West.* Berkeley and Los Angeles: University of California Press.

Ayad, Christophe. 1995. "Le star system: de la splendeur au voile." In Magda Wassef, ed., *Egypte: 100 ans de cinema.* Paris: Institut du Monde Arabe. Pp. 134–41.

Badawi, M. M. 1993. *A Short History of Modern Arabic Literature.* Oxford: Clarendon Press.

Baker, Raymond William. 1974. "Egypt in Shadows: Films and the Political Order." *American Behavioral Scientist* 17 (3): 393–423.

Bakr, Abd al-Wahab. 1982. *Arms Manufacture in Modern Egypt: History and Myth.* Los Angeles: California State University.

Bakr (Muhammad), Abd al-Wahab. 1988. *Al-Gaysh al-Misri wa harb Filastin.* Cairo: Dar al-Ma'arif.

Baron, Beth. 1997. "Nationalist Iconography: Egypt as a Woman." In James Jankowski and Israel Gershoni, eds., *Rethinking Nationalism in the Arab Middle East.* New York: Columbia University Press. Pp. 105–24.

Beinin, Joel. 1998. *The Dispersion of Egyptian Jewry: Culture, Politics, and the Formation of a Modern Diaspora.* Berkeley and Los Angeles: University of California Press.

Berque, Jacques. 1972. *Egypt: Imperialism and Revolution.* New York: Praeger.

Bodnar, John. 1992. *Remaking America: Public Memory, Commemoration, and Patriotism in the Twentieth Century.* Princeton: Princeton University Press.

Brown, Nathan. 1990. *Peasant Politics in Modern Egypt: The Struggle Against the State.* New Haven: Yale University Press.

Chakravarty, Sumita S. 1993. *National Identity in Indian Popular Cinema: 1947–1987.* Austin: University of Texas Press.

El-Charkawi, Galal. 1966. "History of the UAR Cinema." In Georges Sadoul, ed., *The Cinema in the Arab Countries.* Beirut: Interarab Centre of Cinema and Television. Pp. 69–97.

Colla, Elliot. 2000. "Shadi Abd al-Salam's *al-Mumiya:* Ambivalence and the Egyptian Nation-State." In Ali Abdullatif Ahmida, ed., *Beyond Colonialism and Nationalism in the Maghrib.* Hampshire, UK: Palgrave. Pp. 109–43.

Culhane, Hind Rassam. 1995. *East/West, an Ambiguous State of Being: The Construction and Representation of Egyptian Cultural Identity in Egyptian Film.* New York: Peter Lang.

Custen, George F. 1992. *Bio/Pics: How Hollywood Constructed Public History.* New Brunswick, NJ: Rutgers University Press.

Danielson, Virginia. 1991. "Shaping Tradition in Arabic Song: The Career and Repertory of Umm Kulthum." Ph.D. dissertation, University of Illinois.

———. 1997. *The Voice of Egypt: Umm Kulthum, Arabic Song, and Egyptian Society in the Twentieth Century.* Chicago: University of Chicago Press.

Darwich, Mustafa. 1987. "La Censure, le Cinema et d'autres Choses." *Bulletin du CEDEJ* 21 (1), pp. 97–107.

———. 1995. "Al-Riqaba wa al-sinima al-ukhra: shahadat raqib." *Alif: Journal of Comparative Poetics* 15, pp. 91–98.

Daud, Raga'. 1996. "Lughat al-musiqa fi aflam Shadi Abd al-Salam." *Al-Qahira* 159 (February), pp. 142–45.

Dickinson, Thorold and Catherine De la Roche. 1972. *Soviet Cinema.* New York: Arno.

Dougherty, Roberta. 1998. "Good Girls, Gun Molls with a Heart of Gold: Female Dancers in Egyptian Cinema." Paper presented at the Middle East Studies Association meeting.

———. 2000. "Badi'a Masabni, Artiste and Modernist: The Egyptian Print Media's Carnival of National Identity." In Walter Armbrust, ed., *Mass Mediations: New Approaches to Popular Culture in the Middle East and Beyond* (Berkeley and Los Angeles: University of California Press. Pp. 243–68.

Douglas, Allen and Fadwa Malti-Douglas. 1994. *Arab Comic Strips: Politics of an Emerging Mass Culture.* Bloomington and Indianapolis: Indiana University Press.

Elsaessar, Thomas. 1995. "Tales of Sound and Fury: Observations on the Family Melodrama." In Barry Keith Grant, ed., *Film Genre Reader II.* Austin: University of Texas Press. Pp. 350–80.

El Enany, Rasheed. 1993. *Naguib Mahfouz: The Pursuit of Meaning.* London and New York: Routledge.

Ezzedine, Salah. 1966. "The Role of Music in Arabic Films." In Georges Sadoul, ed., *The Cinema in the Arab Countries.* Beirut: Interarab Centre of Cinema and Television. Pp. 46–53.

Fathy, Hassan. 1973. *Architecture for the Poor: An Experiment in Rural Egypt.* Chicago and London: University of Chicago Press.

Farid, Samir. 1993. *Hiwar ma' al-sinima al-Misriya.* Cairo: Mahragan al-Qahira al-Sinima'iya al-Dawli.

———. 1995a. *Fatin Hamama.* Cairo: Sanduq al-Tanmiya al-Thaqafiyya.

———. 1995b. "La censure, mode d'emploi." In Magda Wassef, ed., *Egypte: 100 ans de cinema.* Paris: Institut du Monde Arabe. Pp. 102–17.

———. 1996. "Periodization of Egyptian Cinema." In Alia Arasoughly, ed., *Screens of Life: Critical Film Writing from the Arab World.* Quebec: World Heritage Press. Pp. 1–18.

Fawal, Ibrahim. 2001. *Youssef Chahine.* London: British Film Institute.

Fayid, Ziyad. 1999. *Al-Thawra fi al-sinima al-Misriya.* Cairo: al-Hai'a al-Misriyya al-Amma lil-Kitab.

Gabriel, Teshome H. 1982. *Third Cinema in the Third World: The Aesthetics of Liberation.* Ann Arbor: UMI Research Press.

———. 1999. "The Intolerable Gift: Residues and Traces of a Journey." In Hamid Naficy, ed., *Home, Exile, Homeland: Film, Media, and the Politics of Place.* New York and London: Routledge. Pp. 75–84.

Gaffney, Jane. 1987. "The Egyptian Cinema: Industry and Art in a Changing Society." *Arab Studies Quarterly* 9 (1), pp. 53–75.

Ghanem, Fathi. 1966. *The Man Who Lost His Shadow.* Tr. by Desmond Stewart. Cairo: American University in Cairo Press.

Goodwin, James. 1993. *Eisenstein, Cinema, and History.* Urbana and Chicago: University of Illinois Press.

Gordon, Joel. 1989a. "The False Hopes of 1950: The Wafd's Last Hurrah and the Demise of Egypt's Old Order." *International Journal of Middle East Studies* 21, pp. 193–214.

———. 1989b. "The Myth of the Savior: Egypt's Just Tyrants on the Eve of Revolution." *Journal of the American Research Center in Egypt* 26: 223–37.

———. 1992. *Nasser's Blessed Movement: Egypt's Free Officers and the July Revolution.* Oxford and New York: Oxford University Press.

———. 1997. "Secular and Religious Memory in Egypt: Recalling Nasserist Civics." *The Muslim World* 87 (2), pp. 94–110.

———. 1998. "Becoming the Image: Words of Gold, Talk Television, and Ramadan Nights on the Little Screen." *Visual Anthropology* 10, pp. 247–63.

———. 1999. "Film, Fame, and Public Memory: Egyptian Biopics from *Mustafa Kamil* to *Nasser 56.*" *International Journal of Middle East Studies* 31, pp. 61–79.

———. 2000. "Nasser 56/Cairo 96: Reimaging Egypt's Lost Community." In Walter Armbrust, ed., *Mass Mediations: New Approaches to Popular Culture in the Middle East and Beyond.* Berkeley and Los Angeles: University of California Press. Pp. 161–81.

———. 2001a. "*With God on Our Side.* Scripting Nasser's Mutiny." In Jane Hathaway, ed., *Resistance, Repression, Reinvention: Mutiny in Comparative Contexts.* New York: Praeger. Pp. 253–72.

———. 2001b. "Class-crossed Lovers: Popular Film and Social Change in Nasser's New Egypt." *Quarterly Review of Film and Video* 18 (4), pp. 385–96.

———. 2002. "Days of Anxiety/*Days of Sadat:* Impersonating Egypt's Flawed Hero on the Egyptian Screen." *Journal of Film and Video* (forthcoming).

Gran, Peter. 1978. "Modern Trends in Egyptian Historiography: a Review Article." *International Journal of Middle East Studies* 9, pp. 367–71.

al-Hadiri, Ahmad. 1984a. "Al-Haram: al-tazawag al-murhaf bayna al-rumansiya wa al-waqa'iya." *Al-Funun* 5 (20), pp. 43–50.

———. 1984b [1962]. *"Sira' al-abtal:* indama yartafaq al-waqa' ila mustawa al-fan al-rafi'." *Al-Funun* 5 (20), pp. 68–69.

Hafiz, Abd al-Halim. 1977. *Hayati.* Cairo: Ruz al-Yusuf.

al-Hakim, Sulayman. 2000. *Tahiya Karioka: bayna al-raqs wa al-siyasa.* Cairo: Dar al-Khayyal.

al-Hakim, Tawfik. 1985. *The Return of Consciousness.* Tr. by R. Bayley Winder. New York: New York University Press.

———. 1989. *Maze of Justice: Diary of a Country Prosecutor.* Tr. by Abba Eban. Austin: University of Texas Press.

Hasanayn, Adil. 1995. *Ayyamna al-hilwa.* Cairo: Amadu.

Haykal, Muhammad Hasanayn. 1961. *Azmat al-muthaqifin.* Cairo: Dar al-Udaba'.

Heikal, Mohamed. 1983. *Autumn of Fury: The Assassination of Sadat.* New York: Random House.

Idris, Yusuf. 1984. *The Sinners.* Tr. by Kristin Peterson-Ishaq. Washington, D.C.: Three Continents Press.

al-Imrusi, Magdi. 1994. *A'azz al-nass.* Cairo: Adil al-Balak.

Ismail, Fayiq. 1984. *"Sira' al-abtal."* *Al-Funun* 5 (20), p. 70.

Kassem, Mahmoud. 1995. "Adaptation, egyptianisation et 'remake.'" In Magda Wassef, ed., *Egypte: 100 ans de cinema.* Paris: Institut du Monde Arabe.

Khan, Mohamed. 1969. *An Introduction to the Egyptian Cinema.* London: Informatics.

Lang, Robert. 1989. *American Film Melodrama: Griffith, Vidor, Minnelli.* Princeton: Princeton University Press.

Larkin, Margaret. 1992. "A Brigand Hero of Egyptian Colloquial Literature." *Journal of Arabic Literature* 23, pp. 49–64.

Leff, Leonard J. and Jerold Simmons. 1990. *The Dame in the Kimono: Hollywood, Censorship, and the Production Code from the 1920s to the 1960s.* New York: Anchor.

LeGassick, Trevor. 1977. "Mahfuz' *al-Karnak.* The Quiet Conscience of Nasir's Egypt Revealed." *Middle East Journal* 31 (2), pp. 205–12.

Lohr, William. 1987. *World Cinema Since 1945.* New York: Ungar.

Mahfouz, Medhat. 1995. "Les Salles de Projection dans l'Industrie Cinematographique." In Magda Wassef, ed., *Egypte: 100 Ans de Cinema.* Paris: Institut du Monde Arabe. Pp. 124–29.
Mahfouz, Naguib. 1978. *Miramar.* Tr. by Fatma Moussa-Mahmoud. London: Heinemann.
———. 1993. *Adrift on the Nile.* Tr. by Frances Liardet. New York: Anchor.
al-Malak, Kamal and Abd al-Mun'im Sa'd. 1977. *Abd al-Halim Hafiz wa al-sinima.* Cairo: [?].
Malkmus, Lizbeth. 1988. "The 'New' Egyptian Cinema: Adapting Genre Conventions to a Changing Society." *Cineaste* 16 (3), pp. 30–33.
Malkmus, Lizbeth and Roy Armes. 1991. *Arab and African Film Making.* London: Zed.
Mankekar, Purnima. 1993. "Television Tales and a Woman's Rage: A Nationalist Recasting of Draupadi's Disrobing." *Public Culture* 5, pp. 469–92.
McLeave, Hugh. 1969. *The Last Pharaoh: Farouk of Egypt.* New York: McCall.
Menicucci, Garay. 1998. "Unlocking the Arab Celluloid Closet: Homosexuality in Egyptian Film." *Middle East Report,* Spring, pp. 32–36.
El Messiri, Sawsan. 1978. *Ibn al-Balad: A Concept of Egyptian Identity.* Leiden: E.J. Brill.
Mohi El Din, Khaled. 1995. *Memories of a Revolution: Egypt 1952.* Cairo: American University in Cairo Press.
Moosa, Matti. 1994. *The Early Novels of Naguib Mahfouz: Images of Modern Egypt.* Gainesville: University Press of Florida.
Mumtaz, Itidal. 1985. *Mudhakkirat raqibat sinima: 30 amman.* Cairo: al-Hai'a al-Misriya al-Amma lil-Kitab.
Naficy, Hamid. 1993. *The Making of Exile Cultures: Iranian Television in Los Angeles.* Minneapolis: University of Minnesota Press.
al-Nahhas, Hashim. 1990. *Najib Mahfuz ala al-shasha.* Cairo: al-Hai'a al-Misriya al-Amma lil-Kitab.
———. 1995. "Salah Abu Sayf wa tajdhir al-waqa'iya wa al-tanwir fi al-sinima al-Misriya." *Alif: Journal of Comparative Poetics* 15, pp. 6–21.
———. 1996. *Salah Abu Sayf.* Cairo: al-Hai'a al-Misriya al-Amma lil-Kitab.
Nagib, Muhammad. 1975. *Kalimati lil-tarikh.* Cairo: Dar al-Kitab al-Namudhiji.
———. 1984. *Kuntu ra'isan li-Misr.* Cairo: al-Maktab al-Misri al-Hadith.
Nandy, Ashis. 1998. "Indian Popular Cinema as a Slum's Eye View of Politics." In Ashis Nandy, ed., *The Secret Politics of Our Desires: Innocence, Culpability and Indian Popular Cinema.* London: Zed. Pp. 1–18.
Nasser, Gamel Abdul. 1955. *Egypt's Liberation: The Philosophy of the Revolution.* Washington, D.C.: Public Affairs Press.
Neguib, Mohammed. 1955. *Egypt's Destiny.* London: Victor Gollancz.
Nora, Pierre. 1989. "Between Memory and History: Les Lieux de Memoire." *Representations* 26, pp. 7–25.
Nutting, Anthony. 1972. *Nasser.* New York: E.P. Dutton.
Ossman, Susan. 1994. *Picturing Casablanca: Portraits of Power in a Modern City.* Berkeley and Los Angeles: University of California Press.

al-Quwaysni, Narimin. 1991. *Ihsan Abd al-Quddus: ams wa al-yawm wa al-ghadan.* Cairo: Diyasik.

Rached, Tahani. 1997. *Four Women of Egypt.* Film produced by Eric Michel.

Ramzi, Kamal. 1984a. "*Suwwaq al-autobis:* ingaz gil al-shabab fi magal al-sinima." *Al-Funun* 5 (20), pp. 65–67.

———. 1984b. "Thawrat Yulyu wa harb Suways fi al-sinima al-Misriya." *Al-Funun* 5 (20), pp. 82–88.

———. 1995a. "Le realisme." In Magda Wassef, ed., *Egypte: 100 Ans de Cinema.* Paris: Institut du Monde Arabe. Pp. 144–59.

———. 1995b. "Repertoire des acteurs." In Magda Wassef, ed., *Egypte: 100 Ans de Cinema.* Paris: Institut du Monde Arabe. Pp. 266–83.

———. 1997. *Nugum al-sinima al-Misriya.* Cairo: al-Majlis al-A'la lil-Thaqafa.

Riad, Hassan. 1964. *L'Egypte Naserienne.* Paris: d'Minuit.

Rotha, Paul. 1960. *The Film till Now: A Survey of World Cinema,* 3[d] edition. New York: Twayne.

Saad, Abd al-Mun'im. 1975. *Al-Mukhrig Ahmad Badrakhan.* Cairo: al-Hai'a al-Misriya al-Amma lil-Kitab.

El Sadat, Anwar. 1957. *Revolt on the Nile.* New York: John Day.

———. 1977. *In Search of Identity: An Autobiography.* New York: Harper and Row.

Sadoul, Georges. 1966. *The Cinema in the Arab Countries.* Beirut: Interarab Centre of Cinema and Television.

al-Salamuni, Sami. 1984. *"Al-Haram." Al-Funun* 20 (5), pp. 48–49.

———. 1996 [1986]. "Usturat al-film al-awwal." *Al-Qahira* 159 (February), pp. 122–25.

———. 2001. *Al-I'mal al-kamila lil-naqid al-sinima'i Sami al-Salamuni.* Pt. 1. Cairo: Al-Hai'a al-Amma li-Qusur al-Thaqafa.

Salmawi, Muhammad. 1995. *Al-Ganzir.* Cairo: Dar Alif.

Sardar, Ziauddin. 1998. "Dilip Kumar Made Me Do It." In Ashis Nandy, ed., *The Secret Politics of Our Desires: Innocence, Culpability and Indian Popular Cinema.* London: Zed. Pp. 19–91.

Sayf, Samir. 1984. "Du'a al-karawan: bayna al-ruwaya wa al-sinariyu," *Al-Funun* 20 (5), pp. 56–58.

Schatz, Thomas. 1995. "The Structural Influence: New Directions in Film Genre." In Barry Keith Grant, ed., *Film Genre Reader II.* Austin: University of Texas Press. Pp. 91–101.

———. 1996. *The Genius of the System: Hollywood Filmmaking in the Studio Era.* New York: Henry Holt.

Shafik, Viola. 1998. *Arab Cinema: History and Cultural Identity.* Cairo: American University in Cairo Press.

Sharaf al-Din, Duriya. 1992. *Al-Siyasa wa al-Sinima fi Misr, 1961–1981.* Cairo: Dar al-Shuruq.

al-Sharqawi, Abdel Rahman. 1990. *Egyptian Earth.* Austin: University of Texas Press.

Shebl, Mohamed. 1996. "Scream till you're Sick." *Al-Ahram Weekly,* March 17–23.

Shusha, Muhammad al-Sayyid. 1978. *Ruwwad wa ra'idat al-sinima al-Misriya.* Cairo: Ruz al-Yusuf.

Sirhan, Yahya Shukri. 1999. *Ibn al-Nil: Shukri Sirhan wa khamsun amman bayna al-fann wa al-haya.* Cairo: [?].

Sobchak, Thomas. 1995. "Genre Film: A Classical Experience." In Barry Keith Grant, ed., *Film Genre Reader II.* Austin: University of Texas Press. Pp. 102–13.

Stewart, Desmond. 1957. "Cairo." *Middle East Forum* 35 (10), December, pp. 22–57.

Stewart, Susan. 1984. *On Longing: Narratives of the Miniature, the Gigantic, the Souvenir, the Collection.* Baltimore: Johns Hopkins University Press.

Stites, Richard. 1985. "Iconoclastic Currents in the Russian Revolution: Destroying and Preserving the Past." In Abbot Gleason, Peter Kenez, and Richard Stites, eds., *Bolshevik Culture.* Bloomington and Indianapolis: Indiana University Press. Pp. 1–21.

Sullivan, Earl L. 1986. *Women in Egyptian Public Life.* Syracuse: Syracuse University Press.

Swedenburg, Ted. 1990. "The Palestinian Peasant as National Signifier." *Anthropological Quarterly* 63 (1), pp. 18–30.

Taylor, Richard. 1979. *The Politics of the Soviet Cinema, 1917–1929.* Cambridge: Cambridge University Press.

Thabit, Madkur. 1984. "Mayu 68 wa laylat al-aflam al-ula li-tila'i ma'ahad al-sinima." *Al-Funun* 20 (5), pp. 93–99.

al-Tilmissani, Kamil. 1955. "Al-Film al-Misri . . . ibn haram." *Ruz al-Yusuf,* January 10, p. 38.

Toth, James. 1999. *Rural Labor Movements in Egypt and their Impact upon the State, 1961–1992.* Gainesville: University Press of Florida.

Tudor, Andrew. 1995. "Genre." In Barry Keith Grant, ed., *Film Genre Reader II.* Austin: University of Texas Press. Pp. 3–10.

Ukasaha, Tharwat. 1990. *Mudhakkirati fi al-siyasa wa-al-thaqafa.* Cairo: Dar al-Hilal.

Vitalis, Robert. 2000. "American Ambassador in Technicolor and Cinemascope: Hollywood and Revolution on the Nile." In Walter Armbrust, ed., *Mass Mediations: New Approaches to Popular Culture in the Middle East and Beyond.* Berkeley and Los Angeles: University of California Press. Pp. 269–91.

Wassef, Magda, ed. 1995. *Egypte: 100 Ans de Cinema.* Paris: Institut du Monde Arabe.

Waterbury, John. 1978. *Egypt: Burdens of the Past, Options for the Future.* Bloomington: Indiana University Press.

Wheelock, Keith. 1960. *Nasser's New Egypt.* New York: Praeger.

Wilk, Richard. 1993. "'It's Destroying a Whole Generation': Television and Moral Discourse in Belize." *Visual Anthropology* 5: pp. 229–44.

Wright, Judith Hess. 1995. "Genre Films and the Status Quo." In Barry Keith Grant, ed., *Film Genre Reader II.* Austin: University of Texas Press. Pp. 41–49.

Yusuf, Ahmad, ed. 1992. *Salah Abu Sayf: arba'un filman tawarikh lil-sinima al-Misriya.* Cairo: Abu Lalu.

al-Zayyat, Latifa. 2000. *The Open Door.* Tr. by Marilyn Booth. Cairo and New York: American University in Cairo Press.

Indexes/Encyclopedias/Film Guides

al-Bindari, Mona and Mahmud Qasim and Yaaqub Wahbi. 1994. *Mawsu'at al-aflam al-Arabiya.* Cairo: Bayt al-Ma'rifa.
Cinema Development Fund. 1983. *Panorama of the Egyptian Cinema/Directory of Egyptian Films.* Cairo: Egyptian Film Fund.
Cairo International Film Festival. 1996. *Istifta' mahragan al-Qahira al-sinima'i al-dawli bi-munasibat mi'awiyat al-sinima.* Cairo: Cairo International Film Festival.
Daud, Abd al-Ghani. 1997. *Al-Rahilun fi mi'at sana sinima.* Cairo: Wizarat al-thaqafa.
Hasanayn, Adil. 1999. *Al-Mawsu'a al-musawwara li-nugum wa aflam al-sinima al-Arabiya.* Cairo: Amadu.
Leaman, Oliver, ed. 2001. *Companion Encyclopedia of Middle Eastern and North African Film.* London: Routledge.
Mahfuz, Midhat. 1998. *Dalil al-aflam.* 2[d] ed. Cairo: Ministry of Culture.
Qasim, Mahmud and Ya'qub Wahbi. 1997. *Mawsu'at al-mumathil fi al-sinima al-Misriya.* Cairo: Dar al-Amin.
———. 1999. *Dalil al-mumathil al-Arabi.* Cairo: Magmu'at al-Nil al-Arabiya.
Saad, Abd al-Munim. 1976. *Mawgiz al-sinima al-Misriya.* Cairo: [?].

CD-ROM Programs

MetaMedia Information Technology. 1999. *Al-Andalib al-asmar.*
MetaMedia Information Technology. 1999. *Cinderella al-shasha al-Arabiya.*
MetaMedia Information Technology. 1999. *Isma'il Yasin fi al-kumbyutur.*

Filmography

Abbud on the Borders (Abbud ala al-hudud). 1999. Dir. Sharif Arafa.
Adham al-Sharqawi (Adham al-Sharqawi). 1964. Dir. Hussam al-Din Mustafa.
Africano (Africano). 2001. Dir. Umru Arafa.
Alexandria Again and Forever (Iskandriya kaman wa kaman). 1990. Dir. Youssef Chahine.
Alexandria . . . Why? (Iskandriya lay?). 1979. Dir. Youssef Chahine.
Alley of Fools (Darb al-mahabil). 1955. Dir. Tawfiq Salih.
Almaz and Abduh al-Hamuli (Almaz wa Abduh al-Hamuli). 1962. Dir. Hilmi Rafla.
Amal (Amal). 1952. Dir. Yusuf Maaluf.
Ambulance 55 (Is'af 55). 2001. Dir. Magdi al-Hawwari.
Asphalt Demons (Afarit al-asfalt). 1996. Dir. Usama Fawzi.
Autumn Quail (al-Siman wa al-kharif). 1967. Dir. Hussam al-Din Mustafa.
Beginning and the End, The (al-Bidaya wa al-nihaya). 1961. Dir. Salah Abu Sayf.
Between Heaven and Earth (Bayna al-sama' wa al-ard). 1959. Dir. Salah Abu Sayf.
Bit of Fear, A (Shay' min al-khawf). 1969. Dir. Husayn Kamal.

Bitter Day, Sweet Day (Yawm murr, yawm hilw). 1988. Dir. Khayri Bishara.
Black Market, The (al-Suq al-sawda'). 1945. Dir. Kamil al-Tilmissani.
Blazing Love (Hubb min nar). 1958. Dir. Hasan al-Imam.
Blocked Path, The (al-Tariq al-masdud). 1958. Dir. Salah Abu Sayf.
Blood on the Nile (Dima' ala al-Nil). 1961. Dir. Niyazi Mustafa.
Boss Hasan (al-Usta Hasan). 1952. Dir. Salah Abu Sayf.
Bread and Salt (al-Aysh wa al-milh). 1949. Dir. Husayn Fawzi.
Bride of the Nile (Arus al-Nil). 1963. Dir. Fatin Abd al-Wahab.
Bus Driver, The (Sawwaq al-autobis). 1983. Dir. Atif al-Tayyib.
Cairo 1930 (al-Qahira 30). 1966. Dir. Salah Abu Sayf.
Cairo Station (Bab al-hadid). 1958. Dir. Youssef Chahine.
Call of the Curlew, The (Du'a al-karawan). 1959. Dir. Henry Baracat.
Case 68 (Qadiya 68). 1968. Dir. Salah Abu Sayf.
Chatter on the Nile (Tharthara fawq al-Nil). 1971. Dir. Husayn Kamal.
Choice, The (al-Ikhtiyar). 1971. Dir. Youssef Chahine.
Closed Doors, The (Abwab al-mughliqa). 2001. Dir. Atif Hatata.
Confession, The (al-Itiraf). 1965. Dir. Saad Arafa.
Crazy Youth (Shabab magnun giddan). 1967. Dir. Niyazi Mustafa.
Dahab (Dahab). 1953. Dir. Anwar Wagdi.
Dalila (Dalila). 1956. Dir. Muhammad Karim.
Dark Girl of Sinai, The (Samra' Sina'). 1959. Dir. Niyazi Mustafa.
Dark Glasses, The (al-Naddara al-sawda'). 1963. Dir. Hussam al-Din Mustafa.
Daughter of Nobility (Bint al-akabir). 1953. Dir. Anwar Wagdi.
Dawn of the New Age (Fagr yawm gadid). 1965. Dir. Youssef Chahine.
Day in My Life, A (Yawm min umri). 1961. Dir. Atif Salim.
Day of the Unjust (Laka yawm ya zalim). 1951. Dir. Salah Abu Sayf.
Days of Sadat (Ayyam al-Sadat). 2001. Dir. Muhammad Khan.
Destiny (al-Masir). 1998. Dir. Youssef Chahine.
Determination (al-Azima). 1939. Dir. Kamal Salim.
Diary of a Country Prosecutor (Yawmiyat na'ib fi al-aryaf). 1969. Dir. Tawfiq Salih.
Dispossessed, The (al-Hirman). 1953. Dir. Atif Salim.
Don't Put Out the Sun (La tutfi al-shams). 1961. Dir. Salah Abu Sayf.
Down with Imperialism (Yusqut al-isti'mar). 1952. Dir. Husayn Sidqi.
Duped, The (al-Makhdu'un). 1973. Dir. Tawfiq Salih.
Egyptian Tale, An (Haduta Misriya). 1982. Dir. Youssef Chahine.
Empire of M's (Imbaraturiyat mim). 1972. Dir. Husayn Kamal.
Empty Pillow, The (al-Wisada al-khaliya). 1957. Dir. Salah Abu Sayf.
Fallen Angels' Paradise (Ginnat al-shayatin). 2000. Dir. Usama Fawzi.
Father's Up a Tree (Abi fawq al-shagara). 1968. Dir. Husayn Kamal.
For Men Only (Lil rigal faqat). 1964. Dir. Mahmud Zulficar.
Four Girls and an Officer (Arba' banat wa zabit). 1954. Dir. Anwar Wagdi.
Giants of the Sea (Amaliqat al-bihar). 1960. Dir. al-Sayyid Badir.
Girls' Secrets (Asrar al-banat). 2001. Dir. Magdi Ahmad Ali.
Girls and Summer (al-Banat wa al-sayf). 1960. Dir. Izz al-Din Zulficar, Salah Abu Sayf, Fatin Abd al-Wahab.

Good Earth, The (al-Ard al-tayyiba). 1953. Dir. Mahmud Zulficar.
Guha's Nail (Mismar Guha). 1952. Dir. Ibrahim Imara.
Hamam in Amsterdam (Hamam fi Amsterdam). 1999. Dir. Said Hamid.
Hasan and Naima (Hasan wa Na'ima). 1959. Dir. Henry Baracat.
Heroes' Struggle (Sira' al-abtal). 1961. Dir. Tawfiq Salih.
I Can't Sleep (La anam). 1957. Dir. Salah Abu Sayf.
I Want a Solution (Uridu halan). 1975. Dir. Said Marzuq.
Ice Cream in Glym (Ice cream fi Glym). 1992. Dir. Khayri Bishara.
I'm Free (Ana hurra). 1958. Dir. Salah Abu Sayf.
Impossible, The (al-Mustahil). 1965. Dir. Husayn Kamal.
Jamila (Jamila). 1958. Dir. Youssef Chahine.
Karnak (al-Karnak). 1976. Dir. Ali Badrakhan.
Khan al-Khalili (Khan al-Khalili). 1966. Dir. Atif Salim.
Kilometer 99 (Kilo 99). 1956. Dir. Ibrahim Hilmi.
Lachine (Lashin). 1939. Dir. Fritz Kremp.
Lamp of Umm Hashim, The (Qandil Umm Hashim). 1968. Dir. Kamal Atiya.
Land, The (al-Ard). 1970. Dir. Youssef Chahine.
Land of Hypocrisy (Ard al-nifaq). 1968. Dir. Fatin Abd al-Wahab.
Land of Peace (Ard al-salam). 1957. Dir. Kamal al-Shaykh.
Layla (Layla) 1927. Dir. Widad Urfi and Stefan Rosti.
Layla the Bedouin (Layla al-badawiya). 1944. Dir. Bahiga Hafiz.
Layla, Daughter of Poverty (Layla bint al-fuqara'). 1945. Dir. Anwar Wagdi.
Letter from a Missing Woman (Risala min imra'a maghula). 1963. Dir. Salah Abu Sayf.
Life, My Passion (Ya Dunya ya gharami). 1996. Dir. Magdi Ahmad Ali.
Life or Death (Haya aw mawt). 1954. Dir. Kamal al-Shaykh.
Love Story (Hikayat hubb). 1959. Dir. Hilmi Halim.
Miramar (Miramar). 1968. Dir. Kamal al-Shaykh.
Madam Hanafi (al-Anisa Hanafi). 1954. Dir. Fatin Abd al-Wahab.
Madam Sugar (Sukkar hanum). 1960. Dir. al-Sayyid Badir.
Man in Our House, A (Fi baytina ragul). 1961. Dir. Henry Baracat.
Man Who Lost His Shadow, The (al-Ragul alladhi faqad zilu). 1968. Dir. Kamal al-Shaykh.
Monster, The (al-Wahsh). 1953. Dir. Salah Abu Sayf.
Mountain, The (al-Gabal). 1965. Dir. Khalil Shawqi.
Mummy, The (al-Mumiya'; Night of Counting the Years). 1968/1975. Dir. Shadi Abd al-Salam.
Mustafa Kamil (Mustafa Kamil). 1951. Dir. Ahmad Badrakhan.
My Prince Charming (Fata ahlami). 1957. Dir. Hilmi Rafla.
My Wife and the Dog (Zawgati wa al-kalb). 1971. Dir. Said Marzuq.
My Wife is General Director (Mrati mudir amm). 1966. Dir. Fatin Abd al-Wahab.
Nasser 56 (Nasir 56). 1996. Dir. Muhammad Fadl.
Nights of Love (Layali al-hubb). 1955. Dir. Hilmi Rafla.
Nile Boy (Ibn al-Nil). 1951. Dir. Youssef Chahine.
Noble Thief, The (al-Liss al-sharif). 1953. Dir. Himada Abd al-Wahab.

Open Door, The (al-Bab al-maftuh). 1963. Dir. Henry Baracat.
Our Green Earth (Ardina al-khudra'). 1956. Dir. Ahmad Diaa al-Din.
Our Sweet Days (Ayyamna al-hilwa). 1955. Dir. Hilmi Halim.
Palace Walk (Bayn al-qasrayn). 1964. Dir. Hasan al-Imam.
Papa Amin (Baba Amin). 1950. Dir. Youssef Chahine.
People at the Top, The (Ahl al-qima). 1981. Dir. Ali Badrakhan.
People Below, The (al-Nass illi taht). 1960. Dir. Kamil al-Tilmissani.
People's Idol, The (Ma'budat al-gamahir). 1967. Dir. Hilmi Rafla.
Platform Number 5 (Rasif nimra khamsa). 1955. Dir. Niyazi Mustafa.
Port Said (Bur Sa'id). 1957. Dir. Izz al-Din Zulficar.
Postman, The (al-Bustagi). 1968. Dir. Husayn Kamal.
Prisoner of Abu Zaabal, The (Sijin Abu Za'bal). 1957. Dir. Niyazi Mustafa.
Rains Dried Up, The (Gafat al-amtar). 1968. Dir. Sayyid Isa.
Raya and Sakina (Raya wa Sakina). 1953. Dir. Salah Abu Sayf.
Rebels, The (al-Mutamaridun). 1968. Dir. Tawfiq Salih.
Return My Heart (Rudda qalbi). 1957. Dir. Izz al-Din Zulficar.
Saidi at the American University, A (Sa'idi fi al-Gam'a al-Amrikiya). 1998. Dir. Said Hamid.
Saladin the Victorious (al-Nasir Salah al-Din). 1963. Dir. Youssef Chahine.
Sayyid Balti (al-Sayyid al-Balti). 1969. Dir. Tawfiq Salih.
Sayyid Darwish (Sayyid Darwish). 1966. Dir. Ahmad Badrakhan.
Second Wife, The (al-Zawga al-thaniya). 1967. Dir. Salah Abu Sayf.
Shame, The (al-Ayb). 1967. Dir. Galal al-Sharqawi.
Shepherd and the Women, The (al-Ra'iy wa al-nisa'). 1991. Dir. Ali Badrakhan.
Silent One, The (al-Kharsa'a). 1961. Dir. Hasan al-Imam.
Sin, The (al-Haram). 1965. Dir. Henry Baracat.
Sins, The (al-Khitaya). 1962. Dir. Hasan al-Imam.
Snakes and Ladders (al-Sillim wa al-thu'ban). 2001. Dir. Tariq al-Aryan.
Song of Devotion (Lahn al-wifa'). 1955. Dir. Ibrahim Imara.
Struggle in the Valley (Sira' fi al-wadi; Blazing Sun). 1954. Dir. Youssef Chahine.
Struggle on the Nile (Sira' fi al-Nil). 1959. Dir. Atif Salim.
Sunset, Sunrise (Ghurub wa shuruq). 1970. Dir. Kamal al-Shaykh.
Terrorism and Shish Kabob (al-Irhab wa al-kabab). 1992. Dir. Sharif Arafa.
They Who Missed Their Past (Man fata qadimu). 1943. Dir. Farid al-Gindi.
Thief and the Dogs, The (al-Liss wa al-kilab). 1962. Dir. Kamal al-Shaykh.
Third Class (al-Daraga al-thalitha). 1988. Dir. Sharif Arafa.
Thug, The (al-Futuwwa). 1957. Dir. Salah Abu Sayf.
Today's Girls (Banat al-yawm). 1957. Dir. Henry Baracat.
Too Young for Love (Saghira ala al-hubb). 1966. Dir. Niyazi Mustafa.
Uncle Abduh's Ghost (Afrit Amm Abduh). 1953. Dir. Husayn Fawzi.
Violets are Blue (Lay ya banafsig). 1993. Dir. Radwan al-Kashif.
Watch Out for Zouzou (Khalli balak min Zuzu). 1972. Dir. Husayn Kamal.
Where's My Life (Ayna umri). 1956. Dir. Ahmad Diaa al-Din.
White Rose, The (al-Warda al-bayda'). 1933. Dir. Muhammad Karim.
Whom Should We Shoot (Ala min natlaq al-rasas). 1975. Dir. Kamal al-Shaykh.

Widow Wanted (Matlub armala). 1966. Dir. Isa Karama.
Wife of an Important Person (Zawgat ragul muhim). 1987. Dir. Muhammad Khan.
With God on Our Side (Allah ma'ana). 1955. Dir. Ahmad Badrakhan.
Woman's Youth, A (Shabab imra'a). 1955. Dir. Salah Abu Sayf.
Zaynab (Zaynab). 1930. Dir. Muhammad Karim.

INTERVIEWS AND FORMAL CONVERSATIONS (CAIRO)

Ahmad and Muhammad Abd al-Quddus, December 15, 1995.
Magdi Abd al-Rahman, April 12, 1996.
Mahfuz Abd al-Rahman, April 4, April 11, and June 6, 1996.
Daud Abd al-Sayyid, December 31, 1999.
Salah Abu Sayf, December 19, 1995.
Muhammad al-Bisati, May 10, 1996.
Khayri Bishara, January 2, 2000.
Mustafa Darwish, April 17 and 28, 1996.
Samir Farid, February 7, 1996.
Louis Greiss, November 26 and December 11, 1995.
Baha Jahin, November 27, 1995.
Fayda Kamil, June 5, 1996.
Salah Marii, January 25, 1996.
Galal Muawad, December 12, 1996.
Ahmad Said, January 20 and 24, 1996.
Tawfiq Salih, January 7, 2000.
Farid Shawqi, January 19, 1996.
Kamal al-Shaykh, January 23, 1996.
Kamal al-Tawil, December 10, 1995.

INDEX